This is ou

– a celebration of
the bicentenary of the

Reading British School,
Southampton Street

1811 – 2011

**as seen through the eyes of those
most closely involved throughout its history**

by

Daphne Joyce Barnes-Phillips, MA (Ed), BA (Hons)

Copyright details

Published by:	Corridor Press
	19 Portland Avenue
	Exmouth
	Devon
	EX8 2BS
	England
Tel:	(01395) 263494
E-mail:	corridorpress@yahoo.co.uk

Text and editorial arrangement copyright to:
Daphne Barnes-Phillips © 2011

Cover design copyright to:
James Barnes-Phillips © 2011

ISBN: 978 – 1 – 897715 – 12 – 3

Printed and bound in Great Britain by:
CPI Antony Rowe
Chippenham and Eastbourne

Spring Gardens

Publications

IMPORTANT DATES

1778	25 November	Birth of Joseph Lancaster
1780		Robert Raikes founded first Sunday School in Gloucester
1802		First Factory Act, restricting labour of women & children
1808		The Royal Lancasterian Institution (R L I) founded
1810	31st October	Lancasterian Free School for Boys ready for occupation on east side of Southampton Street, Reading
1811	8th January	Master arrived so School open to pupils
1814		R. L. I. was renamed British and Foreign School Society
1818	30th March	Reading British Girls' School opened
1819		Factory Act stated that no children under 9 be employed and 9 – 16 year olds could only work 12 hours a day
1835		British Infant School in Hosier Street
1836		St. Giles National School founded
1839		Inspectors of Schools first appointed
1840		First postage stamps and Great Western Railway opened
1845		Time standardised in Great Britain (previously Bristol was ten minutes behind London)
1846		Inauguration of Pupil Teacher system
1848		Ragged School started in St. Giles' Parish
1862		Revised Code (Payment by Results)
1870		Forster's Elementary Education Act introduced School Board System in England and Wales
1891	31st August	Holiday to commemorate introduction of free education
1893		School Attendance Act raised age of exemption to 11 years
1894		The Prevention of Cruelty Act
1897		Voluntary Schools Act provided grants for such schools
1898		Still Penny Post to Commonwealth countries
1899		Textile Unions angered by raising Schooling age limit to 12
1901	1st October	Reading British School transferred to Education Board
1902		Balfour Education Act transferred control to Local Authorities, placing all Elementary Schools on the rates
1906		Provision of School Meals Act
1907	3rd October	Pupils & staff transferred from Southampton Street to new George Palmer School, Basingstoke Rd./Northumberland Av.
2000		British School building is grade II listed
2001	March	Reading British School won BBC History Magazine competition to save building of historical importance
2010	26th April	Planning Application passed for Conversion of Building to luxury apartments

3

Acknowledgements

I should like to thank the following:

John Bassett who lent me the information he had collected while researching for his booklet *A Brief History of the Reading British School* (2000).

Sidney Gold who, among other items, came up with the seemingly sole surviving photograph of pupils taken at the British School.

Iain MacNaught of Parkcroft Developments (Old School) Ltd., who, in 2011, showed Jim and me the interior of the building that housed the British School for almost a century 200 years after the first boys were educated there.

Edward Mather of Mather Dew Architecture Ltd. for use of his Design and Access Statement and Photographic Survey of the British School.

Muriel Nutt (née Lodge) who loaned the photograph of the Pupil Teacher Class of 1923, in which her brother, Sidney, featured.

Ann Snowdon, the present head teacher of George Palmer Primary School, for her encouragement in contacting former pupils and members of staff of the George Palmer Schools and help in arranging Reminiscence events, which led to the production of my two previous books about them and the discovery that they had a predecessor in the British Schools in Southampton Street.

Staff of Berkshire Records Office for maintaining original Lancasterian Minute and Visitor Books; Log Books of the Reading British Boys' and Infants' Schools, and of George Palmer Schools; also for their help with locating the relevant sections.

Staff of Reading Central Library for maintaining secondary sources of local newspapers, Education Committee Reports, Street Directories & related books

and finally, my husband, **Jim Barnes-Phillips**, who designed the cover, has helped with research and transcription of original documents and newspaper articles, also the taking and insertion of photographs and sketches and generally been a tower of strength since I embarked upon this project.

Dedication

This book is dedicated
to the memory of
the staff, pupils and all those connected with the
British School,
Southampton Street,
Reading
from 1809
and its successors,
the George Palmer Schools,
Basingstoke Road
Reading
from 1907
and Northumberland Avenue,
from 2004.

It is also dedicated to those
whose vision enabled the schools
to come into being
and provide an education
for the children of south Reading
since 1811.

Finally, it is dedicated to
all those who are being,
and will be
educated,
at George Palmer Primary School,
Reading Girls' School and
the Madejski Academy
that they may appreciate
the tremendous heritage
that is their's.

5

Table of Contents

British School Song

Words composed and specially adapted by former pupil, Mr. **S. Jackson Coleman**, to an old patriotic air of the Transvaal:

Once more from distant hill and plain
We Old Britonians meet;
Too long in silence have we lain,
Too long, save memory sweet.
Schoolfellows since this wide world through
Have wandered many ways,
Try British sons and lassies, who
Would call back happy days.

Those dusty schools produced great minds,
That playground sport with zest,
The old-time forms with well-worn lines
Were used by Reading's best.
The boys then felt dear "Daddy's" stick,
And waited in dismay:
The girls, too, got it fairly thick
From Pierpoint and from Reay.

Prizes and trophies not a few
By "British" lads were gained.
And many know those "British" slew
Teams who at football reigned.
Through many a fierce and eager match
Our boys made fight of old,
And out of each, with scarce a scratch
Came every hero bold.

Here's to the memory of our chief,
Whose fame we would accord,
Known through this town as "Daddy Gleave",
Now passed to his reward,
Enriched with length of days, full bright,
Noble in life and ways,
He is that orb of golden light,
We but reflect his rays.

Now lift we high the social glass,
Success to one and all!
Forget tonight all clans and class,
And join the "British" call.
To sing aloud the glad old song
Of schooldays gone, but dear,
A song to help your way along,
A song that rings – Good Cheer!

This song was first performed by the soprano, Miss Helen Tocock of Beech Hill at the British Schools' Reunion Dinner on 10th February, 1923.

A most important school

As I stated in *So many hearts make a school* (published 2007), the revelation that pupils from the Southampton Street Council Schools had transferred to the newly-opened George Palmer Council Schools on 3rd October, 1907 extended my investigation and led to the writing of this separate book when I discovered that there was too much material for just one. It was the account in the *26th October, 1907 Reading Standard* entitled: *The George Palmer Schools – The Latest Addition to Reading's Splendid Elementary Schools* that first enabled me to recognise the connection between those two places of education from its description of the opening of the George Palmer Schools:

> The new schools are meant to serve the purposes of the old British Schools, which on being taken over by the Council, were known as Southampton-street Schools.

That opened up a whole new vista for me as I had heard that Reading's British School in Southampton Street was possibly the earliest survivor of the British School movement. It also meant that the history of the Infant and Junior Schools, where I had received my Primary Education from 1949 until 1955, was of even more importance to the History of Education in England than I could ever have envisaged.

Unfortunately, by the time I discovered that fact, the original 1810 British School building was shrouded in scaffolding. However, that building has outlived its replacement buildings in Basingstoke Road, despite having been condemned for school use in the early 1900s!

Obviously the format of this book had to be somewhat different to that of *So many hearts make a school* as no former staff or pupils remain alive to give us their memories of the first hundred years of the schools. Fortunately, though, there are Log Books, Attendance Registers, newspaper accounts and census records that have enabled a picture to be pieced together so I have chosen to write this book as if six key figures were telling their stories in the first person.

George Palmer was active in his support of the Reading British Schools for at least 50 years. Since that was for more than half the time the schools were on the Southampton Street site, it became obvious that to tell the story of the schools primarily from his angle would be the best way forward.

10

Another person who was associated with the schools for a similar period of time was **Annie Fabry** as, having been one of its pupils, she was teaching in the Infant School from its British School days through its Board School to its Council School status and finally to the new buildings and totally new name of George Palmer School in 1907 and through until her retirement in 1924.

However, to gain insight into the type of school and the reason for its set up, the story of the London-born innovator, **Joseph Lancaster**, needed to be told. It had been at the Reading home of fellow Quaker, **Thomas Letchworth**, that the initial meeting about the setting up of a Lancasterian School had taken place. Since he was later elected a Trustee and then its Secretary, his story, when combined with that of the Girls' School Secretary, **Susan Champion**, provided the link from Joseph Lancaster to George Palmer.

To balance the male/female ratio, I chose **Eliza Barcham**, who was one of the Committee Ladies who visited both the Girls' and Infants' Schools on a regular basis from the 1860s until 1889 when she moved to Tunbridge Wells.

To round off this glimpse into the life of Reading's British School, the story of the long-standing Master of the Boys' School, **Thomas Gleave**, is told by others who recalled his service to the school in the months following his death in 1923. Annie Fabry had been present at the 1923 Reunion of Old Britishers organised a short time after his death so proved an ideal link character to him, since much of the information I had gleaned came from that Reunion.

The dates given for each character indicate their years of association with the school rather than their total life span. All but Joseph Lancaster were associated with the school for more than 30 years each so, where events span the service of more than one character, I have detailed them under the most appropriate.

Before we start to hear of Joseph Lancaster's innovative ideas that led to the creation of many Lancasterian and British Schools, including the one in Reading, I have produced three tables to summarise those who were responsible for the Schools on the Southampton Street site, plus the uses to which the building has been put over the two centuries that it has stood there.

Daphne Barnes-Phillips

11

The terms Headmaster and Headmistress were not used until later. Initially, a Master or Mistress was helped by Monitors and later by Pupil and Assistant Teachers. Some blanks remain in the following tables as it has proved impossible to ascertain precise dates for some of the Masters and Mistresses who were responsible for the organisation of the schools prior to the keeping of Log Books in 1870:

Masters of the Schools on the British School site

Name of school	Name of Master	Dates of service
Trial for Reading Lancasterian School	James Draper	27 November 1809 – 30 October 1810
Setting up School	Kenneth McRae	8 January – 28 Feb. 1811
Reading Lancastrian School's 1st Master	Nathaniel Higgins	16 February 1811 – 31 January 1815
Reading Free School on the British system	William Gatward	17 January 1815 – 31 May 1826
Boys' School on the British System	Edward Edwards	12 May 1826 until his death on 24 April 1829
	James Cornwall	25 April – 31 July 1829
	Matthew Thompson	24 Aug. 1829–7 June 1839
	Mr. Rodway	19 June 1839 – Sept. 1840
	William Lane	16 September 1840 – 1849
British Boys' School	John Worley	1850 – 1856
	Thomas Gleave	1857 – 23 December 1896
	Edwin Thomas Caton	From 11 January 1897
Southampton Street Board School– Boys	Edwin Thomas Caton B.A.	1 October 1901 – 30 September 1903
Southampton Street Council Sch – Boys	Richard Williams	1 October 1903 – 30 March 1905
	Joshua Swallow	1 April 1905 – 2 Oct. 1907

Mistresses of Reading Girls' & Infants' British Schools

Name of school	Name of Mistress	Dates of service
Girls' School on the	Jane Thomson	30 March 1818 – 23 June 1830
British System	Mrs. Slaughter	24 June 1830 – March 1838
	Miss Ireson	March – 28 October 1838
	Miss Perry	29 October 1838–30 June 1841
	Miss Searle	1 July 1841 – 15 July 1848
British Girls' School	Miss West	17 July 1848 – 1849
	Miss Smith	1849 – 24 March 1850
	Jane Belcher	25 March – 27 September 1850
	Catherine Thompson	28 October 1850 – 1867
	Miss Martin	1868 – December 1869
Reading Girls' British	Mary Ann Reay	10 January 1870 – 26 Feb.1892
	Catherine A. Pierpoint	29 Feb. 1892 – 30 Sept. 1901
Southampton Street Board School – Girls	Catherine A. Pierpoint	1 October 1901 – 8 April 1903
Southampton Street Council School – Girls	Catherine A. Pierpoint	21 April 1903–2 October 1907
Infants' Department	Fanny Anne Ace	10 Jan. 1870 – 14 Feb. 1873
	Myra Janet Stephens	3 March 1873 – 22 Dec. 1880
	Emma Ryder	10 Jan. 1881 – 1 Feb. 1899
	Edith Varley	6 Feb. 1899 – 30 Sept. 1901
Southampton Street Board School – Infants	Edith Varley	1 October 1901 – April 1902
Southampton Street Council School Infants	Alice E. Osman	25 April 1902 – 2 Oct. 1907

Schools/Organisations that have used British School site

Organisation	Dates
The Reading Lancasterian School	From 8 January 1811
Reading Free School on British System	Renamed from 28 September 1815
Reading British Free School	
Reading British Free School – Girls	From Monday 30 March 1818
Reading British School, Southampton-street	From June 1823
Reading British School – Infants	From July 1852
Reading British School and Infants	From January 1870
Southampton Street Board School	1 October 1901 – 8 April 1903
Southampton Street Council School	21 April 1903 until 2 October 1907
Central Kitchen for provision of meals for necessitous school children	1907 – 1917
Southampton Street Feeding Centre	From 1915
Communal Kitchen	From 3 September 1917
Air Raid Precautions headquarters	During World War II
Soup Kitchen	From 1946
Reading School Meals Service	From 1965
Physically Handicapped & Able Bodied Club (PHAB)	From 1957
Apollo Youth Club	Moved there late 1983
Mary Seacole Day Nursery	Moved from Coley Primary School 4 January 2006
MAPP Centre – purpose built to house Mary Seacole Nursery Apollo & PHAB	From 10 January 2006

READING LANCASTERIAN SCHOOL

I. Innovator's Tale: JOSEPH LANCASTER 1809 – 1816

I first visited Reading on 29th of the 8th month of 1809 when I was invited to give a lecture on my Plan for the Education of Poor Children in the town. This had come about as a result of the success of my ideas for providing education free of charge, having opened a small purpose-built school in Borough Road, Southwark in the city of London in 1798 at a time when there was no free system of education. My school grew rapidly and within a couple of years, I was teaching over 1,000 pupils. Since I could not afford to pay any assistants, I devised a plan using a monitorial system. Under such a system, one Master could oversee a class whilst older pupils, known as Monitors, taught the younger children. The system worked with military efficiency.

Members of Society, such as the Duke of Bedford and members of the Royal family, visited my school and offered their support. I even had an audience with **King George III** [1] in 1805. As a Quaker, I believe that all men are equal so I declined to remove my hat in his presence and, to his credit, he liked that. As a result, we got on well and the King told me that it was his dearest wish that every child in his Kingdom should be able to read the Holy Bible. He gave me £100 and promised a similar sum each year. As  a result of his support and that of **Queen Charlotte, the Princesses and Royal Dukes**, I changed the school's name to The Royal Free School.

Although by then a Quaker, I had not been raised as such and, in fact, my father, Richard, had hoped that I would enter the established Church. I had been born in Southwark on November 25th, 1778, the youngest child of devoutly religious parents. As a boy, I believed that I should become a

---

[1] 4 June 1738 – 29 January 1820

missionary and travel to the West Indies so, at the age of fourteen, I travelled to Bristol to catch a boat to Jamaica. However, I could not raise the fare so I found work in that city and remained there. I became attracted to the Society of Friends, a non-conformist religious sect, whose members are often called "Quakers", so joined them. Four years later, I returned to Southwark and started to teach boys from a room in my father's house. That went so well that, two years later, I opened a school in Borough Road. At that time (1798), there were some fee-paying schools but there was no free system of education for the poor. I therefore hung this sign outside my school building:

> All who will may send their children
> and have them educated freely and,
> those who do not wish to have education for nothing,
> may pay for it if they please

The founding of Royal Lancasterian Institution

I believed that God would provide the finances for the important work I was doing so did not concern myself too much with that side of things. However, as a result, I did always seem to be in debt. This led fellow Quakers, Joseph

Fox and William Allen and Moravian, William Corston, to found the Royal Lancasterian Society (The Society for Promoting the Lancasterian System for the Education of the Poor) in 1808. Joseph was a dental surgeon from Guy's Hospital, who had been amazed and delighted to see that, within three weeks of a Lancasterian School for 300 boys being opened by me in Dover, it was being run efficiently by a 17-year-old I had trained. The deeply-respected Quaker Elder, **William Allen**, became Treasurer of the Society, a position he was to hold for the rest of his life. He also travelled throughout Europe promoting both the schools and the Anti-Slavery Campaign.

The involvement of those three allowed me more time to travel the country delivering lectures and advocating the creation of new Lancasterian Schools.

As a result, twenty-five new schools had been founded by July 1810, one of which was the Reading Lancasterian School.

The aim of the Society was to create schools which were not controlled by the Church of England and could provide free mass education to the working classes. Ever since 1668, when **George Fox** established a school for boys at Waltham Abbey in Essex and a school for girls at Shacklewell in East London, the Society of Friends in both England and Ireland had set great store by education but even those fee-paying schools had not on the whole prospered so it was amazing to see how popular my system for educating the poor had become.

As a result of my being invited to give the aforementioned lecture in Reading in 1809, my *Plan for the Education of Poor Children* was considered at a meeting on August 27th in Mr. Letchworth's house. Rev. Dr. Valpy was in the chair at that first meeting and there were thirteen other men present, including two other ministers, Revs. Gauntlet and Marsh, and Dr. Deane. At that meeting, it was resolved that:

> such school be established for both boys and girls and that the same be a free school;
> my offer of assistance be accepted;
> the rev, the rector and vicars of the parishes of St. Lawrence, St. Marys and St. Giles be invited to become Members of the committee and other gents there at hand;
> personal application be made for subscriptions;
> Messrs. Deane, Austwick and Maberley be requested to enquire for a suitable situation for a school;
> the thanks of the meeting be given to me for my benevolent attention to the object of my pursuit in the education of the poor children and my very liberal offer of delivering another lecture gratis;
> tickets to be given to the committee;
> the committee be adjourned to Friday next, the 1st Sept at one o'clock.

In 1801, Reading had a population of just 9,724 and was a small, regional, market town serving an agricultural hinterland. During the whole of the eighteenth century, the population of the town had grown by only 40 per cent, but, by the early nineteenth century, it had developed into a commercial centre. It had long enjoyed a position as a communication point standing at the confluence of the rivers Thames and Kennet and also benefited from the development of an extensive road network.

Edward Simeon's £500 gift

The main business of the second meeting, on September 1st, 1809 seems to have been taken up with naming 30 gentlemen who would be invited to serve on the Committee, including Alderman Blandy but, by the time of the third meeting on 9th, L. Austwick was in the chair with ten of the 30 present. A letter was read from Edward Simeon Esq. tendering a gift of £500 towards the

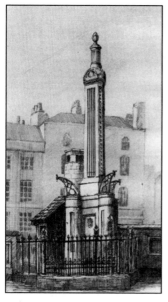 establishing of the school. A letter from Rev. C. Simeon recommended my plan from his own experience and letters from myself to Mr. Ring and to Dr. Valpy were also read. Mr. Simeon's liberal and generous offer was accepted and three were appointed as trustees for that money and any other sums funded for the purpose – Rev. Dr. Valpy, Thomas Ring Esq. and Lancelot Austwick, the latter being appointed secretary and treasurer to the society.

Edward Simeon, son of the Member of Parliament, John Simeon, had become a successful merchant then Director of the Bank of England. Being wealthy, generous and kindly, he funded various institutions in Reading to help the sick, feed the poor and clothe the children. One of his gifts was **the Obelisk in the Market Place**, which was designed by the eminent architect of the day, Sir John Soane, in 1804. He gave an endowment fund for its maintenance and, since its income was larger than that needed, its trustees used the surplus to pay a yearly contribution to the Victoria Nursing Home nurses who visited and tended the sick pensioners in Reading's almshouses.

Edward's younger brother, Charles, who had been born at the old house in the Forbury on September 24th, 1759 was sent as a 9-year-old to Eton and became

18

a Fellow at King's College, Cambridge ten years later. At the age of 23, he was appointed Curate in Charge of Trinity Church, Cambridge and he was the Rev. C. Simeon, who had written of his experience of my Lancasterian Plan. He founded the Simeon Trust sometime later, thus securing the placing of evangelical clergy in Church of England pulpits.

A Trial Run

The Committee next gathered at one o'clock on September 13th and, after considering plans and offers from various proprietors, decided that it would be advisable to have a trial on a smaller scale initially before laying out such a large sum of money. It had been suggested that they consult a Mr. Draper who was already running a school for boys and whose plan of education was somewhat similar to mine. Thus it was that, on 29th, Mr. Draper's offer to instruct 100 children for one year on my plan was accepted.

By October 16th, Messrs. J. Deane, Maberley and Austwick had arranged the business with Mr. Draper and called a meeting of the committee at large. It was resolved at that meeting that Mr. Draper's proposal be acceded to and that he be allowed a cauldron of coals for the use of the school. A cauldron of coals (originally called a chaldron) was a dry measure of volume, not weight, being much more practical than weighing for low-value, high-bulk commodities like coal. It was not standardized, and there were many different regional chaldrons, the two most important being the Newcastle and London chaldrons. A London chaldron was defined as "36 bushels heaped up, each bushel to contain a Winchester bushel and one quart, and to be $19\frac{1}{2}$ inches in diameter". This approximated a weight in coal of around 28 cwt, or 3,136 lb (1,422 kg) and was the legal limit for horse-drawn coal wagons as it was considered that anything heavier would cause too much road damage.[2]

A date – Monday, November 20th – was settled on for me to give a lecture in

---

[2] 1836 Weights and Measures Act legislated that coal should only be sold by weight to prevent unscrupulous merchants from purchasing in lumps as large as possible then selling them in smaller sizes. The cauldron was finally abolished by the Weights and Measures Act of 1963, having been in use from the 13th century.

Reading Town Hall. It was also agreed that each subscriber of £1. 1. 0 per annum be allowed to sponsor a boy so long as he wasn't under six. Prior to that, there was to be a meeting there on 14th when Mr. Ring was requested to write to Edward Simeon, Esq. to ascertain his wishes with regard to the appropriation of the £500 stock.

One guinea
= £1 1s 0d
= £1.05

At the 10 o'clock meeting in the Council Chamber on 21st, it was decided that they should be thinking in terms of a school for 500 children or more eventually. Mr. Holmes, the newly-appointed treasurer had advanced to Mr. Draper the sum of twenty-six pounds five shillings [£26.25] for one quarter according to agreement. The following day at 12 o'clock in the Town Hall, the address to the public was approved and three gentlemen were allocated to distribute said address to each of the three parishes – St. Mary, St. Lawrence and St. Giles. A letter was also sent to the mayor and corporation stating the object of the society and asking for their countenance and cooperation.

Edward Simeon Esq. had naturally been kept informed of all developments. By the meeting of December 1st in the Council Chamber, it had been resolved that subscribers would have the privilege of nominating children for the school according to the amount of their subscriptions – one child for one guinea and so on in proportion. An advertisement detailing the names of subscribers had appeared in the local paper with a request for further support from the public and, the following week, more names were published.

At the meeting on the 8th, it was suggested that Mr. James Draper's other room be fitted up for the reception of the children, and four Visitors (Messrs. Deane, Lovegrove, Shepherd and Holmes) were appointed "till Lady Day next". However, by the following week, those Visitors were asked to remonstrate with Mr. Draper for repeatedly interrupting worship at the Society of Friends Church Street Meeting and, the week after that, the chairman was asked to write to him about his very improper conduct.

Despite such setbacks, the trial did prove successful, so the building of a school was settled upon, and the committee, meeting in the Council Chamber on April 13th, 1810, agreed to purchase a "Lot of Freehold ground containing more or less 45 feet in front and 150 feet in depth" for the sum of £150. Rev. Mr. Marsh and Messrs. Tanner and Ring then submitted to me and my committee Mr. Billing's plan following their meeting a fortnight later.

My bill for sundries amounting to £2 2. 8 was paid after the June 1st meeting. 15 gentlemen were appointed Trustees on 29th and I was then invited to Reading to deliver a lecture on "Wednesday the 11th, Monday the 16th or Wednesday the 18th of July". At the Committee meeting on 20th, it was agreed that the institution should be called The Reading Lancasterian School.

My Lancasterian Plan

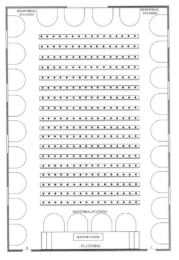

School buildings required certain features for my monitorial system to work. Children would sit on **wooden benches** (called forms) which ran across the classroom. The floor had to be slightly raised at one end so that the teacher could see the class and give commands. On those commands, the children would move to their **monitorial stations** around the room. Semi-circles marked on the floor showed the pupils where to stand so that they could each see their lesson. A **window would be above each station**, letting light in but not allowing the pupils to look

out and so distract them from their lessons.

My system depended on Monitors knowing what they were doing so they were tested before taking up their important position. By teaching others, their own learning was reinforced. Children would learn at their own rates and move on to the appropriate station for their next lesson at a given signal. They did not remain with the same class group for every subject. Children who learnt quickly progressed rapidly and became Monitors themselves.

21

Pupils were taught Reading, Writing and Arithmetic "in order to render them more useful members of society, without any reference whatsoever to sect or party in religious opinions". Lessons were hung on **wooden panelling** round the room at each station. Monitors would then run through the lesson with their pupils.

Boys at a Reading Station

It was important that each Monitor should have a continual eye over every one in the class under his/her care. I believe that the chief offences committed by youth at school arise from the liveliness of their active dispositions and that children cannot talk and learn at the same time. Therefore, when a boy is seen loitering his time in talking and idleness, then the Monitor is duty bound to lodge an accusation against him for misdemeanour. For that to be done silently, the Monitor has a number of **Printed Cards** such as:

"I have seen this boy idle",   "I have seen this boy talking".

Each card has the name of the particular class written on it so, when the defaulter presents it to the Head of School, as he must do, the name of the Monitor making the complaint is immediately known.

On a repeated or frequent offence, after admonition has failed, a **Wooden Log** weighing from four to six pounds is placed around the offender's neck and he is sent back to his seat. While it rests on his shoulders, the equilibrium is preserved, but on the least motion one way or the other, it is lost and the log acts as a dead weight. Thus, he is confined to sit in his proper position and go on with his work.

When logs are unavailable, the legs of offenders may be fastened together with **Wooden Shackles** – pieces of wood, mostly a foot long, sometimes six or eight inches, one or more according to the offence. When shackled, a boy can only walk in a slow measured pace, being obliged to take six steps when confined for two when at liberty. He is then ordered to walk round the school-room until tired out. When he is prepared to promise to behave more steadily in future, he is sent to his seat to continue his work. Should this punishment not have the desired effect, the left hand can be tied behind the

22

back or wooden shackles fastened from elbow to elbow behind the back. Sometimes the legs are tied together – an excellent punishment for boys who offend by leaving their seats to wander about the school-room.

Being a Quaker, I am opposed to any form of punishment that involves inflicting pain. Therefore, my **ultimate punishment** was **the Basket** where a boy was put in a basket or sack and winched to the ceiling where he remained suspended in sight of all pupils who smiled on him much as they would to a **Bird in a Cage**. The punishment was one of the most terrible that could be inflicted on boys of sense and abilities, the name of it being enough to deter Monitors from resorting to its use.

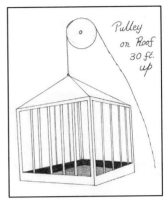

The Caravan was for frequent or old offenders who were yoked together, sometimes by a piece of wood that fastened round all their necks. Thus confined, they paraded the school, walking backwards – being obliged to pay very great attention to their footsteps, for fear of running against any object that might cause the yoke to hurt their necks, or to keep them from falling down. Four or six could be yoked together in this way.

When a boy is disobedient to his parents, profane in his language, has committed an offence against morality, or is remarkable for slovenliness, it is usual for him to be dressed up with **labels describing his offence** and a tin or paper cap put on his head. In that manner he walks round the school, two boys preceding him and proclaiming his fault, varying the proclamation according to the different offences.

Another punishment for slovenliness, when it seems to be the effect of habit rather than accident, is to appoint a girl to **wash the offender's face** in the sight of the whole school. This usually creates much diversion, especially when (as previously directed) she gives his cheeks a few gentle taps of correction with her hand. One punishment of this kind has kept the boys' faces clean for two years!

A **deterrent for truancy** that I found particularly useful was to pit 2 classes against each other. I bet a shilling against an old rusty nail with one of my subordinate monitors that the other class would excel in writing on the slate. Both classes exerted all their powers, including the truants who came to school to aid their companions in securing the honour, which was more than the prize. The most incorrigible boy became reformed and for the two years following that he remained with me, no more was heard of his playing truant.

That brings me to the issue of **Rewards**. Boys were proud to wear Monitors badges and also badges for good work and attendance. Annual Prize-giving days and treats were always anticipated with great excitement. Books and other items such as bats, balls and hoops were given as prizes.

My first lecture in the town

In fact it was Wednesday, August 29th before I could give a lecture to encourage supporters to give money to the cause. My letter, in which I had requested that the proper notice should be given to the public, had been read to the Committee on 24th. The following advertisement then appeared on the front page of *Monday, August 27, 1810 Reading Mercury*:

ROYAL BRITISH SYSTEM OF EDUCATION

JOSEPH LANCASTER, Inventor and Superintendent of the Plan for Educating poor Children under Patronage of the King, Queen, and Royal Family, intends to deliver a LECTURE on his new and original SYSTEM of EDUCATION, at the Town-Hall, Reading, on the evening of the day called Wednesday, 29th of 8th month, (August) at six o'clock – The object of this LECTURE is publicly to explain the manner in which one master may govern and teach one thousand children, with as much facility as twenty, in half the usual time, and at one third the common expence. The principle of order, the method whereby one book will serve for five hundred or one thousand children, and the manner in which five hundred scholars may spell at the instant of time, will be practically elucidated. Tickets to be had at the Printing-Office, price 2s. each, Front Seats – 1s. each, Back Seats.

On the day of the lecture, I also attended a Committee meeting, which was chaired by Mayor Charles Poulton. Mayor elect for 1810/11, William Blandy, was present along with four members of the clergy and 13 other gentlemen. I agreed to supply a master to organise the new school by the beginning of November and, afterwards, a permanent master with full qualifications.

24

Towards the end of October, Mr. Jasper Thos. Holmes wrote to remind me respecting the sending of a master for the new school as the children were being told to attend there on Wednesday, October 31st at 10 o'clock, the society's property having been removed from Mr. Draper's. I had to tell the Committee that I would be unable to send a master before the latter end of December so the children who had assembled on the 31st had been dismissed and it was resolved that the new school be opened on January 1st, 1811.

I was sent a copy of the following article from *December 17, 1810 Reading Mercury*, which showed that the two local Members of Parliament, Charles Shaw Lefevre and John Simeon, were supporting the cause most generously:

The Committee of the READING LANCASTRIAN SCHOOL have the pleasure of informing the Friends of that excellent Institution, and the Public, that the new Building is completed, and will be opened in the first week of January, (under the organisation of a Master immediately from Mr. Joseph Lancaster) for the reception of 350 Boys.

The purchase of the Freehold Land, the Erection of the School, the Inclosure of the Premises, &c. have occasioned an expenditure of about £650.

The following Benefactions and Subscriptions have been already received, and the further assistance of the public is earnestly solicited, as the Committee are desirous that the expenses should be met without touching the funded property, so liberally transferred by Edward Simeon, esq., the half-yearly dividends of which will most essentially subserve its future prosperity.

DONATIONS

Edward Simeon, esq. £500. 3 per Cents. Console standing in the names of Rev. Dr. Valpy, Rev. Wm. Marsh and T. Ring, esq. as Trustees.

	£	s		£	s
C.S. Lefevre, esq. M.P.	52	10	J.B. Monck, esq	10	10
John Simeon, esq, M.P.	26	5	Mr. Ring	10	10
Mr. John Deane	10	10	Dr. Salmon	10	10
Mr. French	10	10	Mr. Tyley	10	10
Mr. Harris	10	10	Rev. Dr. Valpy	10	10
Mr. Holmes	10	10	Mrs. English	5	0
Mr. Hooper	10	10	Mrs. Adams	2	2
Mr. Law	10	10	Rev. Dr. Davies	2	2
Mr. Letchworth	10	10	Rev. A. Douglas	2	2
J. E. Liebenrood, esq	10	10	Mr. Fenton	2	2
C. Lovegrove	10	10	Mr. John Harris	2	2
S. Maberley	10	10	Mr. Sheppard	2	2
Mr. Maddock	10	10	Sundry smaller Donations	3	10

There then followed a list of names of 83 Annual Subscribers of One Guinea of whom a quarter were ladies and some were pairs of people, viz. Messrs. Allaway and Osmond, Miss Chinner and Bewsey, Miss Huntley and Mother, Mr. Millard and Son. Mr. Austwick was detailed as donating two subs and J. B. Monck, Esq. five subs. Finally there was a reminder that:

> Every Benefactor of Ten Guineas, or Annual Subscriber of One Guinea, will be entitled to send two Boys.
>
> Subscriptions are received at the Reading Banks; by the Treasurer Mr. Holmes, Castle-Hill; or the Secretary, Rev. J Maude, in the Abbey; at which places the printed Regulations of this Charity may be had.
>
> Further Benefactions and Subscriptions will be published in this paper.

That spurred more people into action as in the *Saturday, December 29th edition of the Reading Mercury*, further donations of £10 10s and £5 0s and 24 Annual Subscriptions of One Guinea were acknowledged, one of the latter being for five subscriptions from Edward Golding, Esq.

Appointment of Nathaniel Higgins as the first Master

A letter from myself to the treasurer was read on January 4th at the first committee meeting of 1811. In it, I explained that I was sending Mr. Kenneth McRae to open and organise the school until such time as a permanent Master could be appointed. As a result, it was resolved that one guinea and a half should be allowed for Mr. McRae's board and lodging on the school's accounts while he remained in Reading. Even more importantly, it was stated that the school should open the following Tuesday (8th) at nine o'clock and that an advertisement to that effect should be inserted in the paper with a list of additional subscribers.

The first month seemed to go well as, at the February 15th meeting, it was agreed that Mr. McRae should be presented with twenty guineas and that the committee's approbation of his services in organising the school be expressed to him. Since Mr. Nathaniel Higgins, the candidate for the situation of Master was waiting, he was introduced and five questions were put to him:

1. Have you read the rules of the society?
2. Are you willing to comply with them?
3. The committee having resolved to allow the master a salary of seventy pounds per annum for his services, are you willing to undertake the management of the school for the above sum?

4. The committee having also resolved that the master for the time being is on no account whatever to receive either directly or indirectly any pecuniary recompense or gratuity from any of the parents, relatives or friends of the children introduced into the school, are you willing to comply with their resolution?
5. The committee having resolved that the master is to consider his salary as inclusive of every claim except the poundage on the annual subscriptions, are you willing to comply with their resolution?

When he responded in the affirmative to each question, he was told that his salary had commenced from the first day of the month of February.

At the Annual Meeting on March 29th, the Annual Report confirmed that the lowest estimate for the erection of a building to hold upwards of 300 children had been accepted and the structure completed ready for occupation by the end of October. However, it was the organisation of the school that had proved arduous for the committee so the two-month engagement of Mr. McRae, who had been involved in setting up similar schools before, had proved to be money well spent. Thanks were recorded to me for sending him and also for my proposing of Mr. Higgins, who had been engaged as superintendent before Mr. McRae had left Reading, it being recognised that I did not authorise those appointments, simply recommended them.

R.L.S. becomes British and Foreign School Society

That was my last real involvement with the Reading Lancasterian School because the Committee were able to manage the school themselves from then. Between 1798 and 1810, I had travelled 3,775 miles, advocating my views on schooling; delivering 67 lectures in the presence of 23,480 people and helping to form fifty new schools for 14,200 pupils. In 1814, the Royal Lancasterian Society changed its name to the British and Foreign School Society and schools were then established as far afield as New York, Philadelphia and Caracas. The legacy which I had set in motion was to affect the education of

READING BRITISH SCHOOL ESTABLISHED 1810

the poor in many towns in England and abroad for a long time to come. [This **original sign** was found during recent refurbishment work.]

As the *Reading Mercury of December 4, 1815* reported under *London News*:

> At the meeting of the friends and patrons of the British and Foreign School, held on Saturday at Freemason's Tavern, it was announced by Count Lieven that "the Emperor of Russia had given his unqualified approbation to the British system of education and directed it to be adopted throughout his dominions without delay."

Having had a dispute with the trustees of the British and Foreign School Society, I left it in 1816, feeling that I had been driven out of my own institution. I attempted to form my own school in Tooting but it failed and I ended up bankrupt. After imprisonment for debt, I emigrated to America in 1818 to view the progress of my methods in schools in Boston, New York City, and Philadelphia. I tried to establish a school in Baltimore, but was prevented by my failing health from making it financially viable. I published a small book: *The Lancasterian System of Education* in 1821, having previously published two books explaining my teaching methods:

1803: *Improvements in Education* and

1810: *Report of Joseph Lancaster's Progress from 1798*, which revealed that, of the 7,000 children I'd educated not one had become a Quaker.

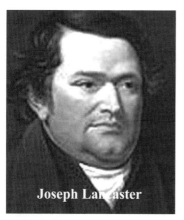

Joseph Lancaster

Having seen my system in operation and sending two Venezuelan teachers to be educated in it, President Simón Bolìvar had invited me to observe the Lancasterian model school set up in Caracas, Venezuela, promising $20,000 for the education of the children of the city so I went there for a couple of years from 1825 to 1827 in the hopes that the warmth would enable me to regain my health. Although I married there with Bolivar presiding over the wedding, I eventually left after falling out with him over the non-payment of the promised sum.

A number of schools using my system had been established in Lower Canada before I settled there in 1828 but, when I opened another in Montreal, my attempts to obtain funding floundered, so I returned to the United States.

II. Trustee's Tale: THOMAS LETCHWORTH 1809–1839

I was a Quaker belonging to the Reading and Warborough Monthly Meeting at the time that great interest was being expressed in Joseph Lancaster's ideas for the education of poor children in 1809. I was very interested in finding out more about his methods so offered my house in Reading for an initial meeting on August 27th, prior to his lecture on the 29th. 14 of us had been present then and, at our subsequent meeting on September 1st, I was one of 30 gentlemen named to serve on the Committee. The next meeting I attended was on 29th when 14 of us heard that Mr. Draper, who had been consulted by the Committee as his plan of education was similar to Mr. Lancaster's, had offered to instruct 100 children for one year on Mr. Lancaster's plan. We accepted his offer and detailed Messrs. Deane, Maberley and Austwick to arrange the business with him. They then called a meeting for October 16th when a proposal from Mr. Draper was read and it was agreed that it should be acceded to for one year and that he should be allowed a cauldron of coals for the use of the school. It was also resolved that each subscriber of £1. 1. 0 per annum be allowed a boy so long as they did not send any under 6 years of age.

On the 30th day of the tenth month, the Committee for conducting the Education of the Poor heard that:

James Draper engages to teach (or cause to be taught) a number of children not exceeding one hundred, in English reading, writing and arithmetic, for one year from the date hereof, for the sum of one hundred guineas, payable one quarter in advance. The committee engage to defray the fitting up of desks (becoming their property, which they will be at liberty to remove), increase of light & other reasonable preparations for the accommodation of the above number of children, and the reinstatement of alterations at the end of the year (or other more or less extended term) if required so to do by the said James Draper.

Slate 1st year 1.0   *Slates, pencils, pens, books and*
Pencils " " -.6   *rewards, not exceeding 5/6 each boy for*
Books " " 1.6   *the year, are to be furnished by the*
Rewards 2.6   *Committee to James Draper.*
     S 5.6

Should any additional Room be required other than that under the immediate and now leasehold occupation of James Draper the committee must engage to pay the charge thereof. Coals being an expensive article in the winter season – 'tis hoped a reasonable and moderate consumption thereof will be supplied by the committee. James Draper.

To give some idea of prices in Reading during years 1809 – 1815, the price of a gallon loaf [3] ranged from 1s. 7d. to 3s. 2d. but, during 1812, the price never fell below 2s. 6d. and, from October 1812 to July 1813, it was 3s. Meat was relatively cheaper – beef, mutton and bacon costing from 6d. to 1s. – 'though bacon occasionally rose to 1s. 6d., whereas butter cost 1s. 3d. to 1s. 9d. per pound. In July 1816, potatoes were 4d. per gallon and beer 5d. or 6d. a quart (though it became much cheaper after 1831 Beer Act). Herrings cost 3d. a dozen when plentiful. Price of Tea varied from 7s. to 14s. per pound in Reading in 1814 but from 5s. 6d. to 6s. in 1826. It was frequently remarked that provisions were dearer in Reading than Newbury. In 1813, candles cost 15s. 6d. per dozen and a long spell of frost, by closing the water-ways, would send the price of coal up to 52s. or 68s. per chaldron. House rent for a wage-earner was estimated at 2s. 6d. weekly in 1815 and 3s. to 3s. 6d. in 1833. [4]

At the meeting in the Town Hall on November 14th, it was requested that Rev. Mr. Stewart act on the Committee, Rev. Mr. Maude be secretary and Mr. Ring write to Edward Simeon Esq. to ascertain his wish and intention respecting the appropriation of the £500 stock. We agreed to act on the engagement with Mr. Draper as a preparatory plan for a school of 500 or more children on the principles of Mr. Lancaster at the meeting held at 10 o'clock on Tuesday 21st in the Council Chamber. Mr. Holmes was appointed treasurer and instructed to advance to Mr. Draper twenty six pounds five shillings for one quarter according to agreement. Mr. Ring was requested to acquaint Mr. Simeon with the appointment of Mr. Marsh as Trustee and other committee proceedings, including the appointment of Messrs. Douglas, Tanner and Lovegrove as a sub. committee to draw up an address to the public on the proposed plan.

I was unable to be at the committee meeting the following day at 12 o'clock at the Town Hall but was soon informed that I had been appointed to distribute said address after its adoption at that meeting. Messrs. Holmes, Tanner and Fenton were to distribute it for the St. Mary's Parish; Messrs. Deane, Hooper and myself for St. Lawrence and Messrs. Lovegrove, Maberley and Law for St. Giles. The following was sent from that meeting:

To the Worshipful the Mayor, the Aldermen and Burgesses of the Borough of Reading
Gentlemen
    The committee chosen for establishing a large charity school in this town on

---

[3] A gallon loaf weighed 8 pounds 11 ounces and was called the half-peck loaf
[4] W.M. Childs: *The Town of Reading during the early part of the Nineteenth Century*

Mr. Lancaster's Plan having resolved that the Mayor & Corporation be applied unto respectfully soliciting their countenance & co-operation in so laudable an undertaking this request is now made in their name. They beg leave to observe they have deferred making this communication till they themselves are satisfied with the practicability of carrying it into effect. The favour of an answer will very much oblige.

      By order of the Committee, your obedient servant

         Signed Jasper Thomas Holmes

            Treasurer

                    November 22nd, 1809.

Sponsoring the first boys

I had proposed to sponsor Josiah George (born 1801 in Reading) very early on and, in fact, his was the 4th name entered on the School Register on the first admission date recorded – November 27th. My son, Thomas, recommended John Rider (born 1804 in Reading) on 28th so his was the 12th on the register:

School Register

Date of Admission 1809	Names	By whom recommended
Nov 27	Henry Slaughter	Rev. J. Maude
	Thomas Wickes	Mr. Maberley
	John Pecover	Rev. A. Douglas
	Josiah George	**Mr. Letchworth**
	William Cox	Mr. Tanner
	Richard Harper	Mr. Shotter
28	Henry Bowden	Mr. J. Deane
	Thos Crop	Rev. W. Marsh
	John Willis	Dr. Salmon
	John Moore	Rev. Dr. Valpy
	Chas Davis	Mr. Law
	John Rider	**Mr. Letchworth junr**
	Thos Castle	Mr. Holmes
29	Josh Spraggs	Mr. Lovegrove
	Saml Stanmore	Mr. Saml. Williams
	John Pocock	Mr. K. Harris
	James Hales	Mr. Greenwood
Nov 29 continued	Thos Monkhouse	Mr. Austwick
	David Bushnell	Mr. Fenton
	John Symmons	Mr. Mitchell

Date of Admission 1809	Names	By whom recommended
30 Dismissed Jan 13, 1810	George White	Mr. Jackson
	Richd Hackley	Mrs. Bevington
	Wm Hackley	Mr. John Harris
	Wm Alloway	A Friend
	Robt Bailey	Mr. Ring
	Wm Lovell	Mr. Maul
Dec 1	Wm Parrott	Mr. B. Simmonds
	Wm Allen	Mr. Simmonds
2	James Hodges	Mr. Stratton
	Wm Hodges	Mrs. Jones
	James Monkhouse	(2) Mr. Austwick
	Peter Lovegrove	Mr. H. Deane
	George Gregory	(2) Mr. Maberley
	Abraham Parry	Rev. Dr. Davies
	Robt Sherwood	Mr. Maddock
4	Charles Parker	Mr. C. Maude
	George Baskerville	Rev. J. Young
	James Shade	(2) Mr. J. Deane
	Jesse Herbert	Mr. Biggs
	Thos Pearce	Mr. French
	James Collier	(2) Mr. Maddock
	George Kift	Mr. J. Newbury
5	John Hodgson	Mrs. Willats
	James Pink	Mrs. Harries
	Wm Evans	Mrs. Mabnab
	Edwd Lovejoy	Mrs. Hooper
	Richd Flower	Mr. Lawrence
6	Wm Brown	Mrs. Adams
	Thos Fidler	Mr. Monck
	Thos Davis	(2) D^o
	David Marshall	(3) D^o
	James Parr	(4) D^o
	George Silver	(5) D^o
	Ambrose Webb	Mr. Stephens
	Isaac Church	Mr. Watkins
7	Thos Pilgrim	Rev. H. Gauntlett
	Thos Brown	Mrs. Mary Deane
	James Ryder	Mr. John Sutton
	Richd Simmonds	A Lady
12	Joseph Allen	Mr. Billing

Date of Admission 1809	Names	By whom recommended
13	John Bond	Mr. Westbrook
	John May	Mr. James Sutton
	John Townsend	Mr. Harbert
14	John Allen	Mr. Wm Stephens
	John Barry	Mrs. Cowslade
18	James Weller	Mr. Billing
	Robt Hall Stevens	Mr. Golding
	John Lockston	Mr. Shepherd
	Wm Waite	(2) Mr. Billing
Drowned	James North	Mr. Liebenrood
19	Henry Wheeler	Mrs. Liebenrood
	Josh Silver	Capt. Bolton
22	Henry Parker	Mrs. Blandy
	George Chappel	(3) Mr. Billing
29	John Walker	Mr. Richardson
1810		
Jan 1	Samuel Ford	Mrs. Johnson
2	Wm Chesterman	Mr. Jas. Tagg
5	Wm Williams	Mr. Douglas
9	Saml Ibbots	Mr. McConnell
	Wm Hudson	Mr. Stacy
17	Francis Saunders	Rev. J. H. Stewart
	Wm Baker	Mr. Tiley
26	Wm Carter	Mr. Fergusson
29	Richd Brittain	Rev. Mr. Thompson

Space for Remarks had been left by the side of each name but only two were entered during the Trial – George White (admitted November 30th) was dismissed January 13th, 1810 and James North (December 18th) drowned. Although, on December 8th, it was being suggested that Mr. Draper's other room be fitted up for the reception of the children, by the following week, the four Visitors, who had all been appointed on the 8th "till Lady Day next" – Messrs. Deane, Lovegrove, Shepherd and Holmes – were asked to remonstrate with Mr. Draper relative to the impropriety of his conduct in the religious assembly of the Friends in the Borough and the following week, the chairman was asked to write to him about his very improper conduct:

Sir,
The Committee for managing the Free School established in the Town, having
received Information that you James Draper the Master have repeatedly
interrupted the Society of Friends worshipping in Church Street Meeting and

33

knowing that subscriptions to this excellent Institution have been withheld in consequence, beg to inform you, that they very highly disapprove of such conduct, and that if you persist in this improper behaviour and it should produce inconvenience to the Society, and the Interference, which is to be expected, of the Civil Powers, they will consider their engagement with you at an end and think it their duty to appoint another Master.

Thos. Ring (Chairman)

Henry Finch Letchworth (Hannah's and my 6-year-old grandson) was already being taught by Mr. Draper at the time of the Trial Run for the Lancasterian School as our son Thomas had chosen his private school in Portland Place for the lad. Henry became friendly with fellow pupil, William Silver Darter [5] so I was able to question the lads about their education.

At the third Committee meeting in 1810 – held January 19th in Town Hall – a letter from Mr. Lancaster was read, in which he stated that it would be some time, probably a month, before he could leave London. Edward Simeon's letter was similarly read at February 9th meeting in the Council Chamber:

Salvador House 7 February, 1810

My dear Sir
 I have this day transferred into the joint names of
   Revd. Dr. Richard Valpy }
   Revd. William Marsh } Reading
   Thomas Ring Esq.   } Berks
Five Hundred Pounds Consols for the benefit of the Free School on Mr. Lancaster's Plan and herewith I send you an order on Messrs. Hepherns & Co. for L6.15 being the Dividend due thereon.
 It will give me sincerest pleasure to hear that this grand undertaking is attended with complete success.
 I beg you will make the above communication to the Committee, & believe me ever.

My Dear Sir
Most faithfully yours
E. Simeon

Thos. Ring Esq.

At February 23rd meeting in Council Chamber, it was resolved that the small temporary Schoolroom belonging to Mr. Draper be filled up with Boys to the

---

[5] He attended a commercial and classical school in Chain Street 1811 – 1818, become an Alderman then Mayor of Reading 1850 – 52 then later wrote *Octogenarian* articles

number of 105 and, in fact, 114 boys were eventually admitted to the Trial, the last being admitted on September 20th. Since 85 boys had been admitted by the beginning of February, a closer note was then kept of numbers:

Date of Admission 1810	Names	No	By whom recommended
Jan 29	Francis Knighton	85	Mrs. S Adams
Feb 1	M. Hills		(4) Mr. Billing
5	Wm. Baggs		Mr. Musgrove Lamb
8	Ephraim Marshall		Miss Taylor
	Saml. Justice		(2) Do
	Geo. Walden	90	Mr. Wm. Blandy
15	John Castle		Mr. Hetherington
17	George Higgs		Mrs. Cummings
	John Roberts		Mr. Jackson
21	John Shade		Hon. Mrs. Cadogan
	Joseph Wood	95	Mr. Henry Simmonds
23	Edwin Poole		Mr. Body
	Wm. Barry		(5) Mr. Billing
	Wm. Ford		}
	Joseph Cockram		}
	George Russel	100	} By The
	William Witt		}
	John Blackman		} Committee
	Wm. Simpson		}
	Richd. Martin		}
March 3	James Lambden	105	Mr. Dorset
5	James Brown		The Committee
15	Wm. Silver		Mr. Bulley
16	Charles Spackman		The Committee
May 14	John Turner		Mr. Billing
July 18	John Kift	110	Rev. H Gauntlett
	John Shackle		Mr. Liebenrood
21	James Wells		Mr. Stephens
August	John Qwelch		Miss Blain
Sept 20	Benjamin Mason		Mrs. Cummings

Location, location, location

When once the Trial was underway and seemed to be progressing well, the Committee spent much of the early part of 1810 searching for a suitable

35

location for the proposed school. The Abbey had been offered by March 9th and, after consideration of that and several other places thought suitable by the subcommittee, those present at the meeting in the Council Chambers on 30th adjourned to Silver Street in order to view that situation.

Mr. Ring reported on April 6th that, as a result of an interview with the Corporation, he had discovered that they had committed themselves to advertising for tenders for the Silver Street building so were ready to receive one from the committee. Katesgrove master builder, brick-maker and architect, Richard Billing, was therefore asked to look at it and report on its value. Another letter had to be sent to James Draper, reprimanding him for his frequent absence from the school and Messrs. Lovegrove, Deane, Fenton, Shepherd and Shotter were appointed Visitors for the ensuing quarter.

At that time, the only buildings of height and mass in Reading were the  Abbey Ruins; the parish churches of St. Mary, St. Lawrence & St. Giles; the Episcopal Chapel of St. Mary in Castle Street; the Baptist Chapel in Hosier Street; Independent Chapel, Broad Street; the Friends' Meeting House, Church Lane & the Catholic Chapel in Vastern Lane. The Town Hall, erected 1785–6, had **Reading School (formerly Hospitium of St. John)** adjoining it. Other schools included: 17th century Blue Coat School at the corner of Silver Street and New Street; Green Girls' School (founded 1782 in St. Mary's Butts, had moved to Broad Street in 1790) and Mrs. Cadogan's School of Industry for poor girls was established in Friar Street in 1802. The poor-house of St. Mary's parish was in Pinckney's Lane [now Coley Street]; that of St. Giles' in Horn Street and St. Lawrence's in Friar Street. The Water Tower by St. Giles' Mills in Mill Lane; County Gaol & the Oracle in Minster Street completed the picture.

It was on April 13th in the Council Chamber that the committee agreed to purchase the Lot of Freehold ground offered by Mr. Warwick on the part of Mr. Davidson, containing more or less 45 feet in front and 150 feet in depth for the sum of £150. I discovered at 4 o'clock meeting the following Friday that a deposit of £15 had been advanced by Mr. Ring as the treasurer was directed to repay that sum to him when the papers relative to the purchase of Mr. Davidson's land were committed to him. It was reiterated that a brick building capable of containing 300 boys and 150 girls should be erected, with Messrs. Holmes and Ring enquiring into a possible opening into Silver Street. Mr. Billing's plan was submitted to Mr. Lancaster and his committee for their opinion, and to Messrs. Maberley and Deane following the meeting on 27th.

Mr. Draper's third quarter salary of £26 5s. was advanced as a result of the May 25th meeting when Messrs. Holmes, Tanner & Fenton were requested:

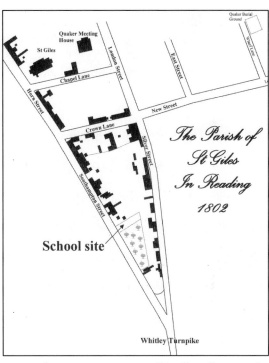

> to wait on the Mayor to obtain use of the Barn in Silver Street in order to make it suitable for the school and to take measures for removing the fixtures belonging to the committee at Lancasterian School.

Of the ten of us present in the Council Chamber on June 12th, Messrs. Jasper T. Holmes, Shepherd, Shotter, Watkins and myself – were elected as a Committee to enquire into the boys' progress at the School and its general management so a Reading Lancastrian School Logbook was started July 27th, 1810 and Mr. Ring was requested to write to Messrs. Fox and Lancaster respecting a plan for the new School and further regulations.

Deed of Trust for The Reading Lancasterian School

Although I was not present at the meeting held on June 29th, it was then that I was appointed a Trustee for the land and buildings with the Mayor and thirteen others. Mr. Ring had reported that Mr. Warwick, as agent for

Mr. Davidson, was ready to convey the land as soon as the writings could be drawn up so Mr. Holmes was requested to confer with Messrs. Blandy and Saunders who were to be employed as the solicitors for that purpose.

By July 20th, a sub. committee appointed on 13th (as a result of the solicitor's suggestion that some rules be inserted in the Deed of Trust that was about to be made of the land and school house to be thereon erected) gave their ideas of some rules which should be submitted at a general meeting of the subscribers for their approbation. I was present at that general meeting of the subscribers on 27th when 16 of us, including three clergy, agreed unanimously to the adoption of the seven rules which had been severally moved and seconded. They then appeared in *July 30, 1810 Reading Mercury*, as follows:

READING LANCASTERIAN SCHOOL

At a general Meeting of the Subscribers held in the Council Chamber, on the 27th inst. J.E. LIEBENROOD, Esq. in the Chair,

It was unanimously resolved,

1. That this Institution shall be called THE READING LANCASTERIAN SCHOOL, the object of which is to educate poor children gratuitously.
2. That the Freehold Land in Southampton-street, and Building to be erected thereon, be vested in the following names, in trust, for this Institution, and when the number shall be reduced to five, a new Trust Deed shall be executed, and the vacancies filled up by, and chosen from the Subscribers at large:-

     The Mayor of Reading, for the time being,

Messrs. Edward Simeon	John Stephen
John Berkeley Monck	Thos. Ring
J. T. Holmes	J. E. Liebenrood
Edw. Law	Thos. Letchworth
Robert Harris	Blackall Simonds
J. S. Jackson	Rev. Dr. Valpy
Wm. Marsh	Archibald Douglas

3. That the entire management of the Charity shall be in a Committee of twenty-one, to be chosen annually; and that five of the Committee be competent to act.
4. That a Treasurer and Secretary be chosen annually.
5. That Subscribers of one Guinea per annum may always have one child or more in the School, and so in proportion to every Guinea subscribed.
6. That a Benefaction of ten Guineas, at one time, shall constitute a Member for life, with the privileges of an annual Subscriber of one guinea, and so in proportion for every ten guineas.

7. That an annual Meeting of the Subscribers be held on the first Friday after the twenty fifth of March, for auditing the accounts, and to choose a Treasurer, Secretary, and Committee.

Resolved,
That a School be erected on the Land purchased in Southampton-street, capable of containing 300 children.
That Subscriptions and Donations be requested of the public, and received at the Reading Banks, and by Mr. Holmes, the Treasurer.
That another general Meeting of the Subscribers and Friends to the Institution be holden on Friday, Aug. 3, at 12 o'clock, to adopt the best plan, that may be offered for the Building.
　　　　　　Signed, J.E. LIEBENROOD
Resolved, That the Thanks of the Meeting be given to the Chairman, for his attention to the business of the day.

You will see that, among the 14 other Trustees appointed with me, was Rev. Dr. Valpy who had moved to Reading in 1781 when, as Rev. Richard Valpy, he was appointed to the headmastership of Reading School. His degree of Doctor of Divinity had been bestowed in 1792 after he had gone on to devote his life to turning round that school and improving its reputation.

The other clergy were: Rev. Archibald Douglas (1769 – 1839) who had come to Reading in 1796 as Minister of the Broad Street Independent Church, and William Marsh D.D. (born July 20, 1775) who eloquently preached his first sermon at **St. Lawrence** at Christmas 1800. "That evangelical young Marsh", as the Vicar of Basingstoke called him, was a friend and disciple of Mr. Cadogan, the famous Vicar of St. Giles, who had passed away three years earlier. Those were the days of pluralities in the Church, and Mr. Marsh, in addition to his curacy, accepted the two small livings of Nettlebed and the adjoining parish, the gift of that liberal-minded Roman Catholic patron, Mr. Stonor. The Catholic Squire and the ultra-Protestant Vicar became warm friends, the latter staying at Mr. Stonor's on his

39

frequent visits to the parish. When Dr. Marsh occupied the pulpit of St. Lawrence's during the eleven years of his curacy there, the fine old Parish Church was crammed to the doors, for his was a ministry of spiritual power, happily combined with a gentle winsomeness and unselfish devotion. "Most heavenly-minded of men" was the description given of him by Charles Simeon. He left Reading in 1811.

At the next general meeting of the subscribers on August 3rd, Messrs. Holmes, Fenton and Deane who had been appointed at July 27th meeting to superintend the building and obtain a plan and estimate of the same, had their plan and specifications adopted. The treasurer was asked to pay Mr. Draper his quarter salary commencing July 30th but to withhold the payment of the remaining £13. 15s. 0d, being a majority of the cost of slates, books etc. until the end of the quarter when they were to be bought up by the society. An advertisement was then placed in *August 6th Reading Mercury*:

TO BUILDERS
It is intended to erect a Building for the LANCASTRIAN SCHOOL: – A Plan and Particulars may be seen at Mr. Holmes's, Castle-Hill. Estimates for the whole, or the different parts of the Building to be sent, sealed up, on or before Saturday the Eleventh instant.
Reading, Aug. 4, 1810

Saturday was a normal working day at that time and, by 13th, sealed estimates from Messrs. Elisha; Thos. Jones; Cooper & Sons; Billing & Sons and W. Winter were being considered. The lowest quote – that of Cooper & Sons – was the one accepted, with the request that the building be completed in two months from that date! Messrs Law & Stoppard were added to sub committee.

Mr. Lancaster attended the Wednesday 29th meeting when the Mayor (Charles Poulton) and Mayor-elect (William Blandy), four clergy and thirteen other Committee members, including myself, were present following his public lecture that day. He affirmed the committee of their cordial co-operation at the meeting, and engaged to supply a proper master by the beginning of November to organise the new school and afterwards one of full qualifications as permanent master. Also at that meeting, Mr. Ring and myself were requested to collect money from the general public in St. Lawrence's parish, as were others for St. Giles' and St. Mary's, to provide a fund to pay for the land and buildings as the generosity of local philanthropist, Edward Simeon, and Committee members, had not provided enough money:

St. Lawrence's	St. Giles'	St. Mary's
Mr. Letchworth	Ald. Blandy	Mr. Tanner
Mr. Ring	Mr. Hooper	Mr. Holmes
	Mr. Stephens	J. B. Monck Esq.

John Berkeley Monck had come to Reading in 1796. When his father died in 1809, he had inherited a fortune of £100,000, which enabled him to become a philanthropist and reformer, and buy **Coley House** in 1810 [6]. A magistrate, poet & sportsman, he stood for parliament in 1812, was eventually elected in 1820 & served until 1830. He died in 1834 but his descendants

Coley House c1823

also turned out to be particularly interested in education. [7]

Mr Lancaster's expenses of £3. 15. were allowed at the meeting on September 7th. On 24th, the sub committee reported that there had to be a slight deviation from the original plan for the better security of the roof. Mr. Draper was up to his tricks until the last it seems as, at the October 12th meeting, Mr. Holmes was requested to inform Mr. John Perry that the committee had nothing to do with the bill delivered by him for work done by order of Mr. Draper. Also, at that meeting, Messrs. Tanner, Holmes and Deane were appointed as a subcommittee for the drawing out of a plan of internal regulations for the new school. By the 19th, a further generous donation of fifty guineas in favour of Reading Lancasterian School had been received from Charles Shaw Lefevre.

At the November 9th meeting, Mr. Holmes reported that Mr. Lancaster could not send a master before the latter end of December, so the children, who had assembled, according to order, at the new school on Wednesday 31st had been

---

6 now part of the Berkshire Independent Hospital (formally Capio Private Hospital)

7 his son, John Bligh Monck was elected onto Reading Board Schools Com; grandson, William Berkeley Monck, mayor in 1887 & 1897, was Education Committee chair

dismissed. The committee therefore concentrated on developing rules for the school's internal management, which were read and approved on 23rd and referred to the meeting a week later for confirmation, recording, then printing and circulating of a sufficient number of copies.

The rules of the Reading Lancasterian School

1. That a school master be appointed.
2. That the committee shall at each monthly meeting, which shall be the last Thursday in the month, appoint two inspectors or visitors for each week in the ensuing month, who shall attend at least twice in the week at the school room for the purpose of ascertaining the progress made by the children in their learning. These visitors, after having received the master's report shall enter any remarks they may deem proper in a book to be kept for the purpose; these remarks are to be signed by them and are to be laid monthly before the committee.
3. That no book of instruction be introduced into the school, but the *Holy Scriptures* (without comments), extracts therefrom, Watt's *Hymns for Children* and lessons in spelling and arithmetic.
4. That children of five years old and upwards be received by a written recommendation from a subscriber, who shall state the name, age and residence of the same and, as it is desirable the small schools already in the Town should be injured as little as possible, it is hoped that such children will be selected whose parents are unable to provide them education.
5. That the recommendation for the admission of children be sent to the secretary or treasurer.
6. That no child be admitted with any infectious disorder; and the parents are required to send them each day washed, combed and decent in their appearance; for neglect of which (if persisted in) the child to be dismissed.
7. That, if any child be dismissed for improper behaviour or other causes (after suitable admonition), the subscriber who represented him shall be immediately informed thereof, that the vacancy may be filled up.
8. That the children attend the school from the first day of November to the twenty fifth day of March, from nine to twelve o'clock in the morning, and from two till four in the afternoon; and from the twenty fifth day of March to the first day of November from eight to twelve in the morning, and from two to five in the afternoon. That Saturday afternoon be considered a half holiday and that there be two vacations in the year; the first two weeks in August and two weeks at Christmas.
9. That, on the children's going from school, both morning & afternoon, master and monitors do attend them to the corner of Crown Lane in Southampton Street, from whence they are to go quietly to their respective homes.

42

10. That the school be open at all times during school hours to visitors, introduced by a subscriber.
11. That the annual subscriptions be collected by the master, who shall pay them into the hands of the treasurer and be allowed sixpence in the pound.
12. That the object of the institution being solely to instruct the children in reading, writing and arithmetic, thereby rendering them more useful members of society, without any reference whatsoever to sect or party in religious opinions, it is expected their parents and friends will see they attend some place of Divine Worship of the Lord's Day.
13. That the committee, for any just cause, may remove the schoolmaster, upon giving him two months' notice in writing. And if the master should at any time be desirous of leaving his situation, he shall be at liberty to do so upon giving similar notice to the committee.
14. That if any additional regulation should be thought necessary for the better management of the school, the same shall, previous to its being acted upon, be submitted to, and approved by a majority of the subscribers, specially convened for the purpose.

Dated this day 30th November 1810

Also at the meeting on 23rd, Messrs. Holmes, Douglas and Deane were appointed as a subcommittee for carrying into effect the agreement made with Mr. Davison relevant to a fence between his ground and that belonging to the school and also for making a fence at the front. A bill for L4. 16. 11. was paid to the glazier, Thomas Behoe, following December 7th meeting and, on 14th, the Treasurer was asked to write again to Mr. Lancaster about his sending a Master for the School. The Collectors from the three parishes had reported and, as a result, an advertisement detailing the Donations and Subscribers was drawn up for the Reading paper. Following the meeting on 21st, Mr. Ring was requested to write to John Simeon Esq. to thank him for his handsome donation of 25 guineas to Reading Lancasterian School and the collectors (myself included) were requested to continue their collections until 28th, after which a list of additional donations & subscriptions was put in the next paper.

The first Annual Meeting

A letter from Mr. Lancaster was read at the first meeting in 1811 – on January 4th – informing the treasurer that he had sent Mr. Kenneth McRae to open and organise the school. The 8 there resolved that one guinea & a half be allowed for the board and lodging of Mr. McRae per week during his continuance at

43

Reading on the school's account. Naturally, though, as well as support, there was also opposition to the school. The *January 5th Reading Mercury* alluded to that when, after giving notice of the opening of the Lancasterian School the following Tuesday (8th) at nine o'clock for those Children who had Tickets and detailing a further eleven subscribers' names, the following was stated:

> It is gratifying to add that the prejudice entertained against those most excellent Institutions for the Education of the Poor are gradually giving way and that the highest Characters in the kingdom, both in Church and State, are encouraging them. With pleasure we present the following extract from the London papers: "The Archbishop of Canterbury has become a subscriber to the Lancastrian School recently established in the town of Leeds. The Duke and his Lady are also contributing to the same Institution."

At the meeting on 11th, Mr. Billing's bill was paid by the Treasurer, after various deductions pointed out by the sub committee had been made. The committee also thankfully accepted Mr. Holmes' offer of the use of a **Buzaglo** [8]. The Treasurer was requested to pay on February 1st, £16. 4. 11 to Mr. Lancaster for articles for the school and the balance due to James Draper. He reported on 8th that there appeared to be a probable deficiency of £300, independent of funded property, so we determined to consider ways of covering that.

On March 8th, the Treasurer was directed to pay Mrs. Jane East at the rate of one guinea and a half per week for nine weeks for the board and lodging of Mr. McRae while he was organising the school and, on 22nd, Mr. Ring reported that he had settled same with her. It was resolved that an advertisement be inserted in the next Reading paper giving notice of the subscribers' Annual General Meeting on 29th inst. for the purpose of receiving the report, auditing accounts and electing committee, Treasurer and Secretary for the ensuing year. A list of Subscribers' names was also to be prepared against that meeting in order to elect 21 to serve on the new committee.

The Master, Mr. Higgins, who had been appointed February 15th, and fourteen Committee members were present at the first Annual Meeting on March 29th.

---

[8] Buzaglo stoves, patented in 1765 by a Moroccan, Abraham Buzaglo, who had moved to London in 1760, were intended for the heating of large public buildings

Mr. Shepherd presented a report summarising the happenings of the previous year, including the fact that Mr. McRae had organised similar schools in various parts of the Kingdom. He said that we:

> had been taught wisdom from the embarrassment, discouragement and expense which the subscribers had been subjected to through Mr. Draper and, although they thought that they were unlikely to meet with his equal in subtlety and impertinence, they were fully convinced that clear and cautious understanding was important when entering upon an engagement with a new teacher. They therefore felt that the appointment of visitors, who were to attend the school twice a week to keep a vigilant eye on attendance and orderliness, were most important.

All those who had held office throughout the previous year were thanked and Mr. Holmes was requested to continue in his office of Treasurer; Rev. Joseph Maude as Secretary and twenty-one gentlemen were voted onto the Committee for the ensuing year. It was considered desirable that E. Simeon's donation of £500 stock be preserved as a permanent fund and that £400 be raised within the following month at either of the Reading Banks or at Mr. Holmes the Treasurer as a voluntary loan free of interest in shares of £5 each to be repaid annually by lot out of the surplus of subscriptions.

Reading's population had increased by just over 1,000 to 10,788 by the 1811 Census (Monday, May 27th). At the meeting held on 30th, the visitors reported that the school was going on exceedingly well. Messrs. Law, Lamb, Holmes, Shepherd and Fenton were appointed as a committee for arranging a procession of the Children through the town on June 4th, being the King's birthday. W. S. Darter recalled [9] in his *1880s Reading Observer* articles:

> I remember that in the year 1810 the Lancastrian School in Southampton Street was built, and in the following year the children were paraded down London Street with the usual demonstrations of joy. David Fenton Esq., a gentleman then living in Castle Street, appeared to take great interest in this movement; but since his time the name of the school has been changed to the 'British School.' If I mistake not, the gentleman here referred to was great-grandfather of the Allnatts of the present day.

At June 27th committee meeting, Messrs. Law and Lamb reported on the school's good order and the master's conduct. However, two boys of the name of Gardner, who had been repeatedly admonished by Master and Visitors, were to be discharged on any future improper behaviour. Considerable

---

[9] which were later published in book form in his *Reminiscences of Reading*

inconvenience had also been experienced from the Chalk Floor so they were asked to obtain by the next meeting, an estimate of the expense of **bricking the paths**. A bill from Mr. Lancaster amounting to £5.3.2 was to be paid.

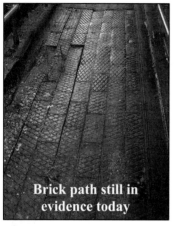

Brick path still in evidence today

On July 25th, go-ahead was given for the floor to be done during the next vacation, along with any other matters that the Visitors deemed necessary and, sure enough, the brick flooring and sundry works were completed by Mr. Cooper by August 29th. It was resolved on September 26th that any boy, who frequently stayed away from school, should be sent by the Master to the subscriber who nominated him so that he might be reproached, then a note could be sent from the subscriber to the boy's parents. At the end of November, the Master was directed to collect the annual subscriptions after an advertisement was placed in the Reading paper announcing to the Friends of the Institution that the Master would call upon them for those.

The success of the British School in educating the poor had led in 1811 to the formation in Reading of a branch of the National Society for promoting the education of the poor in the principles of the Church of England; and on September 6th, 1813, an elementary day-school for boys and girls was opened in two rooms within the walls of the great hall of the Abbey. During the discussion period for the setting up of this National School in Reading, we had inserted in *January 30th, 1812 Reading Mercury*:

> The Committee for managing the Lancasterian School in this Town have heard with pleasure that a general wish is expressed that religious instruction should form a part of the system. Adopting this sentiment in the fullest degree they earnestly request the Clergy of the three Parishes and the Dissenting Ministers to cooperate in this Plan and suggest to the several Gentlemen the propriety of summoning the Boys belonging to their several congregations to attend them once a week for religious instruction.

The Annual General Meeting of the Subscribers was held in the Town Hall on Thursday 26th since the last Friday in March 1812 was Good Friday. It was:

> Resolved that further Subscriptions to the Free Loan be requested in order that the balance due to the Treasurer be immediately paid.

Resolved that in consideration of the faithful & diligent services of Mr. Higgins, the Master, that his salary be augmented from seventy to eighty pounds per annum to commence from the first day of February last.

Resolved that Messrs Law, Lawrence, Fisher, Fenton & Shepherd be a Committee for arranging a procession of the Children through the Town on the 4th June being the King's Birthday.

When the *Reading Mercury* reported on the latter on the 8th, it was mentioned that nearly 300 boys were being educated at Reading Lancasterian School.

The Visitors reported on November 26th that two boys, who had been found guilty of stealing some potatoes, had been punished by the Master. However, their father had afterwards called at the school and exceedingly abused the Master, who had then suspended their attendance at school. Approving the Master's conduct, the Committee dismissed the two boys entirely.

On December 31st, it was resolved that:

every boy leaving the school with the recommendation of the Master & Visitors, shall be presented with a Bible as a token of appreciation from the Committee and that the Treasurer be requested to prepare new Bibles for such donations with a suitable inscription on the cover (a reward of the Charity) & that the boy's name be inserted thereon.

Specimens of writing of fifteen boys were presented at the meeting and the committee resolved that those boys should each receive a Silver Token to the value of one shilling and six pence – a total of 22/6. Richard Flower, aged 8, was the youngest recipient and William Lawrence, aged 13, the eldest.

At January 28th, 1813 meeting, the Treasurer reported on the good Character while in school and highly satisfactory conduct with respective Employers, of: 1. John May 2. William Williams 3. Thomas Davies 4. George Pickover 5. Abraham Perry and 6. Thomas Barkwill. Each was therefore presented by the Chairman with a Bible inscribed on the cover "Lancastrian School" with their names inserted, as a gift from the Committee, following a suitable address by Revd. Douglas. As a result of a holder of a share in the Free Loan making a proposal in May of applying it to become a Life Governor on condition of having the annual subscriptions which he had paid returned, the committee referred the matter to the Annual Meeting. In July, a subcommittee recommended that the remainder of the school flooring be bricked by Mr. Cooper during the ensuing vacation. That expense meant that we judged it expedient not to increase Mr. Higgins' salary but to present him with a gift of £10. In the Autumn, the Visitors (assisted by Treasurer and Secretary) were requested to look into the reasons for several boys leaving the school.

Terrible suffering was caused by 1813 – 14 winter according to W.M. Childs:

> the visitation of frost and snow lasted with little intermission for twelve weeks. Between 25th December, 1813 and 9th March, 1814, no coals reached Reading. Almost every article in life commanded an excessive price. Door-to-door collections were made for the relief of the famishing. For six weeks, bricklayers, shoemakers, weavers, and almost all trades stopt. The great winter having passed, and Europe being at length at peace,[10] the conclusion of peace in 1814 was marked by about 6,000 persons dining in the streets of Reading, and sports, including donkey and sack races, a pig hunt, gingling, grinning and smoking matches, being held in the Forbury.

The suffering of the poor continued because many employers had to discharge their workmen. Although, by Midsummer 1816, food had become cheaper, the overall situation was little changed and the poor-houses were full to overflowing, people having pawned what little possessions they had to buy food. In December 1817, the general prosperity of the town had felt no increase and the poor's rates were higher than they were ever known before, £645 having been subscribed and spent in charity in the winter of 1816 – 17. To give some idea of prices then, about seventy men were paid 9s. a week for road mending in the Forbury at a time when three gallon loaves cost 8s. 3d.

READING BRITISH FREE SCHOOL

The Royal Lancasterian Society had changed its name to British and Foreign School Society in 1814 so we changed the name of our school from Reading Lancasterian School to Reading British Free School. In response to Mr. Higgins' request for an increase in his salary in May, we convened a special full Committee meeting on 26th and expressed our satisfaction in respect of his services but since the Finances of the Institution would not permit an increase, we suggested that if he were willing to continue with us in the current year then a Gratuity of £10:10. would be voted. Mr. Holmes reported on June 30th

---

[10] The first Treaty of Paris had been signed on 30th May 1814 following an armistice signed a week before between France and the allies of the Napoleonic Wars

that he and the Secretary had examined the children and found that all but a few in the lowest classes were able to repeat the Lord's Prayer satisfactorily.

Having received a circular letter from the Parent institution soliciting aid to the general purposes of the British & Foreign School Society, we deliberated their request at our meeting on September 29th but came to the conclusion that the debts outstanding on our own school and the low state of our present fund, did not allow an immediate contribution to the Parent Institution, but that we would wish to support it whenever we were in a position to do so, and hoped that such an opportunity would soon occur.

Mr. Higgins tendered resignation of his office of School Master by letter to the November 24th, 1814 meeting. On its acceptance, he was thanked for the candid manner in which he had made known to us his intention to end quickly his connexion with the school, and the great attention and ability with which he had always conducted the concerns of his office. That meeting also:

resolved that the following boys be each presented with a Bible in testimony of their good character & conduct:

				Where employed
1	William Hope	aged	12 years	at Mr. Richards, King Street
2	John Allen	"	13 "	Mr. H. Simmons "
3	Chas. Davis	"	13 "	Mr. Midwinter, Market Place
4	Ebonige Benvill	"	11 "	Mr. Swaine's Factory
5	James Scouthouse	"	14 "	His Father, Friar St.
6	Geo. Knight	"	12 "	Mr. Moore's, Horn St.
7	Thomas Burchall	"	11 "	" " "
8	James Fruvin	"	13 "	Mr. Horn's, Friar St
9	John Pocock	"	12 "	Mr. Pocock's, London St
10	Richard Simmonds	"	14 "	Mr. Goodman, Brunsdon Pl
11	Wm. Tichner	"	13 "	Mr. Francis, Chain Lane
12	Henry Rivers		13	Faversham
13	Matt. Brambury			Eynsham, Oxford
14	Joseph Form		13	Mr. Turner, Butcher Row

As at the appointment of Mr. Higgins, the Parent Society was requested to recommend a new Master. By December 19th, Mr. Fox's letter nominating Mr. Gatward (born 1789 in London) was read. We then communicated to the London Secretary our acceptance of Mr. William Gatward's services on the same conditions made with Mr. Higgins and requested that he come to Reading about the middle of January to meet the Committee and receive our instructions. Thus it was that on Tuesday, January 17th, 1815, his services were accepted, following his affirmative responses to the questions previously asked of Mr. Higgins. He was told that his salary of £70 per annum had commenced from that day and he would also receive 6d. in the pound for collecting subscriptions. It was also recommended at that meeting that the next general meeting be asked that school do commence and conclude with prayer and with reading a portion of the Holy Scripture.

By Thursday February 23rd meeting, it was resolved that a few Arithmetical Tables be printed upon cards for the use of the boys and that, in future, Children who are absent for a month except in case of sickness or other causes satisfactory to the committee shall be dismissed the school. It was also being recommended to the General Meeting that the school shall not be kept on Saturday, it being Market Day and the attendance always thin in consequence. Mr. Gatward's Report of Progress for March was sent to the Committee:

> 28 boys have been advanced to higher classes and several have repeated the Multiplication and Numeration Tables.
> The Boys in general are much improved and are cleaner in their persons.
> For the order I must beg leave to refer to the minutes of the Gentlemen who have visited the school.

His April report was even more interesting:

> 140 – 170 in daily attendance and now much more punctual for School hours. Out of those in daily attendance there are 130 –140 who constantly attend the different Sunday Schools. This I ascertain by taking a report every Monday morning.

A letter from Mr. Fox stating his wish to inspect the School along with Mr. Allen when passing through Reading to Bristol was read at July 27th meeting. At the September 28th one, it was ordered that the inscription at the school would in future be "**Reading Free School on the British System**" and that the present be altered accordingly. September 1815 Report included:

> Several boys have been enabled (by a simple method used in this school) to enumerate from three to twelve figures.
> It will be seen by the Sunday Report Book that near 200 of the Boys regularly attend the different places of worship in the Town and Country.
> The new method adopted for sending the Boys home is found to answer its intended end extremely well, as it prevents all noise or confusion as they file along the streets.

At the end of November, the following were introduced to the Committee and presented with a Bible each by the Treasurer after a suitable address was given by the Revd. Mr. Watkins.

1	James Ryder	living at Mr. Higgs, Katesgrove
2	John Shackle	at Mr. Hayes, Hill Hall
3	William Stokes	with his father, Silver Street
4	Thos. Dill	at Mr. Macauleys, Oracle
5	James Ford	with his Father, Crown Inn
6	John Lockstand	at Mr. West, Oxford Road
7	Richard Swain	at Mr. King Lambs, Katesgrove
8	John Walton	at Mr. Richard's, King Street
9	Joseph Woods	St. Mary's Butts, now removed near to Newbury and the Bible will be sent there.

It was also reported:

> This Month an Italian Boy has been admitted into the School and although quite ignorant of the English Tongue when he came, he can nearly master all the words in the third class –a striking instance how some knowledge may be communicated to the most ignorant by means of the British System.

On May 30th, 1816, the Treasurer was empowered to present the sum of five guineas as a Gratuity to Mr. Gatward, the Master, who had reported:

> Several of the parents of the boys have called at the school during the preceding and present months to express their obligations for the attention paid to their Children. I have taken the liberty to state thus much as to show the good effect the Institution has upon the minds of Parents as well as Children – at all times much to be desired.

By July 25th, the Treasurer reported that all shares of the Free Loan had been discharged and satisfied. A month later, it was resolved that the School Room should be Lime washed and coloured where necessary by Mr. Cooper and that Mr. Williams be spoken to about the fixing of Tin Shoots and proper drains for carrying off the Rain Water as soon as convenient.

Mr. Gatward was quite complimentary of his pupils in August 1816 Report:

> I hope the Committee will be pleased to hear that the boys are very regular in their attendance at the different places of Worship on the Sabbath Day and their order and attention in school time deserves my warmest praise.

The November Report continued in that vein:

> Our daily attendance for the past month has not been so large as usual, arising chiefly from the Measles being prevalent at the time. I hope that the above

statement will sufficiently prove the diligence of those who have attended.

It should therefore be no surprise to hear that the numbers in the school increased under his leadership reaching 236 by May 1817. The month before:

the Secretary was designated to procure Leather Caps not exceeding 1/3 each in value for the Boys who attended for examination at the General Meeting to be presented to them previous to the Public Procession; Messrs Carter & Thorogood were requested to make enquiries respecting the expense and best materials to be used for repairing the Roof and Floor of the school and the following inscription was to be painted on a board affixed to the walls of the school:
"The Public are respectfully invited to inspect this school any day except Saturday between the hours of 9 and 12 and from 2 to 5."

The Committee was summoned to attend at the School House on Wednesday, June 4th at 10 o'clock for the Anniversary Procession and the Secretary was reminded to provide Cakes and treats for the Boys as usual. The Report for June 1817 showed 288 on the books and 160 – 223 present.

We heard later that Joseph Lancaster left the Society in 1816. In 1818, he travelled to America where he continued his work by establishing new schools in Baltimore, Venezuela and Canada. Unfortunately, he was run over by a carriage in New York in 1838 and died on October 24th of the injuries he sustained. He was buried in a pauper's grave – such a shame as, at the time of his death, between 1,200 and 1,500 schools were said to use his principles.

A National School having been set up in Reading in 1813 for those who attended Church Sunday Schools, we noticed and recorded in the Minutes of March 31st, 1817 that almost a third of Britishers also attended one as follows:

97	attended Church S.S.	25	Silver St. Meeting
54	Castle St. Chapel	4	Wesleyan Chapel
46	Broad Street Meeting	4	R.C. Chapel
37	Salem Chapel	16	Country Schools
32	Hosier's Lane Meeting		

During the preceding year, the State of the School was given as:

113	Admitted
41	quitted for service
40	left town
18	removed by parents
4	Apprenticed
3	Deceased

We were also able to report the following details about the curriculum:

115	Boys have learned to read the New Testament
120	Boys have learned to read the Old Testament
47	Boys have learned to read Selected passages from Watt's Hymns
59	Making progress in junior classes
146	Boys received **copy books**, a great number of whom write good useful hands, and some very neat
196	Boys have been learning the four first Rules, simple & compound; this number includes:
	87 in combination of figures
42	rules from Reduction to Practice
1	has learnt as far as **Double Fellowship**
1	has reached cube root

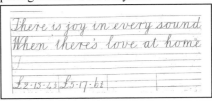

Double Fellowship Example.
A had in trade £50 for 4 months and B £60 for 5 with which their sum gain was £24.
Required each person's particular share.
50 x 4 = 200
60 x 5 = 300
500: 24:: {200:£ 9. 12s. A's gain
{300:£14. 8s. B's gain

The BRITISH FREE SCHOOL for GIRLS

At a committee meeting on August 6th, Mr. John Hooper passed on the Girls' School Committee's request for part of the ground in Southampton Street to be made available for the erection of a Girls' School. We therefore called a meeting of Subscribers to the Free School on the British system for 20th at the Town Hall. In the meantime a letter had been published in *August 18th Mercury:*

> Sir, when the gratuitous education of the poor on the Lancasterian now British System was first set on foot, doubts were here and there raised – by some, of its utility – by others, of its expediency. These details, however, soon gave way and so much did our Reverend Sovereign the Archbishop of Canterbury, the Dukes of Sussex, Kent, Bedford and other exalted Episcopalians, approve of it that they all contributed to its support, the Prince Regent also sends annually a donation of 100 *l.* [11] – The dignitaries of our Church too were in a short time so convinced of the numerous advantages it possessed, that National Schools on a similar system as recommended by Dr. Bell were, soon after, generally established for the promotion of the same beneficent object; schools whose chief variety is (as might naturally be expected) the education of poor children agreeable to the ritual of the Church of England.

---

[11] One hundred pounds – the *l* standing for the Latin *lira*

The education of the poor on the British system, a system which includes children of every religious denomination, was first established in this town about 7 years ago. The original design was to include both Girls and Boys but the heavy expense attending the purchase of ground and erecting a suitable Building for the Boys School only obliged the subscribers, much against their inclination to defer the consideration of a School for Girls to some future period – This period I trust is now arrived – The advantages predicted of this mode of educating Girls as well as Boys having been amply confirmed in the National and British Schools in other parts of the Kingdom as well as in the National School in this town, a strong desire has been expressed that an endeavour should be now made to complete the plan originally projected and I am happy to find that this endeavour has every prospect of success.

A meeting of Ladies has taken place, Rules and Regulations have been printed and circulated and personal application for Subscribers and Donations are raising. In the meantime, measures have been adopted for securing a suitable room, or for erecting an appropriate Building as circumstances and means may point out.

The number of poor Girls in this town of a suitable age for reception in gratuitous schools is calculated at about 700 – of this number, not more than about 280, including the National and Green Schools, are receiving the advantages of education so that there still remains at least 400 nurturing up in lamentable ignorance and all its sad, vicious and demoralising effects. This consideration ALONE, even were the number but half what is here stated, comes home with irresistible force to the feelings of a generous and benevolent public.

In addition to the rudiments of learning common to both sexes, the Girls are also to be instructed in Needlework, Knitting, the mode of making and mending their Cloaths; &c. an advantage that cannot fail to add greatly to the subsequent comfort and happiness of this class of society through life.

As well as that difference, it had been realised that the twelfth Rule of the original Rules of the Boys' School had needed to be adjusted:

In the first formation of the British Schools, it was considered, as the least open to objection, to leave the peculiar religious tenets of the children under the direction of their respective parents in conforming with the liberal principle on which they were established. The motive was correct but, after some time, a defect was acknowledged. The patrons of this Institution found they had given too much credit to the parents by supposing they would so far improve the advantages of their education as to take care that their children regularly attended some place of worship on the Sabbath and otherwise duly observed this Holy Day. In this, however, they were, in too many instances, mistaken. A new Regulation was adopted by which this defect was rectified at the same time that the PRINCIPLE was preserved.

This Regulation consists in assembling the Children every Sunday morning and conducting them to that Place of Worship which the parents prefer, and where an indifference is manifested by them, they are entered in the Register kept for that purpose to go to their Parish Church. Another Regulation is that the Clergymen or Ministers of the Places of Worship where the Children are to attend, shall be at liberty to appoint any one day in the week to afford them such further religious instruction as they shall severally deem proper.

The following week (August 25th) the Conclusion of the Address to the printer on the subject of **BRITISH FREE SCHOOL for GIRLS** appeared:

In the preceding observations, I think it may safely and with great truth be said that the Schools on the British System are, at this time, raised on a basis as unexceptionable as benevolence, philanthropy and Catholicism can make them. I do not say this with the most distant wish to derogate from the just value attached to the National Schools in this and other places to which I am myself a Subscriber but as they are expressly set apart for those children whose parents are desirous of bringing them up in the principles of the Church of England it necessarily follows that, as the object is of a definite and limited nature, the extent of the benefit of an education on such a plan must be proportionally limited. Much then as I admire the aggregate of its forms and much as I rejoice in every manifestation of zeal for its vital prosperity yet I hope never to measure worth, as to suppose no other human institution or religious creed can be equally acceptable to HIM who is no respecter of persons but in every nation he that feareth him and worketh righteousness be accepted by him.

The establishment of a Girls' School in this Town on the British system in connection with the Boys' School must necessarily be of paramount importance.
Signed R.
Reading, August 7, 1817

At the August 20th meeting, the resolution passed at the very first meeting on August 27th, 1809, that girls should be educated as well as boys, was therefore ratified and a subcommittee (Messrs. Hooper, Dyer and Farmer) was appointed to co-operate with the committee of ladies as far as was deemed expedient and report back to the general committee at their next meeting on Thursday 28th. It was then that the unoccupied plot of ground adjoining the boys' school was offered to the ladies for their purpose and it was resolved unanimously:

That the sum of £100 3 per cent Consuls and the further sum of £15 remaining from the donation of the late Edward Simeon Esqre be appropriated towards the erection of a Female School provided that a sufficient sum be obtained by other means to complete the same.

You will see from the letter received August 30th that my son, Thomas; his father-in-law, Mr. Finch; and myself were among the twelve Gentlemen the Ladies' Committee wished to help them in the erection of the Girls' School:

Reading Free School for Girls on the British System.
Sir
At a meeting of the Ladies Committee on Friday Aug 29th the following resolution was unanimously passed.
That in order to carry into effect the designs of this Committee with as much expedition as possible, the following Gentlemen are earnestly and respectfully solicited to favor the committee with their assistance with procuring estimates, receiving subscriptions etc. towards the erection of a school sufficient to contain 200 children.
*Messrs. Hooper, Tanner, **Finch**, Fenton, Ring, Marsh, Shepherd, Buncombe, **Letchworth, T.Letchworth**, Maddock and Lawrence.*
And that they be empowered to add any other Friends to their number.

Signed   J. Tanner   Secretary Pro tempore

It wasn't until September 25th meeting that we were told that that letter had been intended as a personal invitation to Mr. Shepherd and other Gentlemen from the Ladies' Committee and had been entered by mistake in the Minutes of this Institution, but it was to be left as a document. Around that time, I accompanied **Sir Francis Burdett** to the Market Place where a large crowd heard him speak. He was Member of Parliament for Westminster and very popular in 1817. Snuff and tobacco boxes made of brass were cast with his profile on the lid and the words "Westminster's Pride and England's Hope" on the rim. He spoke from the balcony of Marsh's bank, addressing his hearers as "Men of *Barkshire*" then left for his home in a post chaise from the Bear Hotel.

Accommodation for Teachers

At the October 30th meeting, Mr. Hooper and I were appointed Visitors for the coming month and the Treasurer was requested to transfer the money received from the sale of the funded stock into the name of the Treasurer of the Girls School on the British System. However, it was also resolved:

That a Plan and estimates be obtained for erecting a Building in front of the School for the purpose of accommodating the Master & Mistress and that Messrs. Ring & Hooper be appointed to procure the same in order to being submitted to the next meeting of this Committee.

Although the ladies were keen to proceed with the school for the girls, us gentlemen were just as keen to get accommodation for the master and mistress underway so, that day, it was resolved that a plan and estimates for erecting a building in front of the school for the purpose of accommodating them be obtained by Messrs. Ring & Hooper. The requested plans were duly presented on December 5th when it was resolved to build two homes in front of the school for the accommodation of the Master and Mistress. A subcommittee of seven, including the treasurer and secretary, was delegated to look into the plans. However, by the meeting on 30th, Mr. Ring reported that a conference had taken place with the ladies committee. Due to the unfinished state of the building for the girls' school, they felt that they could not cooperate with the plan for creating the houses at that time. It was therefore resolved to postpone the erection of those buildings for three months.

As a result, the Girls' Department opened Monday, March 30th, 1818 and the Rules & Regulations for that school were published in *March 30 Mercury*:-

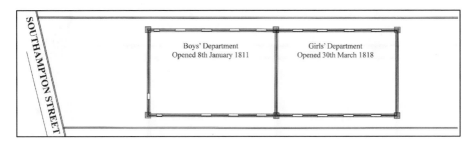

READING LADIES' FREE SCHOOL SOCIETY
𝔣or 𝔊irls'
ON THE ROYAL BRITISH SYSTEM.

At a GENERAL MEETING of the Subscribers and Friends of this Institution held (by permission of the Mayor) at the TOWN HALL on FRIDAY last, the 27th March – a communication having been made by the sub-committee, that the NEW SCHOOL, in Southampton Street, was ready for the admission of Girls; the following Rules and Regulations were moved and resolved:-

RULES and REGULATIONS.

1. – That this School be opened on Monday, March 30th at nine o'clock, for the Gratuitous Instruction of the Female Children of the Labouring Classes in this Town, and its immediate vicinity.

2. – That the School shall be open to the Children of persons of EVERY Religious Denomination. No book, except the Holy Scriptures of the authorized Version, shall, on any account whatever, be introduced into the School; and the reading lessons shall consist, exclusively of extracts from the authorized Version of the Holy Scriptures.

3. – That a regular Register shall be kept of all Children admitted into the School, in which it shall be noted, opposite each Child's name, what place of Religious Worship her parents or guardians prefer. The Children who do not attend Sunday Schools, shall be mustered in the School every Sunday morning, and conducted to their respective places of Worship; and those Children whose parents are indifferent on the subject, shall be entered to go to their Parish Church.

4. – That no Religious Tenets, peculiar to any denomination, shall be taught in the School, the Clergymen and Ministers of the places where the Children attend, according to the Register, being at liberty to afford to them, respectively, such further religious instruction as those pastors may severally deem correct.

5. – That all persons subscribing one guinea per annum, or ten guineas or upwards at one time, shall be Members of this Society; and that all Ladies whose families subscribe to this extent, shall be eligible to election on the Committee.

6. – That the business of the Institution shall be conducted by a Treasurer, two Secretaries, and a Committee, consisting of not less than twenty-four other Ladies, eligible to re-election; that five Members be empowered to act, and that the Committee be authorized to procure such patronage as they deem suitable.

7. – That the Committee meet at least once a month, to examine into the general management of the School, and to transact all other business relative to the Institution.

8. – That the Committee divide the town and its vicinity into Districts, and appoint two or more of its members for each, for the purpose of soliciting and annually collecting Subscriptions and Donations from the inhabitants.

9. – That all money paid or received on account of the School, together with every other transaction, shall be regularly entered in a book kept for that purpose and that the accounts be laid before the General Meeting.

10. – That a General meeting of the Subscribers and Friends of this Institution be held annually, on such a day as the Committee shall appoint, when the accounts as audited shall be presented; the proceedings of the past year stated; a new Committee chosen; and a report agreed on to be printed under the direction of the Committee, and circulated among the Members.

11. – That every Subscriber have the privilege of recommending in the proportion of two Children for each guinea annually subscribed.

12. – That every person subscribing half-a-guinea annually shall have the privilege of recommending one Child to the School.

13. – That no child be admitted under the age of six years, nor continue after thirteen, without special approbation of the Committee.

14. – That the school open at *Nine* in the morning and close at *Twelve*, and open again at *Two* and close at *Five* in the afternoon, except in the months of November, December, January and February, when it shall close at *Four* o'clock, subject to future regulation by the Committee.

15. – That no money be paid by the Treasurer, except the order be signed by Three Members in Committee.

16. – That the Committee shall nominate Visitors at every Monthly Meeting, who shall engage to attend in rotation at the School, daily, for at least one hour; and should any Visitor be unable to fulfil her duty, she shall find a substitute from amongst the Members of the Committee.

17. – That the Girls shall be instructed in Spelling, Reading, Writing, the elements of Arithmetic, in Knitting, the mode of making and mending their own Clothes, and other kinds of plain Needle-work.

Donations (continued)

	£. s. d.		£. s. d.
Mr. Maddock, 2d. donation	5 0 0	Mr. Josh. Vines, 2d. don	1 1 0
S. Maberley esq. 2d. don	5 0 0	Mrs. Hatt	1 1 0
Mr. Brown	2 0 0	Collections at the Hall	8 5 6
Mr. Cockel, 2d. donation	1 1 0		
Annual Subscribers (continued)			
Mrs. Burchetts, by Mr. Fuller	1 1 0	Mrs. H. Marsh	1 1 0
M. Annesley, esq.	2 2 0	Mrs. Compigne	1 1 0

Less than a week before that, Subscribers and Friends of Reading Boys' Free School on the British system had been invited on page 3 of *Monday March 23 1818 Reading Mercury* to attend its eighth Annual meeting:

READING BOYS' FREE SCHOOL
ON THE BRITISH SYSTEM

The anniversary of this most excellent Institution, will be held (by permission of the Mayor) at the Town Hall, on Wednesday next, the 25th instant, at twelve o'clock precisely.

In addition to the usual transactions of an Annual meeting; much information will be given on the state of the Parent Society, and the progress of Education in general; by the Rev. Dr. Schwabe, the Foreign Secretary, C. S. Dudley, esq, and other gentlemen who have promised their assistance.

A full attendance of the Subscribers and Friends is requested, accommodation will be provided for Ladies.

Thomas Ring Esq. was in the Chair and thanks were expressed to him; Treasurer J. E. Liebenrood Esq; Secretary Mr. Shepherd and the Gentlemen of the retiring Committee who, in turn, commented on the vigilance and exertion of the Master, W. M. Gatward, whose report for 1817 followed:

State of the Reading Free School on the British System, March 24th, 1818

From the commencement to the present time, 1623 boys have been admitted. During the past year, 166 scholars have been received, which added to 235, the number remaining from last Report, make the total admissions for the year now completed (being 45 more in number than the last year)   401

Quitted School for apprenticeships and other services	53
Removed by parents, no return made	30
Left the town	35
Deceased	3
	− 121
Remain in the school	280

Taking this number from 1623, it will be seen that 1343 boys have quitted the Institution from its commencement.

Progress in Reading

128 boys have learned to read the New Testament; 160 have been exercised in reading the Old Testament; 69 are now learning to read selections from Scripture, with Watts Hymns; and 58 are making progress in the four junior classes.

WRITING – 130 boys have received copy books, a great number of whom write a good hand.

ARITHMETIC – 230 boys have been learning the four first Rules, simple and compound; this number includes 104 in combination of figures – 81 have been taught the different Rules from Reduction to Exchange, most of whom can repeat the Rules they have passed through and solve the questions with the greatest facility and exactness.

RELIGIOUS INSTRUCTION – prayers are daily read in the School; and a great number of the boys can repeat the Lords Prayer and the Ten Commandments; and are frequently exercised in repeating portions of Scripture. Three fourths of the whole School are in possession of a copy of the Scriptures, purchased by their own small subscriptions, through the medium of the Bible Association established in this town. On any boy being taken into the School, it is enjoined on his parents, that he regularly attend some place of worship, if not in a Sunday School; and it is obvious (from a Register kept for the purpose) that very few instances of neglect occur.   W. M. GATWARD, Master

A week later, the meeting of Subscribers and friends held at the Town Hall prior to the opening of Reading British Free School for Girls was described in the *Reading Mercury*:

Having been unanimously called to the Chair, J. HOOPER Esq. opened the business of the meeting by detailing those causes, which had hitherto prevented the completion of the original design of the Institution formed in 1810. The Rev. J. DYER then read a code of Rules and Regulations for the government of the proposed Institution and refuted the objection that education was of less importance to females than to boys. His motion was seconded by J. TANNER, Esq. in a brief address, expressive of his warm interest in the success of the Society. The Rev. A. DOUGLAS, in moving the appointment of Officers and Committee, made many judicious observations on the benefits, which had already resulted from the Schools established in this town, especially in giving a character to female servants.

He was followed by C. S. DUDLEY, Esq. who traced the history of the British and Foreign School Society, from its origin, and explained the nature of the system. He ascribed its success to the purity and simplicity of its design as it took the Bible as its basis and secured the support of the various denominations of professing Christians while the pupils found themselves interested in the "amusement blended with instruction" plan of tuition. He then proceeded to detail, in his usual style of lucid and able illustration, the progress of Universal Education – France, Russia, Spain, etc. had adopted the system, which was rapidly spreading, not only in the continent of Europe, but in other quarters of the globe.

HENRY MARSH, Esq., in moving a vote of thanks to the Rev. John Dyer, and Messrs. Hooper and Tanner, for their kind and effectual assistance to the provisional Committee of Ladies, alluded to those arguments, which shewed the absurdity of the idea that education would render our poor Girls less fit to discharge the duties of their station. He was followed by the Revs. J. WATERHOUSE, and G. LAURIE, who made some judicious observations on the contrast between the habitations of the poor who cannot read and the comfortable abodes of those who gain satisfaction from reading at home.

The report concluded with the following:

At six o'clock in the evening, a meeting of the children, with their parents, was held in the Town hall, which was crowded to excess, and never do we recollect a more interesting and gratifying scene. The parents and children were ably addressed, with reference to their relative duties as conducted with this Institution, by C. S. DUDLEY, esq., Rev. J. DYER, T. RING esq., Rev. A. DOUGLAS, Rev. J. HASLOCK etc. and the numerous assembly dispersed under a suitable and evident feeling, that the events of this memorable and interesting day, were calculated to elevate the moral character, and promote the best interests of our native Town.

Having seen the Girls' School duly completed, the trustees of land and premises belonging to the Lancasterian School again recommended on

April 8th that the places of residence for the teachers in the school be erected in front of the present building. As a result, the boys' school committee, which also met that day, resolved that the submitted plan and specifications should be accepted and an advertisement for estimates based on them be inserted in the Reading paper. The estimates should be delivered to Mr. Gatward's house where the plan and particulars might be seen for the following fortnight. Estimates had been presented by Messrs. Billing, Cooper and Elisha by April 30th meeting in the Council Chambers. After determining that the work would be performed by the person whose estimate was the lowest and that the committee reserved the right to appoint a surveyor, they were examined and that of Billing and Sons was found to be the lowest.

However, by May 21st, the report made by the Secretary and Visitors of the progressive increase of scholars to the Boys' School and the probability of its being necessary to lengthen the buildings, John Hooper Esq. moved and Revd. Archibald Douglas seconded the motion that the proposed erection of cottages be for the present postponed. It was also resolved that:

> Mr. Hooper & Mr. Buncombe be appointed to confer with Messrs. Alexander & Leach and to superintend the erection of a fence between the front of the schools.

Mr. H. Shepherd had received the following from the Marquis of Downshire:

Hanover Square
14 June 1818

Sir
  I have been favoured by the receipt of your letter enclosing a copy of one of the reports of the progress of the Reading Free School over which the superintendent Mr. Gatward conducted me.
  Approving highly of the liberal and tolerating System upon which it has been established, I was pleased to see the good conduct of the boys, & the care and attention manifested by Mr. Gatward & the Girls School particularly attracted my attention from their general very orderly appearance & the arrangement and plan of the schoolroom.
  I should have been happy to have had the pleasure of meeting you, and may perhaps have a future opportunity to do so.
  Should it be necessary I shall certainly avail myself of the obliging consent you have stated the Committee of your school will no doubt give to placing the School Master of West Shefford for a short period under Mr. Gatward to learn the mode practiced by him in the instruction of the Boys under his care.

The education of the children of the lower order in these countries is a measure of which the advantages are now so generally admitted, that it is unnecessary to say more upon it, than that I consider it the duty of every Person to find his aid in forwarding such an object.

In Ireland great progress is making in it, and I read with great pleasure the proceedings of the truly benevolent society you have in your town for the encouragement of education in Ireland.

I remain Sir
Your obedient serv
Downshire

At July 23rd meeting, the visitors appointed a three-week holiday commencing Monday night 27th instant and gave the usual present of £5. 5. 0 to Mr. Gatward. He reported that attendance during that month had not been as large as usual as most of the Country Boys had been employed in the fields, but those who had come to school, had behaved well and been diligent.

The following boys were introduced to the Committee on October 29th and, after a suitable and impressive address delivered by the Chairman on the importance of the Scriptures and exhorting them to a practical regard to their contents, were each presented with a Bible:

Thomas Beckett	aged 11 years	Mr. Thos. Davis, Board lane	Weaver
Benjamin Davis	13 do	Mr. Smith, Southampton Street	Weaver
William Knight	11 do	Mr. Ruskin's	Bookseller
James Lavell	14 do	Mr. Willis, Butcher Row	Shoemaker
Samuel Rous	11 do	Mr. Goodman, Brunsdons, Broad St.	Weaver
John Parker	11 do	going to a situation at Coventry, Worcs.	

Mr. Gatward then reported that:

Total number of boys on the lists up to the present day is 305 and there are about 6 applications for admission, all of whom will be taken into the school during the following week, the Vacant Tickets not being yet delivered to the subscribers.

In November, the funds of the Institution were again being addressed, partly because a further request had been received through Mr. Fenton from Mr. Miller, Secretary of the Parent Institution. It was resolved that:

the Secretary do write to Mr. Miller stating that the increased expenses of our own school are such as to absorb all our resources, so that however desirable we may find it to be, we are unable to send in pecuniary assistance either to the Parent Society or to the proposed School in Thatcham.

63

Following on from the discussion on October 29th about Insurance for the School Buildings and the asking of the Ladies Committee as to whether the whole premises should be insured in one policy or in operating parts, it was resolved on January 28th, 1819:

> That an Insurance be effected on the Buildings and furniture of the Boys School at the County Finance Office to the amount of £300 and that Mr. Fenton be requested to get the same done accordingly.
> A letter from Mr. Hooper was read intimating that the Ladies Committee declined cooperation in Insuring the whole premises not thinking it necessary.

There were 312 boys on the books of the Institution by April 1819 report so it was resolved at June 4th meeting that:

> in consequence of the increased number of Boys it is become necessary that some method be adopted to carry off the heated air.
> Afterwards the Gentlemen accompanied the Boys in procession around the Town (as the Annual Custom) being the occasion of His Majesty's birth day: there were present on the occasion 280.

Mr. Dyer was requested to confer with the Ladies Sub. Committee on 14th to ascertain if the same inconvenience was found which our Master complained of – want of sufficient ventilation in hot weather. However, when it was found that they did not require ventilation, us gentlemen referred to Mr. Billing to execute in the most economical way a more effective ventilation of the Boys' School. At July 12th meeting, it was resolved that two senior monitors should be appointed to conduct the school under the directions of Messrs. Fenton and Cockell who kindly conceded to attend on the absence of Mr. Gatward when he was at Abingdon Assizes.

On November 8th, the Committee met in the Jury Room rather than in the Town Hall Council Chamber as previously, and it was ordered that Messrs. Billing  & Sons' bill of £6. 13. 4 for the **Air Chimney**, Plumbing and Painting work be paid and that the Treasurer make the usual compliment of five guineas to Mr. Gatward for July last. In his October 1819 report, he stated:

> The number in daily attendance continues to increase. Many have returned who were ill last month and others employed in the fields and gardens have come back to their school.

The 1819 Factory Act had introduced an age limit of nine years for employing children and ensured that 9 to 16 year olds could only work twelve hours a day. This had followed on from the 1802 Act which stated that:

- Children between the ages of 9 and 13 could work up to 8 hours a day, whereas for 14 to 18 year olds, the maximum was 12 hours, between 6 a.m. and 9 p.m.
- Children under 9 years were not allowed to work but had to be enrolled in the elementary schools that factory owners were required to establish. They had to be instructed in reading, writing and arithmetic for the first four years of work.
- On Sundays children were to have an hour's instruction in Christian Religion.
- Male and Female children had to be housed in different sleeping quarters and were not allowed to sleep more than two to a bed.
- Mill owners were also required to tend to any infectious diseases.

Although fines of between £2 and £5 could be imposed on factory owners, the 1802 Act established no inspection regime to enforce conditions so it had been largely ignored by factories but it did pave the way for further Acts.

A fifth of Reading's population educated by British School by 1821

The Reports of the Boys' and Girls' Schools in *Monday May 1st, 1820 Reading Mercury & Oxford Gazette* seemed to place more emphasis on the deaths of George III (Britain's longest reigning male monarch – 1760 to 1820) and of the Duke of Kent, than of the progress of the schools themselves:

READING BRITISH FREE SCHOOL
At a numerous and respectable Meeting of the Subscribers and friends of this excellent Institution, held by the permission of the Worshipful, the Mayor, in the Town Hall, on Tuesday 25th inst. John Hooper Esq. in the Chair;
After reading the Reports of the Boys' and Girls' Schools, the following motions were submitted and unanimously carried:-
Resolved – That while the meeting gratefully acknowledges the zeal and diligence manifested by the Committees, it relies upon their continued and preserving attention to the important object of their appointment; and that the respective Officers and Committees be requested to continue their valuable services during the ensuing year.
Resolved – That the meeting avails itself of the opportunity now afforded, to add their public testimony of its participation for the loss of our late beloved and valuable Sovereign, the earliest Patron, and a very munificent Supporter of that System which is now applied with such efficacy in Great Britain, and rapidly extending throughout the world.
Resolved – That we felt it due to the great and important design for the promotion of which we are this day assembled, to record the expression of our deep and

unfeigned for the loss which the Parent Institution and the cause of benevolence in general has sustained in the lamented Death of his Highness the Duke of Kent and Strathern, a Prince in whom universal education found a warm and dedicated friend, a zealous and eloquent advocate, and a firm and intrepid defender.

Resolved – That the thanks of this Meeting be presented to the Worshipful the Mayor for his readiness in granting use of the Town-hall on the present occasion.

Resolved – That the cordial thanks of this Meeting be presented to the Chairman for his obliging conduct in the Chair.

Signed,   JOHN HOOPER, Chairman

However more details about both Schools were given the following year when an invitation to the annual meeting appeared on *Saturday, 19th May, 1821:*

READING BRITISH FREE SCHOOLS

The annual meeting will be held, by permission of the Mayor at the Town-Hall on Tuesday next, the 22nd of May. On this interesting occasion, the diffusive and philanthropic nature of the British System of Education will be explained and the increasing progress of Universal Education detailed. Several zealous and active friends of this excellent Institution have engaged to attend – Doors to be opened at five and the chair taken precisely at six – Upwards of six hundred Children will be present.

In May 28th edition of the same paper, actual details were available:

The Annual Meeting of the Reading British Free Schools was held in the Town-hall, on the evening of Tuesday last, the 22nd instant, and it was with pleasure we observed the attendance more numerous and respectable than on any preceding occasion. The north and south ends of the spacious hall were respectively appropriated to the Boys and Girls belonging to the School, amounting in number to nearly five hundred, and it was well observed by the worthy Chairman J. E. Liebenrood Esq. that "it was impossible to direct a glance, either towards the right or left, without being convinced of the value and importance of such Institutions." The Annual Reports were presented from both Committees, each containing the most gratifying evidence of the satisfactory state of the Schools, and of the beneficial effects which have resulted from their establishment. As it was unanimously resolved that these interesting statements should be published, it is only necessary to present the following abstract to our readers –

Total number of BOYS admitted since the establishment of the School in 1810	1958
Total number of GIRLS admitted since ditto in 1818	447
Total	2405
Total number of BOYS now in School	292
Total number of GIRLS ditto	176
Total	468

When it is considered that this important and extensive benefit to our native Town and to Society at large, has been conferred at an average expense not exceeding twelve shillings for each child, including the charge for clothing sixty girls in a remarkably neat and appropriate manner – we cannot help agreeing most cordially with one of the gentlemen who addressed the meeting on this occasion "that it is difficult to imagine any circumstance under which such a sum can be more profitably bestowed" – It was peculiarly gratifying to find another and decisive proof of that liberal and Catholic spirit by which these Institutions are distinguished. More than half of the BOYS, and considerably more than a third of the GIRLS, regularly attend Divine Service in their respective Parish Churches, while their School-fellows are divided among not fewer than eight other religious denominations. This fact and the uninterrupted harmony which characterises these Institutions, sufficiently indicate the unexceptionable nature of that principle by which the system is governed, while it confirms the claim of the exemplary Committee on the benevolence of the more affluent classes of Society. Institutions like these, which confer no common honour on the public spirit and liberality of Reading, can never fail to receive that support to which they are so eminently entitled.

We cannot close this brief sketch, without adverting to another subject of a kindred nature. Whoever is acquainted with the state of our labouring population (and never was that state so accurately known as at present) must be painfully sensible of the necessity which exists for an ADULT SCHOOL in this populous and increasing town. We have heard with much satisfaction, that measures are now in progress for forming such an Institution, and from the zeal and energy displayed in other works of benevolence and the success which has attended the design in neighbouring districts, we entertain the most sanguine hopes with regard to the results. It would be difficult to find a town of similar extent, wherein more abundant means are provided for improving the condition of the labouring classes, and we are convinced that it is only necessary to direct the attention of our enlightened townsmen to the object which will be shortly submitted to their consideration, in order to secure their countenance and cooperation.

Reading's population had increased by over 1,500 from 1811, reaching 12,367 by 1821. Thus, it will be realised that around a fifth of the town's population had attended one of its British Free Schools by that time. In 1822, the Annual Meeting did not take place until June as *June 3rd Reading Mercury* indicates, and Hay making thinned boys' attendance from 230 to 180 by 8th:

READING BRITISH FREE SCHOOLS

The annual meeting of the Subscribers and Friends to this interesting Institution will be held by permission of the Mayor at the Town-Hall on TUESDAY next, the 4th of JUNE. The Chair to be taken at half past five o'clock precisely.

67

The Children of both Schools amounting nearly to five hundred will be present on the occasion – The punctual attendance of all classes is particularly requested.

On July 18th J. Cockell and David Fenton finding numbers at 130 commented:

The harvest so general & forward in the neighbourhood. We think it prudent to dismiss the Boys till 19th next month. We hope by the blessing insistence of the great Author of Providence that the school will then commence.

However August 19th proved too early as only 119 attended that day. On September 6th, the distribution of rewards amounting to £1 – 9 – 6 afforded much pleasure to 81 boys, who were all neat and clean and very orderly. On 16th, J. Watkins stated:

Monday morning all regular and attentive. 2 boys that misbehaved the last time I attended I examined and found the admonition I gave them had a good effect as the Master says they have expressed their sorrow & have behaved very correct ever since. I called them up, expressed my approbation & commended them before the school. No. in attendance 216.

A Boy was in disgrace on November 8th for playing truant then, on the 29th:

I gave the children admonition respecting their disorderly behaviour in singing at persons doors at Night prophaneing the Lords name & using sacred words improperly preaching it upon them to Abstain in the future. J. Watkins J. Cockell.

By December 17th, J. Cockell complained that many were troubled with Chilblains then commented that the School started 1823 thinly attended – 126 on January 21st – most probably from the severity of the weather and had dropped to 86 by 24th. Later in the year, he described June 4th:

Being the anniversary day for the Procession through the Town. 244 Boys attending. Messrs Fenton, Buncombe, Letchworth Jun. & J Cockell. The weather being unfavourable we were under the necessity of doing it partially after taking the usual route from King Street we took shelter in the Market House and distributed the cakes as the boys entered the Market Place, they formed a circle there and were dismissed.

A change in funding was suggested by A. Shepherd on October 15th:

Had the pleasure of paying a short visit to the school this morning and to see the attention of the children to their respective duties, the cheerfulness & activity of the pupil monitors was also very agreeable to me. A School at Maidstone has lately been visited in which 300 Children are in constant attendance & even if the Room would hold 50 more so many would doubtfully be added. These pay one penny each per week during the whole year – 4/4 each boy. Have found that this

68

small contribution in no way affects the attendance of the children & is most cheerfully contributed by their Parents and Friends. I hope a similar method will be established here for it tracks the value of education while it assists the finances of the school. It is upon the precept of this plan that we have intended to construct a New School Room & we hope it will succeed. I ought to mention with respect the pleasure I experienced in meeting Mr. Gatward at his important post & wishing Committee & all the Constituents of the Society every blessing. I beg to add my name.

J. Watkins was equally complimentary on June 15th, 1824:

How pleasant to see Youth so orderly attentive and clean, rescued from ignorance superstition and vice; instructed in Knowledge Virtue and Truth. Thanks be to God our saviour & the instrumentality of benevolent & Liberal minded friends. Amen.

Mr. Cockell and myself were Secretaries and Mr. Richard Becher, Treasurer and therefore Chairman, in the 1820s when my son, Thomas, was also on the Committee. By 1826, his son, my grandson, Henry Finch Letchworth, had joined us on the Committee, which met the second Monday of every month.

On January 30th, 1826, Mr. Gatward informed George Laurie that there had been more absence through sickness during the previous six months than during the previous eight years. Shortly after this, he informed us that he wished to resign his post, so it was at the May 9th Committee meeting that Edward Edwards was appointed Master of the Boys' School. Revd. Mr. Douglas was in the chair and Revd. Mr. Watkins, Messrs. Fenton, Cockell, Rusher and myself were present when letters, dated April 10th, May 1st and 10th, relative to a new Master were read. After referring to the Minutes of December 1814 (Page 99) upon the subject of appointing a new master, Mr. Edwards was called in. The rules and regulations of the School were read to him, together with the terms upon which he should enter as Master, namely upon a salary of Seventy Pounds a year in commencement, subject to such increase as his good conduct, and the finances of the School might authorize. Upon his agreeing to such terms, and engaging to comply with said rules and regulations, his engagement as schoolmaster was confirmed as commencing May 8th. Since Mr. Gatward had offered assistance and direction to his successor, I, as secretary, was asked to write to him. Naturally, I also had to procure from the Treasurer £41. 13. 4 in payment of salary due to him and acknowledge by letter the sense the committee entertained of his faithful service:

Sir,

In noticing to you the appointment of Edward Edwards as your successor to the conduct of the School upon the British System, I am desired by the committee to express to you, their consideration of your faithful and intelligent services. Their regret at parting with you is only lessened by the hope that the institution may still derive advantage from your continued interest and occasional oversight. Uniting with the committee in good wishes for the success of your future undertakings.

I remain Sir,
Respectfully Yours
Thomas Letchworth Secretary.

Revd. J. Watkins saw Mr. Edwards conduct school on May 12th and gave a few words to the Children about their Obedience to their new Master. 159 were present and all were "attentive to business, clean and decent". J. Cockell described the Anniversary Day on July 17th as:

> Messrs. Fenton, Letchworth, Cockell & Edwards took the boys on London Road, down London Street, through Dukes and King Street, Minster Street, Gun Street, The Butts on Oxford Road, through Thorn Street & Friar Street to Market Place and distributed cakes to 183 boys. After usual formalities we dismissed them.

W. Bramley, an agent of the British and Foreign School Society, visited the Reading Boys' School on August 18th, heard some of the boys read and examined their copy books, was pleased with the Discipline of the School and suggested some improvements which were attended to. There were about a hundred Boys present, many being at Harvest. However, when J. Cockell visited on 22nd, 142 were there and many boys answered questions relating to the Multiplication Table and Money beyond his expectation. On December 15th, 17 boys were absent from illness and want of shoes but 134 were present – a good number for so dull a morning.

By July 26th, 1827, J. Cockell was very displeased with his fellow Committee members as no-one had thought as to when the holiday should commence:

> The number 166. As usual not having any one of the Committee to consult on the subject of dismissing the Boys this week for the holidays during the Harvest. My opinion is that it be so and that to recommend that Mr Edwards acts accordingly unless any of my Colleagues should disapprove that may happen to see this.

Robert Rhodes heard the boys reading the 1st Chapter of John when he visited at 3 o'clock on October 2nd and commented that Mr Edwards was taking great

> pains to make the boys understand what they read by asking them questions etc.

When he visited again on the 8th, he gave Mr. Edwards an order for a ream of utility paper and some pencils and the latter brought the three boys forward that were to be dismissed by order of the Committee. They expressed sorrow, particularly Lambourne, but, on 11th, John Smallbone, Samuel Matthews and William Lambourne were dismissed despite their expressions of much sorrow, tears etc. Afterwards they applied to Mr. Edwards for readmission. The Monitors were very attentive to the Master. When I returned on 29th at ½ past 11, I enquired respecting their subsequent behaviour and Mr. Edwards reported that they were going on very well.

However, when he visited on November 29th and enquired into absence of Mr. Lambourne on 28th, it was discovered that he had played Truant. He therefore dismissed him according to the Committee's 3rd resolution on December 10th even though Mr. Cockell did not turn up as expected. On the 12th, the latter mentioned boys being admonished for "singing (as they term it) Christmas Carols" and by 17th, he had recorded them as John & Philip Chapman, Wm. & James House, James Saunders, Wm. King, Geo. & Thos. Ricketts.

By 1829, David Fenton and Robert Rhodes were suggesting:

> The visitors respectively recommend to the Committee that a sort of Box be put up in the School for Boys to stand in as a punishment. The same be 5 foot 6 high.

Unfortunately, less than three years after his appointment, Mr. Edwards died on Friday, April 24th, 1829, following a short illness. At our Committee meeting on 28th, I reported that a young man of the name of James Cornwall had arrived on the 25th with a recommendation from the Parent Society: and I had engaged temporary accommodation for his board and lodging with Mrs. Coles at 74 Southampton Street at 15/0 per week. We resolved that four weeks' pence on an average of 10/0 a week should be added to £3. 14. 4 salary due to the late Mr. Edwards, plus a further allowance of one pound for destitute children taught by him, but whose names he had omitted to send to the committee. Disbursements of £1. 2. 4 made by him upon account of the society made the total £7. 16. 8 to be paid by the Treasurer.

Henry was at our Special Committee Meeting on July 30th when a letter from the Parent Society was read and Mr. Thompson was requested to come down on August 22nd for one month on probation as a schoolmaster ready for the start of term on 24th. He was to be told that:

71

the sum of 5 guineas would be allowed for the month to cover every expense except travelling: and that should he desire to have a lodging sought out previous to his arrival, the committee on receiving a line from him will do their best to meet his wishes.

Since Mr. Cornwall would no longer be required following the boys' dismissal for the holidays on July 31st, he was to be paid one pound for his travelling expenses and presented with a gratuity of Five Pounds for his services in addition to the payment of his board and lodging. A subcommittee for dismissing the boys, directing necessary repairs and attending the opening of the school was appointed and at September 14th Committee meeting, it was reported that the Revd. Mr. Watkins had delivered a suitable address to the boys upon the latter occasion. Mr. Laurie and I were requested to examine Matthew Thompson on his attainments and qualification for teaching prior to a special Committee meeting on 28th when his suitability as a permanent master was considered. In the meantime, the visitors

were requested to obtain a sufficient number of **slates**, cases and reading cards as he had reported a deficiency. The photo shows the **markings** on the outside wall brickwork where the children sharpened their slate pencils.

1831	Area in acres	Inhabited houses	Families	Houses being built	Uninhabited houses
St. Giles	2,640	997	1,086	24	43
Reading	4,870	3,170	3,593	47	234

The 1831 census on May 30th showed that Reading's population had increased by 3,500 to 15,950 since 1821. At the time of *1833 Berkshire Commercial Directory*, Mr. Cockell and myself were still the Boys' School Secretaries and John Hooper, M.D. its Treasurer while, in the Girls' School, the Mistress was Mrs. Slaughter; Treasurer, Miss Harris and Secretary, Miss Sewell. I was also Treasurer of the Reading Philosophical Institution, which met at 36 London Street. Its president was J. B. Monck, Esq. and its aims were:

> to promote the cultivation of Science, the Arts, and all branches of Literature connected therewith, by Lectures, the provision of a Philosophical Apparatus, a Library of Scientific Works, and a Museum of Natural and Artificial Curiosities.

That year was when the Government first gave grants towards the education of the poor but it was 1839 before Inspectors of Schools were first appointed and Schools had to accept annual Inspections by Her Majesty's Inspectors prior to being given a government grant. We had continued to conduct the Reading British School with economy. The total cost of running the school of around 350 boys, including the Master's stipend, was less than £110 which equated to an annual cost for each boy's education of just six shillings in 1835. In 1837, some of our British School Committee meetings, viz. those of October 16th and November 6th, were held at the Counting House of Letchworth & co. Both Henry and myself were present at the latter meeting.

Other Schools in Reading

Reading's National School remained in the Abbey rooms for many years after 1813 but, gradually each parish developed its own schools and St. Giles' National School was opened in Crown Street in 1836. By 1839, some 200 children were receiving an education there on Dr. Bell's plan and an Infants' School run by Mrs. Coles was then opened in Fount Court, London Street based on Mr. Wilderspin's plan "the utility of which is very highly spoken of." Amongst the St. Giles' Church papers, there was the first draft to an education questionnaire, which described the area in 1811 as having:

> "the day school on Lancaster's Plan, containing 226 boys, no girls", there were also in St Giles' Parish, two Sunday Schools belonging to the Establishment of 40 boys and 40 girls, which had been in existence from the first beginning of Sunday Schools in 1780, and were supported by voluntary subscription. There was also a School of 36 boys belonging to the Methodist Meeting in the parish. Some considered there to be a "danger that education would result in the plough and the loom standing still and the spade would be laid aside for the pen". Others saw Lancaster's methods as deficient because they "did not inculcate in the minds of the children any peculiar system of religion."

Early in 1839, it had been announced that **The Royal Berkshire Hospital** would cost about £12,000 out of £13,000 subscribed to build and maintenance would absorb £2,000 a year. The first court of governors was held on May 6th then, on 27th, a service was held in St. Lawrence's

Church, at which Rev. Hulme preached. It was attended by Mayor and Corporation and followed by a procession through crowded streets to the new hospital in London Road. More than 300 persons of position in county and town dined in the Town Hall under the presidency of the High Sheriff of Berkshire, Mortimer George Thoyts, Esq. of Sulhampstead House, sitting down about 3.30 p.m., and, owing to speeches, not rising till 8.15 p.m. Richard Benyon De Beauvoir, who had contributed £5,000, was elected president and Rev. George Hulme (vicar of Holy Trinity, who had actively aided the movement for a hospital) and my son Thomas were appointed secretaries. During June, the medical staff was appointed. By the end of July, there were 33 patients and, in 1841, it was observed that, owing to the opening of the Great Western Railway, patients were then able to come from distant parts of the county, and its resources were being taxed in consequence.

I had tendered my resignation at the April 15th Committee Meeting, stating that, as I was about to remove from Reading to the St. Sidwell area of Exeter, I must necessarily relinquish my office, leaving the nomination of a successor to the consideration of the next meeting. At that Committee Meeting held on May 15th at the Boys' School, I was thanked for my long and efficient service as Secretary. As Mr. F. P. Everitt was then proposed and seconded as my replacement, I was able to hand over my bills and accounts, which were then examined and passed and the Balance £26. 7. 11 paid into the Bank of Messrs. Stephens, Harris & Co. One of my last jobs was to solicit Mr. Buncombe to accept the office of Treasurer in place of Mr. Hooper. It was suggested that to improve the school finances:

> For teaching geography an extra charge of 2d a week shall be made, and for teaching grammar an extra charge of 3d. and that the master shall retain the half of such extra charges for his own emolument. Some additional payment to monitors to be considered at next meeting.

Son, Thomas, was still living in the St. Giles' area of Reading in 1841 while grandson, Henry Finch; his wife, Maria Elizabeth, and their three children – Edward, Ellen Maria and Henry Howard (born 1833, 1834 and 1836) were in the St. Lawrence area.

III. Secretary's Tale: SUSAN CHAMPION 1830 – 1879

You could say that my involvement with the British School in Southampton Street, Reading began at or prior to my birth as I was born in 1809 on the 20th November. My parents, Benjamin Champion and Susanna (née Taylor) had married in the St. Mary's area of Reading on 11th January 1791, when he was 18 and she was 27. They were devout Baptists and early became involved with Reading British School, both serving on its Committees – my father on the Boys' and my mother on the Girls'. I was the youngest of their children and they brought us all up to believe that we should help all mankind, especially those less fortunate than ourselves. It was their influence that persuaded me to become involved with the Girls' British School.

After their deaths, I come across newspaper articles which showed their earlier financial involvement with the British Schools, especially in connection with the instigation of the Girls' School. Among the 76 Annual Subscribers listed in *Reading Mercurys* in September 1817 were: Mrs. B. and Mrs. Champion, who, like most of those on the list, had donated a guinea. The latter was my paternal grandmother and the former my mother because, at that time, married women were known by their husband's names hence the B. for Benjamin!, and the most senior in age did not require an initial.

In the same article was a further list of 19 names of those who had donated towards the building of the School Room. 15 donations were of £5 0s, and Mrs. W. Champion was one of those donors. That may well have been Mary Anna Wayland's first donation to any cause under her married name as she had married my brother, William, on 7th August that year in Reading and he had subscribed £5 towards the Free Loan for the Boys' School as reported at its Annual General Meeting on 26th March 1812. They lived at Calcot Mill, Tilehurst and their first child, Mary Anna Wayland Champion, who died 12th March 1819, was buried in Church Street Baptist Burial Ground.

My mother's name, Mrs. B. Champion, also appeared among £3. 3s. entries in another *Reading Mercury* account later in September 1817 under the heading:

Reading
FURTHER DONATIONS towards erecting a
Royal British Free School for Girls

At the first Annual General Meeting of the Boys' and Girls' Schools held at the

Town Hall on Wednesday 7th April 1819 – a year after the latter had opened – my mother's name was among the 26 requested to render their services on the Girls' School Committee while my father's was among the 21 for the Boys' School for the ensuing year. As well as Subscribers and the Public in general,

> the children of both schools were seated on the south and north ends of the Hall, upon a sloping scaffolding with the Company placed in the middle. The Chairman, seated opposite the entrance door with other friends, after a suitable and appropriate introduction, called upon the Secretary to read the Annual Reports, and at the desire of the Treasurer his account also, which being done, Mr. Hooper read that of the Girls' School and each Account.

Following the adoption of the reports, Revd. William Gurney, Rector of St. Clements Danes, London, moved and Revd. G Laurie seconded the following:

> That while this meeting rejoices in the rapid progress of the great cause of Universal Education, not only on the Continent of Europe, but in the other quarters of the Globe, it desires to congratulate this ancient and opulent Town of having provided the cause of moral and religious Instruction for every poor Child within its extensive district and thus done its part towards realizing the benevolent wish of our excellent and beloved Sovereign.

Revd. J. Edwards of London moved and Mr. Miller seconded the resolution:

> That this Meeting desires to record this public expectation of its ardent hope that under whatever form or designation the various schools for the education of the Poor may be conducted, those who are charged with their executive details will ever cherish and wince a spirit of Conciliation and love towards each other. Having the Bible for its basis, the British and Foreign School Society disclaims the imputation of being the rival of any other excellent and kindred institution, and is the Enemy of ignorance alone.

The meeting was then adjourned to 6 o'clock in the evening when:

> Rewards were distributed to the Girls and they, with the Boys, were respectively addressed by the Revd. William Gurney. The Parents and Children were then addressed upon their several duties by the Revd. J. Edwards. Several proposals of thanks were then given. After the meeting collections were made at the door and the sum of £16: 9: 9 contributed.

Father's name was again mentioned as on the Boys' School Committee from 1822 – 4 inclusive. At that time, as well as the monthly Committee meetings, Mother often attended special extras such as the one on 12th June 1822 at Bath Court when she and other members of Committee granted Revd. H. R. Dukinfield's request to use the Girls' Schoolroom for his Sunday School

76

children at a rental of £5. At 2nd July meeting, she was appointed Visitor for Fridays until School broke up on 22nd as, on the 13th, it was resolved:

that the holidays commence on 22nd inst. & continue for 6 weeks to 3rd September for the recommendation of the Mistress who has exprest her desire of visiting this vacation her friends in Scotland.

At the 5th November meeting, Mother heard that the state of the school during the previous month, as given in the Remark book, had been:

Numbers of Girls on the Books	144
Proportion of absentees	one third
Number Admitted	10
Dismissed	11

and the Treasurer's report was as follows:

General Account	£ 16 " 5 " 5
Reward Fund	£ 4 " 6 " 5½
Working Fund	£ 3 " 17 " 6
Total	£ 24 " 9 " 4½
Clothing Fund	£ 1 " 7 " 11

According to the report of 7th October meeting, Girls who left the school (termed *Dismissed*) were either *Going into Service* as no. 22, N. Littlewood, did; or to other types of work – S. Allaway *Gone to Silk Factory*; or to other schools – S. & M. Foster *Gone to Mrs. King's School*. Mother was detailed as School's Wednesday visitor at 3rd December meeting, when it was resolved:

that the Xmas holidays commence on the 23rd inst. and close on January 6th unless it should be deemed expedient from the state of the weather or any other circumstance to lengthen one week in addition.

In fact by 7th January 1823 meeting, School reopening was deferred to 13th as:

a request from the Mistress to have the holidays prolonged one week on account of domestic affliction in the family where she resides.

You're probably wondering how I could have remembered so much detail about Mother's involvement with the Girls' School Committee when I was only 13 in 1822. Well, I had been elected onto that same Committee by 1830 and was Assistant Secretary by 1835. Eventually I became Senior Secretary and held that voluntary post for many years. Since I had to record Minutes of each Committee meeting into the Trustees' Minutes Book prior to reading them at the next meeting, I was able to look back at previous entries when I became interested in finding out more about Mother's involvement.

At 4th May 1823 meeting at Bath Court, Mother was designated Visitor for Thursdays. The probable advantages attending the weekly payment of a small sum by the children to the school having been suggested to the Committee, it was resolved at that meeting and later added to the By Laws by 9th June that:

> every child shall weekly contribute the sum of one penny & never be more than one week in arrears. That in consequence of the above plan not being originally adopted every child also subscribing shall have the privilege of the Clothing Fund

They heard at the meeting held on 3rd June that, although no communication had been received from the Gentlemen's Committee as to the deferring of the Anniversary meeting because of the Hibernian Society Anniversary being fixed for 3rd June, the Secretary understood it to be their intention to defer the Anniversary meeting but to parade the Town on 4th as usual, distributing buns to the Boys in the Market Place and dismissing them. The ladies therefore adopted the same plan with respect to meeting in the Market Place but left the dismission of the Girls there, or returning first to the School House, to depend on the state of the weather. The Misses Sewell and Miss George were requested to accompany the School to the Market Place on the 4th.

The following Rules respecting Subscribers to the Clothing Fund were also adopted and hung up in the School Room for general information:

I   That the normal Spelling hour on Monday Morning be devoted to the receiving and entering the weekly payments to the Girls.

II   That the admission of fresh girls, after the lapse of 3 months from the 4 of June of each year the choice be allowed the Parents of paying up the deficiency or receiving only an article equivalent to the sum paid in.

III Any girl neglecting to pay for one week is to be refused attendance at the School til the arrears be duly paid in.

IV   No money paid into the fund will on any account be returned.

1830 saw many changes in the Girls' School so it was an interesting time for me to become involved, having been appointed a Visitor for Wednesdays.

Jane Thomson's health

At 15th June Committee meeting at Bath Court, a letter from Miss Thomson, who had been the Mistress since the Girls' School inception, was read and entered in the Minutes Book in the hopes that it would prove a stimulus to an increased interest in the concerns of the Institution:

Reading British School
9th June 1830

To the Ladies of the British School Committee

Ladies

As the period for resigning the Official duties of your School now draws near I have deemed it proper to embrace this opportunity to lay before you a brief statement of the present circumstances of the Establishment in as far regards my sphere in connection with it.

In respect to the number of daily attendants the School may be pronounced in a flourishing state – And considering the large proportion of very young children whose names are now on the Books, it may be added also, that in point of attainments, they are forward.

The children on the whole appear to be well satisfied with their new Governess. And very little is to be apprehended I think now from acts of insubordination in the first risings of which have been met with a degree of firmness that is likely completely to repel any future attempt of the kind.

The number of Children that have been admitted since the formation of the Institution amounts to nine hundred and ninety-one. One hundred and forty nine of whom are at this time under regular instruction . . . . .

I take the liberty to congratulate the committee on the election they have made for a future Mistress and to assure them that it is my candid opinion that she is quite equal to the important responsibility that must devolve upon her in the discharge of the duties incumbent on the situation. And I feel peculiar pleasure in saying that from her punctual and diligent attendance she has acquired such knowledge of the System as will enable her to conduct the School with comfort to herself and satisfaction to your committee. . . . .

With sincere thanks for the sympathies concerning my health . . . .

Your most obedient humble servant

Jane Thomson.

Mother had been at the special meeting of the Committee at Bath Court on 22nd March 1830 when she had been appointed Visitor for Thursdays. She told me that the Ladies' Committee had tried to persuade Miss Thomson to remain longer in office following her original letter expressing her wish to resign from her situation as Mistress of the British Girls' School but, when they realised that the principle cause of resignation was that of greatly impaired health, which would not permit it, they were grateful for her training of her successor, Mrs. L. Slaughter The latter had requested the same salary as given to Miss Thomson as she had a truly crippled sister whose increasing debilitation necessitated more expenditure. She was offered £40 per annum to be increased at the discretion of the Committee should the state of the funds at any time permit.

79

The Committee had taken the earliest opportunity of bearing unqualified testimony to Miss Thomson:

> the punctuality, zeal & superior ability with which during the 12 years of her superintendence she has uniformly and conscientiously discharged the Duties of her situation.   And when the Committee also bear in mind that the first establishment of the Girls' School in this Town was wholly entrusted to and organised by Miss Thomson with so much credit and discretion, they cannot but more sincerely lament the loss of such valuable service . . . .

She was presented with £20 by our Treasurer, Mrs. Hooper, on the day of the examination with the accompanying letter:

> *The Treasurer of the Girls' British Free School has had assigned her by the Committee the agreeable office of conveying to Miss Thomson their warmest and most grateful sense of the propriety, fidelity and Christian principle which have marked her services in connection with this Institution since its establishment in the year 1818.*
>
> *The Treasurer, Secretary and Committee in taking leave of Miss Thomson, which they do with lively regret, beg to subjoin a sincere desire for the complete restoration of her health, blended with a prayer, that the brightest beams of Providential benediction may eradiate her yet untrodden path. If to this be added another hope more future still it is, that life, when extinct in the body, may be swallowed up of that "immortality" brought to light by the Gospel".*
>
> *S. Hooper*
> *Treasurer.*

The girls had been encouraged to contribute towards a Bible to present to Miss Thomson and the Committee determined to supply her with 12 dozen buns (or more if needed) to present to the children at parting. Mrs. Hooper, Treasurer for the past 12 years, also wished to resign at that stage as did her daughter, Miss Hooper, who had acted as Secretary but was precluded from any further service as she had removed from Reading. Mrs. J. Harris was requested to fill the office of Treasurer and Mrs. N. Sewell, that of Secretary.

Following her term of probation under Miss Thomson from March 1830, Mrs. L. Slaughter was regarded as acting in connection with and under the control of the Ladies Committee on the terms before proposed from mid-summer day.

Grandma Champion was in the chair at the special meeting of the Subscribers at Bath Court on 1st February 1831 and three of the 12 Committee members were members of the Champion clan, including my mother and myself. We were all at the special Committee meeting on the 14th when The Rules & Regulations of the School had been revised and altered for future government:

> The funds of this Institution being in a depressed state, the secretary was requested to draw up letters addressed to Chas Russell Esqr. and Mrs Shaw Lefevre soliciting their pecuniary assistance. Likewise to the Ministers of the different Dissenting Congregations requesting them to preach a Sermon in aid of the same aspect.

Mother and Mrs. J. Champion were absent through indisposition from 5th April meeting in the Schoolroom though I was present and appointed to visit on Thursdays. I did find the discipline of the meetings rather rigid at first and ended up being fined along with Mrs. Whatley and Misses Letchworth and Williams for being absent without reason from the meeting in the Schoolroom on 3rd May 1831. Mother and Mrs. J. Champion had been present, and appointed Visitors for Thursday and Wednesday respectively.

However, by 1835, I had been appointed Assistant Secretary while Mrs. T. Letchworth was Secretary and Mrs. S. Workman, Treasurer. I had been given the office of Collector in district 4 at the 27th October meeting although I had not been present, being absent from home. Mother died, aged 71, on 3rd November 1835 and was buried in Church Street Baptist Burial Ground. I could not attend the 24th November meeting through illness but was at the one on 29th December and delegated to visit the School on Fridays during January, 1836 although I was absent through indisposition from 26th January meeting.

It had been in 1835 that we decided on the **By Laws of the Committee:**

1st That the committee meet on the last Tuesday of every month at ½ past 12 o'clock precisely, and as soon after that time as the present business shall commence.

2nd That the chair be taken by the Treasurer, and in her absence the committee shall appoint a Lady to the chair from amongst themselves.

3rd That the order of proceedings shall be:
  1st To call over the names of the committee and fine the absent
  2nd To read the minutes of the preceding Meeting and to dispose of business arising there from
  3rd To read the observations entered in the "Remark Books"
  4th [mainly crossed out]
  6th (no 5th!) To receive any communications from the Secretary after which any fresh Propositions may be taken into consideration

4th That the Collections shall be made after the Counter Meeting in October annually.

5th That the books to be called the "Remark Books" be laid on the desk of the School-room, one for the observations of Strangers, the other for those of the appointed visitors, which remarks shall be read at the monthly Counter Meetings.

6th That the visitor for the day enter into the Remark Book:
1st The time of her attendance
2nd The number of Children present
3rd Any observations arising out of the School

7th That the school be opened and closed every day by reading a portion of the Holy Scriptures.

8th That the Secretaries be authorised to procure every requisite article for the use of the Society and report what they have ordered.

9th That no girl shall be expelled for Misconduct until the effect of our administration in the presence of the Committee shall have been tried.

10th That the General Examination of the Children be held in October annually, to which all the Subscribers shall be invited. Some Gentlemen shall be invited to address the Children after their examination.

The opening of St. Giles' National School in 1836 produced a letter from Mrs. Slaughter wherein she informed the Committee that she had in positive terms declared to the Children that she would not receive back any Girls who leave the British for that School, and that she would prefer resigning her situation to receding from this determination. From 2nd August meeting, we replied:

That the Committee though they sympathize with Mrs Slaughter in the desertions of the School and in the circumstances of other Institutions reaping the benefit of her labours, nevertheless cannot concur with her in the propriety of the Rule of exclusion which she has laid down and do regret it, since they fear that it may be construed as a mark of hostility to other schools and resentful towards the parents of the Children who may have left, feelings which the Committee do not desire to entertain, but they wish that the British School should be as superior in liberality, as it has been under Mrs Slaughter's care in discipline and efficiency. They can not wish Mrs Slaughter to forfeit her word, but beg that in future she will be careful not to establish any new rule without consulting the Committee thereupon, in order that the unity of feeling and action between the Committee and the Mistress, so desirable to both, may be preserved.

Despite having the school room cleaned and partially whitewashed in May 1837; the clockcase converted to a bookcase and a stool ordered for the Mistress in June, Mrs. Slaughter wrote a letter on 28th September declining her situation as Governess to this school. Mrs. Letchworth as Secretary was asked to acknowledge it, express the Committee's thanks for her energetic services and write to the Secretary of the B. & F. School Society requesting him to select a suitable Governess to supply Mrs. Slaughter's place. At our 26th October meeting, we acceded to Mrs. Slaughter's application for an advance of five pounds of her salary.

During March 1838, the new Governess provided by the Borough Road Committee, Miss Ireson, arrived with a satisfactory recommendation from that establishment and I was requested to draw up a testimonial of support from the Committee for presentation to Miss Slaughter and submit it at the 24th April meeting. We granted Miss Ireson's application for a Black Board for Writing and, also at that meeting, received Mrs. Letchworth's letter signifying her wish to resign her office of Secretary in consequence of Arthritic Affliction and considerable absence from home for several months. Therefore, although I was still termed Assistant Secretary on 28th September 1837, the posts were recorded a year later by the 25th September 1838 Open Committee meeting as:

Treasurer: Mrs. Workman; Secretaries: Mrs. Letchworth and Miss Champion

We had to call a Special Committee Meeting on 26th July as a letter had been received from the Governess expressing her wish to resign her situation in consequence of her finding herself in ill health and incapacitated from the exertion that the school at present requires. Miss Ireson's communication stated her desire to leave as soon as possible so I immediately sent to the Secretary of the Borough Road School, London making application for a suitable Governess to supply her place as early as possible. At 28th August meeting, we requested that Miss Ireson remain until after the examination and sent another immediate application to the Borough School to supply her place. On 30th October, I reported that the Governess (Miss Perry) provided by the Borough School had arrived and commenced her duties on Monday 29th.

I had continued living with my father in Eldon Square after Mother died. The *1833 Berkshire Commercial Directory* showed him as an Assessor for the Parish of St. Giles along with Messrs. R. Billing and Micklem. At the Boys' School Annual Meeting on 23rd October 1838, he was again elected onto the Committee and, on 15th May 1839, he seconded the motion that Dr. Ring be requested to accept the office of Treasurer, to which that gentleman kindly acceded. At the meeting at the school on the 29th, he heard that the Master, Mr. Thompson, had an offer of a Boarding School so was resigning his situation as Master and the Secretary was to write to the Parent School in

London respecting their capability of supplying another suitable one. Also at that meeting, a note from the Committee of the Girls' School was received respecting the Legacy left by the late Mr. Watkins.

It was at the next meeting – on 5th June – that the several applications for the Mastership were read. After considering them, it was resolved that:

> the Secretary invite Mr. Rodway to supply Mr. Thompson's place during his absence after the 7th in order that they may judge of his capabilities.

Then, on the 19th, it was decided that:

> Mr. Rodway be engaged to conduct school till the Holidays & that Mr. Thompson be requested to give him information as to his method of instruction during the remainder of his stay.
>
> That members of this committee be requested to pay a visit to the school during the ensuing six months in order to make observation as to the manner of Mr. Rodway's conducting it.

Father was probably more conscientious than the others on the Gentlemen's Committee in 1840 as the Secretary, F. P. Everett, recorded in Visitors' Book:

> May 25th 1840 Present only 60 Boys – the School in good order. Mr. Rodway reports he has about 80 pupils when all there. Mr. Champion called this morning but no Visitor has been to see how the School goes on since 24th March.
>
> September 16th 1840 Mr. Wm. Lane entered upon the duties of Master of the Boys' British School, Reading this day – the number of Boys having been much reduced through the inefficiency of the former Master, the Committee have since made considerable improvements in the Schoolroom in the expectation of an increased number and with the view of affording greater facility for the instructing of the Scholars under Mr. Lane's superintendence and they earnestly solicit their friends and Visitors frequently to inspect the School and examine the Boys in order to express their opinions as to their proficiency in this book.

When Father visited a month after William Lane's arrival, he wrote:

> Visited the School this morning. There were 42 boys present. The Master and boys were all attending to their duties. B. Champion. Friday October 16, 1840.

The Ladies Committee had a similar change of principal teacher around that time as on 27th April 1841, a note addressed to us from Miss Perry expressed her intention of being married shortly and her wish to resign as Mistress of the Girls' School. We naturally asked her to remain in office for two months as agreed at appointment. By 1st July, we agreed that Miss Searle, the Mistress sent by the Borough School, be retained on probation until after the holidays.

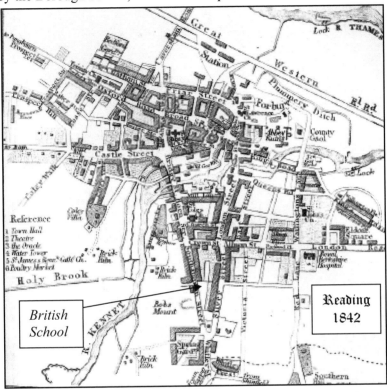

By the time of the *1842 Post Office Directory*, Father was the only Champion in the A – Z compilation of names:

Champion Benjamin, esq. 6 Eldon square

Snare's *Post Office Reading Directory 1842-3* mentioned both him and myself as connected with the British School on page 81:

BRITISH SCHOOL, SOUTHAMPTON-STREET
For Children of all Religious Denominations. Established 1810.
BOYS' SCHOOL
Treasurer, Mr. Goodchild   Secretary, **Mr. T. Letchworth**

COMMITTEE

Andrews Mr.	Cuff Mr.	Legg Rev. W.	Statham Rev. J.
Boorne Mr.	**Curwen Rev. S.**	**Letchworth Mr. T**	Tutty Mr. Henry
Buncombe Mr.	Davies Mr. P.	Maurice Rev. M.	Tyler Mr. John
Champion Mr.	Everett Mr.	Rhodes Mr.	Vines Mr. J.
Corbett Mr.	Laurie Rev. G.	Shedlock Mr.	Young Mr.
Master, Mr. W. Lane			

GIRLS' SCHOOL

Treasurer, **Mrs. Boorne**   Secretaries, **Mrs. Curwen & Miss Champion**

Mistress, Miss Searl

By then, the other Secretary of the Girls' School was Mrs. Curwen, and the Treasurer was Mrs. Boorne as had been the position since 1st October 1839. Like my father and myself, you will notice that they had other family members on the Boys' School Committee at that time – in their cases, it was their husbands, Rev. S. Curwen and Mr. Boorne. There were also two Mr. T. Letchworths – father and son – the elder of whom was the Secretary of the Boys' School as Mrs. T. Letchworth had been of the Girls' until 1838. The British School was one of twelve Reading Public Schools:

> PUBLIC SCHOOLS:
> Royal Grammar School, Forbury
> Diocesan School, Russell Terrace
> Blue Coat School, 31 Albion-street
> Green Girls' School, Broad-street
> **British Schools, Southampton-street**
> Boys' National School, Hosier-street
> St. Giles's National School, Crown-street
> St. Lawrence's Girls' National School, St. Lawrence's Churchyard
> St. Mary's Sunday and Weekly School
> School of Industry, Friar-street
> Infant School, Upper Hosier-street
> St. Giles's Infant School, Font Court, London-street

along with twenty Ladies', nine Gentlemen's and four Preparatory Schools.

Rusher's *Reading Guide 1843* provided the initials for the Boys' School treasurer – J. D. Goodchild – and the Christian name for the secretary – Thomas Letchworth – but was similar in other respects. However, it did also give the 1843 dates of the four fairs held each year in Reading:

READING FAIRS, 1843

Candlemas:	2 February	– horses, cattle and pigs
May [Feast of St. Philip]:	1 May	– horses and cattle
Feast of St. James:	25 July	– horses, cattle and cherries
Michaelmas Cheese:	21 September	– cheese and cattle

An annual melon and carnation feast was mentioned in 1826 and the first show of the Reading Horticultural Society had been held in 1834.

My father died, aged 70, on 9th December, 1843 and was buried alongside my mother in the Baptist Burial Ground in Church Street. By the time of Rusher's *Reading Guide 1845*, Miss Reid had become the treasurer of the Girls' School and, a year later, Mrs. Exall replaced Mrs. Curwen as the other secretary since the latter had become secretary of British Infants' School in Hosier-street. However, although Mrs. Curwen and I were only secretaries together at the Girls' School for a short time from 1839 – 1845, they were eventful years in her life so I'd like to share them with you.

The Sound of Music – Tonic sol-fa developed by John Curwen

She had only moved to Reading in 1837 when her husband, Spedding Curwen was appointed the first Minister of a new chapel in Castle Street. That chapel had been built to seat approximately a thousand people almost opposite the similarly-sized evangelical independent Anglican Chapel. The Rev. James Sherman, who had been Minister at the latter chapel from 1820 until 1836, had taken the opening service, being very sad about the split within the congregation that had brought about the new Chapel.

Mary and Spedding had come to Reading from Zion Congregational Church, Frome where he had been the minister from 1828, following a ministry at the Barbican Chapel, Hackney, London. No fewer than 228 members were added to the Frome Church during his ten year ministry there and he was described as a gifted and earnest preacher. [12]

Spedding and Mary (née Jubb) had married in Leeds on 10th August 1814 and their son, John had been born at Heckmondwike, West Yorkshire on 14th November 1816. When 16, John entered Wymondley College, Hertfordshire

---

[12] By W. J. Harvey, Deacon and Secretary, in his 1918 guide

to prepare for the ministry. A few months afterwards, the college moved to Byng Place, London, where it was renamed Coward College in 1833. [13]

In 1838, **John Curwen** was appointed assistant minister at a Congregational Church in Basingstoke, where he also kept a small school. Three years later, he held a similar post at Stowmarket, then lived with his parents in Reading for a year before being ordained May 1844 to the charge of an independent chapel at Plaistow, where he remained for 20 years. He married Mary Thompson of Manchester in 1845 and their children were: Margaret, John Spencer, Spedding and Thomas Herbert.

I am telling you a lot about John as he was to become well-known nationally for his work on music education, particularly the development of a distinct method of applying Sol-fa, including both rhythm and pitch. Naming it Tonic Sol-fa, it became widely adopted as an easily teachable method in the reading of music at sight. It had resulted from a discussion about congregational singing at a Sunday-school teachers' conference at Hull, which John had been addressing, in the autumn of 1841. The chairman commissioned him to under-take a review of available methods of teaching singing and to recommend the best and simplest way of teaching music. 55-year-old Sarah Ann Glover was recommended to him as a teacher who had employed a very successful system of musical instruction in a school where she taught. Her father had been curate of St. Lawrence, Norwich since 1811 and she and her sister had led the unaccompanied singing there. While trying to teach a young Sunday School teacher the tunes so that he could teach the children, she developed a system of notation, in which DOH is always the first note of the scale, RAY the second, and so forth and called it "the Norwich Sol-fa". She had used the system with great success in a school for poor girls that she had opened in

---

[13] The London merchant William Coward died in 1738, leaving considerable property in trust "for the education and training of young men aged 15 – 22, to qualify them for the Ministry of the Gospel among protestant dissenters."

Black Boy Yard, Colegate. Her *Scheme for Rendering Psalmody Congregational* went through four editions. John altered her Norwich Sol-fa, writing a series of articles on *Singing* in the Independent Magazine for 1842, which advocated what he called the Tonic Sol-fa system. By then, he had already written:

1. *Nelly Tanner*, 1840.
2. *Child's own Hymn Book*, 1841
3. *Look and Say Method of Teaching to Read*, 1842.

His mother brought copies of them along to show me when I showed interest. In June 1843, he brought out his *Grammar of Vocal Music*. Ten years later, I heard that he'd started the Tonic Sol-fa Association then, in 1858, he published his *Standard Course of Lessons on the Tonic Sol-fa Method of Teaching to Sing.*

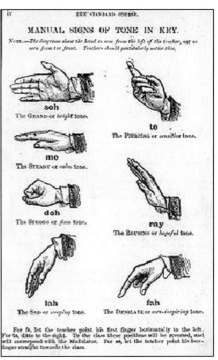

With his eldest son, John Spencer Curwen (who had been born in Plaistow 30th September 1847), John started printing music with tonic sol-fa notation in 1863. He changed his former idea of using the Sol-fa system as an aid to sight reading in 1872, when that edition of his *Standard Course of Lessons* excluded the Staff and relied solely on his Tonic Sol-fa system. John had published a periodical called the *Tonic Sol-fa Reporter and Magazine of Vocal Music for the People*, and, in his later life, was occupied in directing the spreading organization of his system. J. Curwen & Sons Publishing Firm in North Street, Plaistow became a large music and general printing business, specialising in high quality work. [14]

In May 1879, John laid a stone in memory of Miss Glover, the originator of Tonic Sol-fa system. She had died of a stroke in 1867, while staying with

---

[14] Curwen Press continued into the 1970s, when it was closed

friends in Great Malvern, so was buried there. From Norwich, she had moved to Cromer then to Reading then Hereford. Having acquired land in Earlham Grove, the stone was the start of the **Tonic Sol-Fa College,** which John had erected. The first wing of the College was opened on 7th July by the 8th Earl of Kintore and John Spencer became its principal in 1880, having devoted his musical career to forwarding

the Tonic Sol-fa movement. He had lectured on the system all over the United Kingdom and visited the Continent and the United States to research the systems of musical education there. In 1882, he founded the Stratford and East London Music Festival while living in the Upton Lane area where many well-to-do Quaker families lived.

Interestingly in the 1881 census, Mary and Spedding's 32-year-old grandson, Spedding Curwen, who was living at 8 Park Villas, Margery Park Road, West Ham, Essex with his wife, Mary (aged 21) and had a female visitor and two servants (one a nurse) staying with them described himself as:

> Music Printer & Publisher of Firm Curwen & Sons, employing 25 Men, 18 Boys & 14 Women

Although the Tonic sol-fa became popular, it was not until the 1880s that it was actually used at the Reading British School. In the Infant School Log Book, Emma Ryder recorded that, when school reconvened after the two week Christmas holiday in 1882, there was further training for the teaching staff. A singing class commenced 13th January and was scheduled to take place each Friday afternoon after school so that they might be instructed in the New Notation (Tonic Sol-fa) by Mr. Moss. It was a year later that the Tonic Sol-fa system was first mentioned by Mary Ann Reay in the Girls' School Log Book. School had reopened Monday, 8th January, 1883 after three weeks vacation and Mr. Ryder commenced teaching it on 26th. It was mentioned again in 1889:

Examination papers for approximate numbers came on Monday, September 9th. On 16th, I had notice of Inspector's visit on October 18th and 21st. At 9.30 on 27th, Mr. Pearce came to examine the Tonic Sol-fa. The children seemed to do very well. Mr. Boorne visited on afternoon of Monday October 7th (average 215).

Mistress changes until Catherine Thompson appointed

I had remained as Secretary for the Girls' School even though the post of Treasurer and that of the other Secretary changed periodically. In 1848, there was another change of Mistress as, on 28th March, a letter from Miss Searle was read expressing her intention of resigning from that office around 15th July though she was willing to acquiesce in our wishes should we consider a few weeks earlier or later more in the interests of the school. As her resignation was accepted, I, as Secretary, was requested to write to Borough School making application for a Mistress to be sent. On 24th April, I was able to report that my letter had been acknowledged and that it would meet with the early attention of the Committee. A reply had been received by 30th May meeting stating that they had a Miss West who had been for the last three years at a School at Staines and she had good testimonials. It was unanimously resolved that she be offered the situation of Mistress of the Reading Girls' School at a salary of £50 and that the three months' trial commence when she enter on her duties on 17th July.

At 18th December 1849 meeting, I brought in £12 " 3 " 6 from my Collecting Book; there was a Subscription from Mrs. Egerton; 10/- belonging to account from late treasurer; and Mrs. Morley in the chair also transmitted ten pounds to me from a collection made in the Congregational Chapel, Castle Street in aid of the funds of the school. After the usual business had been transacted the present state of the school and the qualifications of the Mistress were considered. The general feeling of the committee appeared to be that Miss Smith, with the sincerest desire to do her duty to the school as far as her ability extends and possessing many of the qualifications in a teacher is materially deficient in many points essential to the work of education. Under those circumstances we resolved unanimously "That it is in the best interests of the school to make a change of Mistress" so I was requested to give Miss Smith three months' notice from that day and open communication with a young woman who was Mistress of the School at Chesham. Her qualifications appeared so satisfactory that the sub Committee met with her when she came to Reading Monday 7th January 1850. At our meeting on 29th, the Committee

91

unanimously decided that Miss Belcher should be appointed to succeed Miss Smith at a Salary of £50 per year and that I should notify that to her at once.

I read both my letter and Miss Belcher's reply at the 26th February meeting and we agreed that she should enter on her duties on 25th March, with Elizabeth Burdler filling in for the week between Miss Smith's leaving, if necessary. I had to furnish Miss Smith with a testimonial to the effect that, during the time that she had had the charge of this school, her general deportment had secured her the respect of the Committee and that they considered her diligent, active and painstaking and that the needlework department was satisfactorily done. In fact I was able to report on 2nd April that the new Mistress entered for her duties on 25th March, Miss Smith having agreed to remain until that time. I then passed on Miss Belcher's application for a supply of several books and was then requested to order the books in her list from the Borough School.

Various other changes took place that year. At the 25th June meeting, it was unanimously agreed that an estimate for whitewashing, painting and repairing, where required, the whole of the schoolroom, cloakroom and other buildings were to be obtained before the next Committee meeting. The desks were to be taken up and made of sufficient height and width for writing and eight boxes to hold books for Monitors to sit upon were to be bought. The store was to be attended to and the desks immediately behind it removed and a passage left in their stead. Although the number present were within capacity of a class-room, it was thought that a gallery (which could at any time be easily enclosed) might be an advantage at the upper end of the room.

By 6th August, I had received a note from Miss Belcher giving notice of her resignation from the office of Mistress three months from then. However, at 29th October meeting, I was able to report that her replacement, Miss Thompson, had commenced work on 28th when school re-opened following the erection of a new classroom.

Mrs. Boorne was Treasurer again in 1851 when my Assistant Secretary was Miss Gantry. By 27th July 1852, the Sub-Committee appointed by the Boys' Committee agreed with the Ladies' Committee on the subject of an Infant School in connection with the British Schools. I was therefore asked to form a Sub-Committee from the Girls' School similar to the one from the Boys' to look for a building suitable for furnishing it.

As with Mary Curwen, Mary Boorne's eldest son was to become well-known – only in his case, it was more locally than nationally as he became mayor in 1861 at the time of the opening of the Public Recreation Grounds and Drinking Fountain at the Forbury Gardens. Like John Curwen, he was also genuinely interested in education.

Huntley, Boorne and Stevens Factory

Born in Cheltenham in 1798, Mary had married fellow Non-Conformist James Boorne, who had been born in Deptford, Kent in 1790. Their son, James, was born in Reading in 1824 and had early joined the Society of Friends, having been attracted by the simplicity of the Quaker mode of life and worship. In 1846, he had entered into partnership with 39-year-old Joseph Huntley, ironmonger, second son of Joseph Huntley, who had opened a tin making and ironmongery shop opposite his father's bakery in London Street in 1832. Huntley & Boorne was to develop into Huntley, Boorne & Stevens in 1872 and become well known as makers of tin boxes for Huntley & Palmers' biscuits. [15] Although very occupied in business, James was deeply interested in all social and political questions that concerned his fellow-townsmen and, as early as 1848, he was writing tracts in defence of Quakerism. He married Ellen Whiting [16] in 1850 and they started married life at 68 London Street – not far from his parents, who lived at 4 Mill Lane.

At the age of 36, James was made Mayor of Reading. During his mayoralty, he opened the Forbury Gardens on 16th August 1861. With his commanding presence; alert, well-stocked mind and rich, well-modulated voice and gift of humour, he was considered a fine speaker. A strenuous Liberal, his tall figure was for many years, both metaphorically and physically, a rallying-point for the men of his party. He was justly proud of the part he took in securing the election, as one of the members for Reading, of Sir Francis Goldsmid, the first Jew to take his seat in the House of Commons. He was also one of the ablest and warmest supporters of George Shaw-Lefevre, later Lord Eversley, who represented Reading for 20+ years and was a member of many Liberal governments at a time when vast numbers of our countrymen were not

---

15 James did not retire from the business until 1893

16 Born Newbury in 1830, daughter of Samuel & Susannah, niece of Joseph Huntley

enfranchised; seats were sold to the highest bidders and there was much bribery, intimidation and corruption.

James' presidency of the **Reading Literary and Scientific Mechanics' Institute** (imposing building seen here on the left-hand side of London Street in 1843) brought him into close association with some of the most distinguished men of letters of our time. Dickens, Thackeray and Kingsley were his personal friends and, it was at his invitation, that **Charles Dickens** was a guest of the Boornes when he gave his first public reading from *Oliver Twist* at the Institute. In 1865, he published *The Friend in his Family*, an exposition of principles as depicted in the writings of early followers of George Fox. He was also a frequent contributor of brightly written articles on religious and literary subjects to the *Friends' Quarterly Examiner*.

In 1868, as a Minister of Reading and Warborough Monthly Meeting, James visited, under religious concern, every Friends' Boarding School in England as part of his Ministry. He was described as "a vigorous and striking personality, an earnest champion of religious freedom and a stalwart pioneer of social and political progress".

Perhaps now is a good point to revert back to the Reading British School and describe how the area round 51 Southampton Street (then called the Lancasterian School with Mr. M. Thomson, the Master of the Boys' School, and Miss Perry, the Mistress of the Girls' School) had changed from E. Yorke's *Reading Street Key 1839*. At that time, it was next to Rose Court then there were seven houses before Lily Court, Mr. G. Baggs owning the first two (numbers 56 and 58) and Mr. Exall the next (number 60) as can be seen here:

Southampton Street
45.   [Rose Court
51. **Lancasterian school,   Mr. M Thomson, master**
                                       Miss Perry, mistress
56. Mr. G. Baggs
58. Mr. G. Baggs
60. Mr. W. Exall
61.
62.
63.   [Lilley Court

Much more in-filling of property round the British Schools occurred between Snare's *Post Office Reading Directory 1842-3* and *1865 Macauley's Reading Directory* as this comparison of addresses in Southampton Street shows:

1842	1865
Southampton Street	*Southampton Street*
[Rose Court	[ROSE COURT
46. Grubb Isaac	46. Chalk Henry
47. Winter Joseph	47. } Lascelles Thomas
48. Bowler Isaac	48. } grocer and beerseller
49. Wallden Josiah	49. Benwell George
50. Steward Mrs.	50. Arman Charles
51. Warner George	51. Wheatley Thomas
[Pink Court	[PINK COURT
British Schools:-	**British Schools:-**
Master, Mr. William Lane	**Master, Thomas Gleave**
Mistress, Miss Searle	**Mistress, Catherine Thompson**
53. Collins Thomas	53. Pocock George
54. Flowers Joshua	54. Ford William
55. Munday William	55. Short William
56. Baggs Mr. Joseph	56. Dobson William
57. Long Edward	**57. Long Edward**
58. Alexander Mrs.	58. Quelch Henry, boot and shoe maker
59.	59. Barkshire Mrs.
60. Exall Mr. William	60.
61. Netherclift Mr. Matthew	61. Crawley Mr. E. T.
62. White Mr. John	62. Litchfield Sarah, milliner/dressmaker
63. Ward Mr. John	**63. Gleave Mr. Thomas**
[Lily Court	[LILY PLACE

Interestingly, only Edward Long seems to have remained in the same house during those 23 years. By the *1865 Macauley's Reading Directory*, I was the

4th named *Champion* mentioned and was living at 5, Eldon Square whereas, at the time of the 1851 census, I had been living at 6 Albion Place with my 24-year-old Lady's maid, Ann Dyer, who had been born in Caversham. I was a Fundholder which meant that I received an annual income from an investment of money (stocks and shares) in Public Funds.

The other Champions living in Reading in 1865 were my older brothers:

1. John Champion, living at Caversham mill – he died that June in Reading.
2. William Champion, esq. (who had married Mary Ann Wayland 7th August 1817) was at Calcot mill with their son and my nephew,
3. William Wayland Champion esq. (born 15th September 1821 in Tilehurst and christened at Kings Road Baptist Meeting). He didn't marry Anne Day until 1869 in Marylebone, London and they then had Rose Annie (1870), Edith Mary (1873) and William Wayland (1875). By 1881, the family were living at Maner Farm House in Reading St. Giles, where William was a Farm Steward of 688 acres, employing 54 men and 2 boys.
5. Joshua Champion, another of my nephews, having been born to John (no. 1 above) and Mary on 3rd November 1822 in St. Mary's district of Reading, was at Southcote mill. By 1881, he was a 57-year-old retired miller living alone at Thames Bank, Caversham, Oxford.

Macauley's Reading Guide, 1867, shows that we had had a period of stability in both schools during that decade as Mrs. Deane and I were still the Secretaries; Mrs. Boorne the treasurer and Miss Thompson, the Mistress of the Girls' School as we had been in 1859 and the Boys' School officers had also remained the same. Mrs. Boorne, 'though, was a widow by 1869 so was detailed as Mrs. Mary Boorne of Cadogan house, Mill Lane as she had remained in the marital home while her son, James and his wife Ellen had moved to Sydenham house, King's-road. Committee meetings were still held once a month – usually on the last Tuesday morning of the month – but June's meeting was held on Monday 27th as Queen Victoria's Coronation Day was to be celebrated on 28th with a feast for 2,200 Sunday and Charity School children in the Market Place (her coronation having taken place on 28th June 1838). The Prince of Wales also visited the town Friday that week and, as so often happened when such events occurred, school attendance was only 60. Several Committee ladies & myself went into Girls' School after that meeting. Many British School children attended the Reading Sunday School Union Festival on 16th July, a report of which appeared in *Reading Mercury* of 18th:

96

FESTIVAL OF THE READING SUNDAY SCHOOL UNION

The annual festival of the Schools of this Union took place on Thursday at Whiteknights Park, kindly lent for the occasion by C. Easton Esq. The weather was exceedingly fine, and the children of one of the schools were conveyed to the park in vans. The Union was established in 1860, and includes the following schools:- Broad-street, Castle-street, Coley-street, Church-street, Hosier-street, King's-road, Silver-street, London-street, Spring Gardens and Trinity. The teachers number 240 and the children about 2,000. All Sunday schools and friends of religious education holding evangelical doctrines are eligible for admission to the Union. The children assembled at their respective schools at one o'clock and at two o'clock a procession was formed in London-street. A large number of flags and banners were displayed, and two bands of music engaged. Along the whole line of the route large numbers of spectators were assembled. Arrived at the Park, each of the schools took up the places assigned to them under the shady trees, the names of each school being affixed to a tree. Cricket, archery and all kinds of field games were commenced, and numerous visitors arrived from Reading during the afternoon and evening. At five o'clock the children were supplied with tea, and after tea the games resumed till eight o'clock when preparations were made for returning to Reading. Messrs. Margrett Brothers made three attempts to obtain water by means of the Abyssinia pump, but without success. Some of the school obtained water from the residence of Mr. Easton, and the refreshment tents of Mr. Hemmings, confectioner, Broad-street were crowded during the day. The Bands of music were stationed in the Park and played a selection of music till eight o'clock, when the National Anthem was the signal for departure. The procession was soon re-formed, and the children arrived at their homes before nine o'clock and at that hour the park was entirely cleared. Several ministers of the various Dissenting congregations were present in the park. The festival passed off well and afforded the highest gratification to all present especially to the youthful members of the schools of the Union.

Although not directly connected with the British Schools, the following article in *Saturday October 23rd 1869 Mercury*, gives an idea of a major change that was affecting life for families living near the schools in the ensuing decade:

READING AND BASINGSTOKE TURNPIKE TRUST

The public will be somewhat interested in knowing that this Trust will expire on 30th June next. The Toll Gates at Whitley, Whitenights, Shinfield, Basing, and Four Lanes End, will then be removed, and the turnpike road thrown open to the public toll free. But this boon will cast upon the parishes, through which the road passes, the entire expense of its future repair. It has often been remarked that this turnpike road is one of the best in the country, and though it will ere long be

97

mixed into the highways of the parishes, yet it is to be hoped the day is far distant when any other remark will be made respecting its condition than that of approbation.

1870s saw many changes

By the time of the 1869 Report of the Reading British Girls' and Infants' School, Mrs. Jas. Boorne was Treasurer, I was Secretary pro tem. and Miss H. Williams was my Assistant. Other members of the Committee were:

Mrs. Andrewes	Mrs. Burgis	Mrs. Gostage	Miss Ridley
Mrs. Arrowsmith	Miss Colebrook	Mrs. S. Gostage	Mrs. Spokes
Mrs. Barcham	Mrs. Collier	Miss Kidgell	Mrs. Siliar
~~Mrs. Barter~~	Mrs. J. O. Cooper	Mrs. Long	Miss Tutty
Miss Boorne	Miss Gilbert	Mrs. Potter	

In accordance with their accustomed habit, the Committee present the Annual Report of the above institution. They regret to state, that the average attendance in both Schools, more especially in the Girls' has been less than during several preceding years. The Committee attribute this to circumstances over which they have had no control, a principle one being the unusual amount of illness among Children in the early part of the year; a secondary one, the opening of another School in the neighbourhood; the attendance has however increased the last few months.   Miss MARTIN has worked with assiduity and diligence, but the Committee prefer giving the opinion of the Inspector rather than their own; the following is an extract from his Report:- "These Schools appear to be worthily performing the functions required of them, in proper, cleanly, and useful habits, and by imparting the knowledge which is likely to be wanted when they are called upon to fill their places in mature life."

It will be remembered that this School has, since its formation in 1818 been supported by Voluntary Subscriptions and the Weekly Fees; and the Committee think they can say with truth that it has been efficiently sustained, and has held a good reputation among kindred Institutions of the town.   But in the altered state of public opinion, with respect to education generally, and the growing conviction that Government should take some part in it, the Committee have this year felt they would fail in their duty if they did not take this subject into consideration, as bearing on the interests of the schools.   They are strengthened in this opinion by some practical difficulties.   In the normal schools for the training of Teachers, there are now found comparatively few who are uncertified, and these are, for the most part, of an inferior class; those certified are generally unwilling to take office in a Voluntary School: again, – the salaries required are much higher in amount than formerly, and the expenses altogether of keeping a School up to the desired level are greatly increased.   When the question was definitely brought before the Committee, whether or not the Schools should accept Government Inspection and a Grant, it was found they were about equally divided in opinion, and on all grounds they considered it desirable to ask the mind of the subscribers on the question. This was done, as far as possible, individually, and the result was, that indifference characterized the answers of many; from twenty to thirty decidedly objected, and consistently promised an increased subscription; and about half the whole number pronounced in favour of Government Aid and Inspection. The Committee then felt justified in taking the primary measures to secure the object contemplated, and, on a certificated Teacher being appointed for each School at Christmas, they believe the required conditions will be complied with, and the Schools accepted by Government.

The certificated Teachers included 33-year-old Mary Ann Reay, a teacher of eight year's standing, whose first words in the Reading Girls' British School Log Book on 10th January 1870 were:

> This Establishment has recently been accepted as a Government School, and will shortly be placed under Government Inspection. Mary A. Reay, formerly of the Girls' British School Tottenham has entered upon the office of Mistress today. Attendance 104 both morning and afternoon.

The following day, Fanny A. Ace from Stockwell Training College, whom we had appointed Infants' School Mistress, commented in Infant Log Book that:

> the school had not yet been visited by an Inspector. About 85 in attendance. Took first class for reading, writing and arithmetic. Children backward in writing.

When I visited the Infants' School during the afternoon of 15th September, I was able to comment on how pleased I was with the appearance of the room. The children semed very orderly and attentive throughout my visit. Miss Ace told me that the previous morning she had had to dismiss a boy from school as his mother complained of his going out for recreation bareheaded although she had not previously requested that he might be allowed to have his cap on. She also commented that Ellen Maggs from the Girls' School had commenced duties as a Monitor on the 13th.

Helen Williams, who had been born in Glamorgan in 1837, took over from me as Secretary of the Girls' and Infants' Schools and, in May 1871, she called in to both schools with the Inspector's Reports and entered them in the respective Log Books. The Public Examination had been held Tuesday, 2nd May with G. Palmer Esq. in the chair – from 10.30 to 11.30 a.m. for Infants. No school was held Monday and Tuesday afternoons and all day Wednesday.

Attendance was very good – average of 122 and 104 Infants – despite many children being absent, the measles being in their families, and the Pupil Teachers and Monitors were also absent several times in consequence of illness. Miss Williams visited on 15th, having the Inspector's Reports with her:

Summary of the Inspector's Report on Reading Girls' British School, 1871

> "The order of the School is excellent. The work of the Standards is very neat and accurate throughout. The elder Scholars answer readily in the Geography of England but do not show any striking proficiency in it."
>
> Copied from Inspector's Report by Helen Williams Secy

Summary of the Inspector's Report of the Reading Infants' School, 1871

> "The Infants' School is managed with a good deal of care and spirit. The efficiency with which it is taught is commendable."
>
> Copied from Inspectors Report by Helen Williams, Sec.

By then, 28 Infants' School children were absent with measles so average attendance had dropped to 91 despite 21 scholars being admitted since the beginning of May.

After I had ceased to be Secretary of the Girls' School, I returned to an annual Prize Giving at three o'clock on Friday, 17th January 1879. The current Committee Ladies had invited myself, along with other friends, and we were all highly delighted with the order, and very much praised it. The children seemed very much pleased with their prizes which were distributed by Mrs. Reaney to those who had passed in every subject at the Inspection. They sang several pieces and eight of them gave recitations. There had been a good attendance all that week, average being 178. It had been good to see that one of the former Pupil Teachers, Annie Spencer, had commenced duties as Assistant Mistress that term. Born in 1858, her father, William, had died, aged 44, in 1874 when she was in her second year as a Pupil Teacher but her widowed mother, Elizabeth, had managed to bring up Annie and her two sisters, the elder being already a certificated teacher of pianoforte.

I had moved to Hastings, Sussex by 1881 and was living at 50 Warrior Square – a Boarding House kept by 51-year-old Anna Jenkins, whose husband, Joseph (54) was a Baptist Minister. A solicitor, his wife and six-month old daughter; four other ladies and Joseph & Anna's son, 19-year-old Stanley, an Ironmonger's Apprentice, lived there. Six female Domestic Servants in their teens or twenties were employed to look after us.

100

IV. Chief Officer's Tale: GEORGE PALMER 1847–1897

I first became involved with the British School in Southampton Street in the 1840s, having moved to Reading in mid-1841 when I was 23 to go into partnership with my 38-year-old cousin, Thomas Huntley. His father, Joseph (1775 – 1849), a yeoman and schoolmaster, had moved to Reading from Sibford Gower, Oxfordshire in 1811 and started a biscuit bakery and confectioner's business here in 1822. In Horniman's *Reading Directory 1826*, it was listed under BAKERS as:

Huntley Joseph, 72 London-street.

By 1832, Joseph's second son, also named Joseph (1807 – 1895) had opened a tin making and ironmongery shop opposite the bakery. That later became Huntley, Boorne and Stevens. My copy of Snare's *Post Office Reading Directory 1842-3* shows that the population of Reading at the time of the 1841 census on June 7th was 19,512 and was split between the three parishes:

	Houses			Persons enumerated		
	Occupied	Unocc.	Build	Male	Female	Total
St. Giles	1,350	120	27	3,144	3,593	6,737
St. Lawrence	756	46	4	1,900	2,117	4,017
St. Mary	1,650	77	14	3,700	4,620	8,320
Total	3,756	243	45	8,744	10,330	19,074

With the following 438 others, the overall total was **19,512**:

Royal Berkshire Hospital	64
St. Lawrence's Poorhouse	91
St. Mary's Poorhouse	106
County Gaol	169
Borough Bridewell	8
Total	438

Prior to 1840, Reading had communicated with the outer world by four principal routes – two by water (the Thames, and the Kennet & Avon Canal, an extension of which united Newbury and Bristol in 1810) and two by land (the London – Bristol road and, of inferior importance, was the Southampton Road, which linked Reading to Portsmouth and Southampton). Naturally,

101

with the opening of the **Great Western Railway station** on March 30th, 1840, Reading became even more accessible. Almost a third of Berkshire's attorneys and solicitors were resident here and it was home to five of the county's 18 bankers at that time.

I had been born in Long Sutton, Somerset on January 18th, 1818, as was my brother, Samuel, in 1820 and sister, Mary Ovens, in 1822. By the time our youngest brother, William Isaac, was born in 1825, the family had moved to Elberton, Gloucestershire where our father, William (born in 1788), died in 1826. Although I was only eight when he died, I was still sent, a year later, to Sidcot, a Quaker boarding school (established near Weston-super-Mare in 1808). My siblings eventually joined me and we each spent five years there from ages 9 – 14. However, in those days, brothers and sisters only saw each other for half an hour a week under strict surveillance. Both the boys' and girls' schools were in the same grounds but the sexes were taught separately and not allowed to mix outside school. Even after 1838, when the two schools were under the same roof, they were in different wings.

From 1832, when I was fourteen and a half, I was apprenticed to an uncle (my father's sister's husband), Robert Hitchcock, in Taunton to learn the trade of confectioner and miller. When my indentures finished in 1840, my widowed

mother, Mary, assigned the lease of the Farm at Elberton to her brother-in-law, Joseph Evans, and she and my sister accompanied me to Cardiff. In mid 1841, the three of us moved to Reading and, on Midsummer Day – June 24th – I went into partnership with Thomas Huntley, a fellow Quaker. The partnership was set up to run for 14 years until Midsummer Day 1855. It was agreed that my mother, sister and myself should live above the shop at **72 London Street** at a net rent of £20 a year while the Huntleys rented a house in a nearby street, still within walking distance of the Quaker Meeting House in Church Street.

Huntley and Palmer Biscuit Factory

After only three years in Reading, my sister (Mary Ovens Palmer) died here of consumption on September 6th, 1844, aged just 22 as she was born on May 17th, 1822. She had been a shop assistant for the business, one of just seven employees when Thomas and I became partners. The others were two journey men, two apprentices and two boys who carried out packing and deliveries. Journey men were normally employed by a master craftsman and had the right to charge a fee for each day's work (French *journée* means *one day*). They could not employ others and would often live apart, possibly with their own family, whereas an apprentice would be bound to a master, living as a member of his household and receiving most or all of his compensation in terms of food or lodging usually for a fixed term of seven years.

Following Mary's death, Mother and I continued living in London Street. She had been born in 1786 to William and Elizabeth Isaac in Somerset. Her mother's maiden name had been Clark and it was her cousins, Cyrus and James Clark (also Quakers), who founded C. & J. Clark, shoe manufacturers, of Street, Somerset. Originating from Cyrus' tanning business, which started in 1821 and concentrating on producing wool rugs and using off-cuts to make slippers, this developed into the renowned Clarks Footwear and Cyrus was eventually in a position to make his brother James a partner in 1833.

In 1846, five years after I arrived in Reading, Thomas and I bought, for £1,800, Messrs Baylis' silk crepe factory which had remained empty for three years or so. It was situated in King's Road and provided an ideal site for our **Huntley and Palmer Biscuit Factory.** Although I spent a lot of time planning and moving into the factory and was obviously absorbed in gradually evolving the mechanical operations there, I did have time for other interests. Like most Quakers, I believed that we should all be helping our fellow human beings and was therefore pleased to see that the builder Richard Billing was conducting a survey into the Sanitary Condition

103

of the Borough of Reading in 1846 as the water supply was irregular, insufficient, expensive, partial and impure. Even after Cubitt's improvements in 1818, the supply was limited to alternate days. I had complained that, if I ordered the filthy gutter in front of my shop in London Street to be flushed, an officer of the Water Company cut off my water supply. Many houses had no supply from wells or pipes and, in 1847, many people were compelled to go 400 yards to fetch water from the Holy Brook. Richard's statistics about the sanitation and ventilation showed:

Richard Billing's 1846 analysis of houses and courts in Reading

Parish	Courts	One Entrance	Houses	No rear Ventilation	Restricted Ventilation
St Giles	42	35	268	153	123
St Mary	60	48	499	360	184
St Lawrence	27	26	211	143	166
Total	129	109	978	656	473

Mary Lobel's 1800 map had given clear evidence of back-to-back building in just 17 courts so Richard's identification of 129 courts and 656 houses (16% of total housing stock) as back-to-back or without rear ventilation, showed a significant increase. The largest number of back-to-backs in any Reading block was 56 in the courts of Somerset Place, Chatham Street, built during the 1820s in St. Mary's parish. **Crane Court, Silver Street** was next largest with 24. However, smaller blocks of back-to-backs were preferred and were more suited to infilling in built-up areas, so 7.6 was the average per court.

In Silver Street, the sewage discharged into a ditch without outlet. Down London Street ran a black open gutter, which was very offensive in hot weather but that Street was not exceptional in that respect. The Town Clerk assessed that there was not a single street in a proper state and the *Reading Mercury* affirmed in August that:

> no one could pass down a by-street without being offended by some stagnant pool of putridity, the insufferable stench of a slaughter-house, or the foul air of a half-choked drain; even the Market Place was often barely endurable.

In 1847, there were forty foul open drains in St. Lawrence parish and, in the poorer quarters there was almost no means of carrying off filth and impurities. The cleansing of the streets was still very imperfect in 1849. Those conditions coupled with the defective water supply, resulted in fevers and a high death-rate. The surgeon, Mr. Frederick B. Hooper drew the attention of the Town Council to the prevalence of typhus fever in August 1846. In a subsequent letter, he stated that he had attended 100 cases of fever among the poor alone in the previous twelve months. In 1848, there was a fresh outbreak and, in 1850, it was officially stated that, whereas the general death-rate was 16 per 1,000, the rate in Reading had risen from 24 in 1841 to 30 in 1849. There had also been several cases of cholera in 1848/9. The medical men – Dr. Cowan, Mr. May and Mr. Hooper – used their authority and position as members of the Corporation to impress the gravity of those facts upon the public mind at a time when the nation was becoming increasingly interested in the principles of public health. Following the 1846 report on the sanitation of the Borough, the Town Council Committee resolved to ask Parliament to sanction a measure called *Reading Improvement, Market, Water Works, & Sewage Bill.*

Pupil Teacher system inaugurated

In 1843, the Council on Education Committee had agreed that the British and Foreign School Society should be consulted on the appointment of inspectors for British Schools and, when grants were extended to Wesleyan and Roman Catholic Schools from 1847, the same right was given to those denominations. Grants additional to those for erecting schools had been inaugurated in 1846:

- for well qualified teachers (those who obtained Certificates of Merit)
- for a new category of apprentice teacher (pupil-teachers or stipendiary monitors) and
- for those who instructed the apprentices.

Obviously schools had to fulfil certain conditions with regard to organisation, discipline, qualified staff, buildings and equipment if they wished to be involved. A system of Queen's Scholarships was also set up to assist the entry of ex-pupil teachers into training colleges so a much greater importance was attached to the role of inspectors.

Nationwide, 1846 had seen the inauguration of the Pupil Teacher system in Schools. The intellectual defects of the Monitorial System had gradually manifest itself and the newly-constituted Education Department decided that Monitors should be superseded by Pupil Teachers, all of whom would be required to pass through the elementary course before receiving regular instruction while training for the office of Teacher under a five-year apprenticeship scheme from the age of thirteen. If they completed their term successfully they could go to College to qualify as Certified Teachers.

It was about that time that I was asked if I could use my business skills for the Reading British School and I willingly agreed. My own education and that of my brothers and sister had taken place at Sidcot from ages 9 – 14. When I went there in 1827, the curriculum consisted of Grammar and Geography, with experimental lessons in Chemistry, Electricity and Acoustics added later. I found the practical nature of the curriculum quite stimulating and it was enough to awaken in me an interest in Science which never left me and which soon developed into a practical skill in Engineering and a mechanical insight later recognised as exceptional in a layman. I willingly continued my Science studies outside school hours as I derived such enjoyment from them. However I did regret that no History, English literature or Foreign Language was taught because I never acquired the ability to speak either in French or German.

My first comments in the British Boys School Visitors' book in 1847 were:

10 Mo 4   Visited the school and am pleased with it but wish the Master had some good help.   Geo Palmer

11 Mo 3   Looked in when the school was going on about as usual at a.m. yesterday.   Geo Palmer

A "Ragged School" for Reading

I realised that education is an extremely important issue and my involvement with the British School meant that I became even more aware of those children that did not seem to have the advantages of an education. I often came across children who were so hungry that, even if they had had a school place, they would not have benefited properly from it. Others had recognised this before me but I determined to make my fellow Readingensians aware of the problem so I wrote a letter to the *Reading Mercury*, in which I showed my concern for the children who were not receiving any education because a "hungry barrier" in them frustrated all "efforts to feed the mind". I suggested that a school should be set up for the very poor, similar to those already established in Aberdeen where the children could be provided with one or two good but plain meals of oatmeal porridge and soup each day, as well as facilities for bathing themselves. The letter appeared in *Saturday, December 18th, 1847* edition and seemed to be directly responsible for the town's first Ragged School being founded a year later, so here it is in its entirety:

To the EDITOR of the READING MERCURY
    RESPECTED FRIEND, – There are in Reading as in most other towns a great

106

number of children untaught and little cared for, whose parents are altogether unable to provide for their animal much less for mental wants. These children are to be found at all hours of the day roving about our streets, at play, or doing nothing, and sometimes worse than nothing. These are the children who will be found crowding the workhouses and the gaols at some future day, so completely untrained to any useful application that as men and women they grow up unfit for service either as domestics or as artisans, useless in this country and altogether unfit as emigrants to another. We have in Reading an abundance of schools to take in all these destitute children, both on Sabbath and other days; there is no lack of teachers belonging to the different sections of the Christian Church to teach those truths which would, if received even by children, elevate their tastes and understandings, or to teach them their duties of man to man, and their duties towards themselves, and yet with all these advantages these children are not taught, and are altogether beyond the reach of the present system of teaching and training. [17]

The simple fact is this – there is a hungry barrier resisting our efforts to feed the mind: our addressing the understanding of the child while he is feeling the cravings of hunger is unnatural and preposterous. If we can direct the child or the man where or how to find food or clothing, that would be the proper plan; but to do this in numerous cases is impossible, and common sense confirms the course a benevolent heart would at once conceive to relieve the pangs of hungry stomach before we can hope to have a willing learner.

A great number of schools under the banner of "Ragged Schools" have sprung up in most parts of the kingdom, probably from the example of Aberdeen and some other Scotch cities, whose municipal authorities have taken the matter up, and by their police regulations sent every begging boy and girl to their "Ragged Schools," where they have not only been *taught* but *fed*. It is for the purpose of calling attention to this mode of treating destitute children that I take the pains to fill up a few leisure moments and trespass on your space. I am myself constantly told by poor children at school that they are hungry and their looks confirm the statement – they do not and cannot listen, they come to school to fill up a tedious hour, and go away to reflect that the teachers are kind – but it is food they want. To a benevolent and Christian public I appeal. Is it not worthwhile to copy the Aberdeen plan of Ragged Schools? Provide a school room well-warmed and ventilated, open to any children who would be sulkily and hungrily wandering about the streets; during the day give them one or two good meals of oatmeal porridge, or soup; let there be a bath attached to the room, and let one of the conditions of being there be the frequent use of it; and at night, after a day's

---

[17] Yes, that sentence really did contain 92 words, 450 characters or 543 if spaces are included!

discipline and a good supper, let them go home to carry into their wretched dwellings those ideas of their duties acquired during the day.

Of course the carrying out such a plan will involve expenses; and an expense well worth incurring too. It can be done effectually by the parish or borough authorities only, and if by doing this we clear the streets of begging children the benevolent will save many pence, which were better spent in poor or borough rates, and if by this regulation the workhouses get some relief, and the police office is troubled with fewer juvenile delinquents, all will have cause to be satisfied as to the cost, and the friends of humanity would lend cheerfully a helping hand in so good a project. The great object of such an establishment as this should be to elevate the minds of those who come; they should be treated with great kindness and forbearance, yet with great firmness, a strict conformity to the rules of the institution should be the condition of being allowed to be there, and if the police authorities had strict charge to prevent any children from being about the streets, but to send all such to the Ragged School, there will at once be in operation a principle to prevent imposition out of doors, at the same time that a good meal and a generous reception will attract these very mendicants to the school room. The scholars going home at night, the whole expense of such a school will be the room, the master, and a few incidentals, besides the food, and this should not be thought too much of, it should be *plain*, while it should be *good, if not very plain* there will be an inducement to stay at school when their own industry might procure a living; for this reason I propose oatmeal porridge and soup, either of which may be made very cheep and quickly. There is, no doubt, many objections can be raised to these brief remarks. I do not presume in this space to lay down a plan, my object is to throw out an idea for the reflection of those who may think the matter worth notice.

Respectfully,

GEORGE PALMER

Other articles in that same newspaper gave some idea of how important the feeding of children was at that time when stealing items such as cabbages, carrots and turnips could render a prison sentence of fourteen days' imprisonment with hard labour:

BERKS POLICE

Fanny Devonport, Martha Devonport and Ann Vickers, for steeling cabbages and carrots, the property of Mr. Cannon, were severally sentenced to 14 days' punishment with hard labour at Reading gaol.

On Monday, Thomas Parker, for steeling turnips from a field belonging to Mr. Hughes of Clewer was committed to the House of Correction at Abingdon for 14 days.

BUCKS POLICE

On Thursday, Henry Stent, for steeling turnips, the property of Mr. Powell of Denham, in default of paying the fine inflicted, was committed to prison for one month.

When I called into the Boys' British School in February 1848, I was surprised to find very few comments had been made in the Visitors' Book. I recorded:

18/2/48 3 oclock found the School in active operation learning the Multiplication table all was going on satisfactorily.   Geo Palmer

Calling in again on 23/2 Mo/48, I found that the Master had written:

Several of the Committee looked in between 15th of November 1847 and the 28th January 1848 but did not enter their names.   Wm Lane.
NB One of the Committee requested me to make the above entry.

I was able to add:

23/2 Mo/48 15 minutes to four oclock found the Master very properly giving the boys ideas of great importance on ventilation space air and its effect on health, did not feel certain that it was necessary for him to stand where he did but felt that his object would have been more easily and effectually carried out had he been standing on a platform. Geo Palmer

Many of my future comments only gave date, numbers present and signature:

4 Mo 18th 1848. 100 Boys Present this morning.   Geo Palmer

although there were occasionally extras, such as:

5 Mo 4 1848.   About 90 present this morning. It being Fair week will account for a less attendance.   Geo Palmer

Later that month, I visited the School in company with James H. Juke on 16th.

In 1849, I was appointed Secretary of the Boys' School on the British system. My predecessor, Mr. Thomas Letchworth, had been involved with the School since its inception, his father having been one of 15 Trustees for the freehold land on which the Boys' School was built, then Secretary, so was a hard act to follow. Fortunately, Mr. J. D. Goodchild continued as Treasurer and Mr. Lane as Master, both of whom had been in post since at least 1842 according to my copies of *Snare's Post Office Reading Directory 1842 – 3* and *Rusher's Reading Guide 1847 – 49*. However, Miss West had replaced Miss Searle as Mistress of the Girls' School in 1848 and John Worley was soon to replace William Lane who wanted to start up his own school at 23 Crown Street.

109

Marriage and starting our own family

I began the 1850s by marrying Elizabeth Sarah Meatyard in Alton, Hampshire on January 17th, 1850. Elizabeth had been born to Robert and Sarah in Tooting, Surrey on November 16th, 1825. Her family were Quakers and her father a druggist agent for Huntley and Palmer in Basingstoke. Later that year, I was elected to Reading Town Council representing Church Ward.

Mother decided to continue living at **72 London Street** after I married as she had a Shop Assistant, Louisa Fear (aged 29) who had been born in Shiplott, Oxfordshire – and a House Servant, 21-year-old Elizabeth Dutch, living there with her. In 1851 census, she described herself as a 64-year-old Farmer's widow who had been born in Sturminster Newton in Dorset whereas I described myself as a "Biscuit baker employing about 130 hands", being a 33-year-old married man living at 1, Wilberforce Place. The only other person in the household on the night of Sunday, March 30th was our 21-year-old servant, Mary Smith, who had been born in Wokingham. At the time of that census, 575,162 females and 74,323 males were in service in England. [18] The number of servants employed ranged from 50 or so in a great house to a single maid-of-all-work (who tended to be girls of 13 or so) in a lower middle class home. Only the working class did not employ servants. The senior female servant was the Housekeeper who was always called Mrs. by the other servants regardless of whether or not she was married. Her male equivalent was the Butler. Housemaids and Footmen were responsible to the Housekeeper and Butler respectively. In the ten years from 1841, the working population increased from 37.8 to 48.2 per cent. The modal occupation at 17 per cent, especially among females under 20, was that of domestic servant, but there were 14 per cent employed in the manufacture or retail of clothing goods, including 445 shoemakers and 465 milliners.

Elizabeth was pregnant with our first child at the time of the 1851 Census and George William was born on May 23rd. That year, *The Great Exhibition of*

---

[18] Details in Visiting Maids' Bedroom at Nunnington Hall on 1 May 2008

the Works of Industry of all Nations had started in the Crystal Palace in Hyde Park, London on May 1st and continued until October 15th based on Prince Albert's idea of a self-financing collection of works of art and industry 'for the purposes of exhibition, of competition and of encouragement'.

In 1801, St. Giles had been the largest Reading parish although the population of the parishes of St. Mary and St. Lawrence were not far behind. During the next 50 years, St. Mary grew the fastest and St. Lawrence the slowest, so, by 1851, about 42 per cent of the population lived in St. Mary's parish, 36 % in St. Giles and just over 21 % in St. Lawrence. The reasons for the different rates of growth were mostly to do with the topographical and geographical aspects of each parish which dictated the availability of building land.

Huntley & Palmer was already the biggest employer in the town by 1851. The number of agricultural labourers living in Reading had increased by over 100 % since 1841 – an indication of the trend for urban living and the move away from the countryside. The head of house in the courts identified in the Census, showed that the unskilled worker was in the majority at 56 %. At that time, an agricultural wage in Berkshire was on average 7s. 6d. per week, low even for the southern counties, and in Willow Court – where all but one of the heads of house was an agricultural labourer – 2s. rent was more than a quarter of the weekly income.

Catherine Thompson appointed Mistress of Girls' school

The Crimean War took place from 1854 until 1856. During that time, I had to combine the role of Treasurer with that of Secretary of the Boys' School on the British System when Mr. John Worley was the Master and Miss Catherine Thompson the Mistress of the Girls' School. John had been born 1816 in Bermondsey and was living with his wife Ann and their young daughters, Elizabeth and Mary, while Catherine (born 1830 in Leeds, Yorkshire) was staying at 33/34 Southampton Street, the home of 62-year-old widowed Sarah Matthews, a Baker employing one man; her daughter, Elizabeth (26), and her niece, Eliza Shade (15), all Reading-born.

However, whereas the Secretary was described as Mr. G. Palmer as for 1848 and 1849, the Treasurer was recorded as Mr. George Palmer! In *Rusher's Reading Guide & Berks Directory, 1857*, that was also the case but, by the

111

time of *Macauley's Reading Directory, 1859*, Mr. C. J Andrewes [19] had been appointed Treasurer and I was able to revert to being just the Secretary again.

That was just as well as I was certainly having a very busy time around then. After being pressed several times to take the office of Mayor, I eventually accepted in November, 1857. Thomas Huntley had died in March that year and his only son, Henry Evans Huntley, decided not to become involved in the business. When I offered him almost £34,000 for his half, he accepted and, with his new wife, bought a country estate in Dorset. Obviously, though, I was committed to continue using the Huntley name and, in fact, sent an annual Christmas cake to Henry from the company for the rest of his life.

My brothers, Samuel and William Isaac Palmer, joined me as partners with an entitlement to a quarter of the profits each so we renamed the business **Huntley and Palmers** on October 19th. I decided to waive the initial premiums of £5,000 each that my brothers should strictly have paid since I wanted to be granted 'liberty to decline taking an active part and absent myself partly or entirely as I think fit' so that I could pursue my interest in public affairs. At that time the annual net profit of the firm had risen to £18,000. It rose to more than £84,000 during the 17 years that our partnership lasted and we enjoyed great personal wealth. However, my younger brother, William Isaac, was also very interested in education and had been elected onto the Boys' School Committee by 1860.

Alfred, our second son, had been born in 1852, just a year after his brother. Our first daughter who was to live was born towards the end of 1856. Emily's birth was a great joy to Elizabeth and myself as, having two healthy sons, we had hoped that we would be blessed with a daughter. I had become a Liberal Councillor in 1850 and, during the Municipal Year of 1857–8, while Mayor of Reading, I had the honour of presenting on January 25th, 1858 at St. James' Palace the Corporation address of congratulation to the Queen on the marriage of Princess Royal (Victoria Adelaide Mary Louise) to Crown Prince Friedrich Wilhelm of Prussia (who was later to rule as German Emperor briefly in 1888 before his death on June 15th that year). Since Queen Victoria and myself are a similar age, we were able to converse briefly about our respective children,

---

[19] Charles James Andrewes of Barrett, Exall & Andrewes' Iron Works, later called Reading Iron Works

especially since her ninth child, Beatrice Mary Victoria Feodore, had been born on April 14th, 1857 so was only a few months younger than Emily.

Elizabeth had been unable to accompany me on that occasion as our third son, Walter, was born around that time. However, she was able to join me when the Queen opened **Aston Hall People's Park** in Birmingham on Tuesday, June 15th, 1858 during a three-day  visit to the Midlands. Reading's own Pleasure Gardens had been opened Easter Sunday, 1856. Mr. Wheble had sold Forbury Hill and the eastern section of the present gardens to the town in 1854 and work began on laying out the area as a pleasure garden, including a fountain and summer house, in 1855. The planting of shrubs and deciduous trees had been  supervised by Suttons Seeds. In 1857, a Battle of Sebastopol gun was placed at the top of the Hill. Jokers fired it off at night and broke windows nearby.

It was the experience of being present at the opening of both the Forbury Gardens in Reading and Aston Hall People's Park in Birmingham that inspired me to give 14 acres of King's Meadow beside the River Thames for use as a recreation ground in 1875 and 49 acres of land in east Reading in 1889 for the future enjoyment of all those living in the Town. I had the latter planted with trees to provide a much-needed park and space for sporting activities. By the time it had been handed over to the Mayor of Reading on November 4th, 1891, it had been named Palmer Park. That evening, a banquet was held in my honour with fireworks in the park and free entertainment for the public. A **statue of myself** was also erected by public subscription and unveiled in Broad Street. However, I'm racing ahead so let's return to the 1850s. Towards the end of 1858, I had to complete an Education Commission form in my role as Secretary of the British School:

British Schools Details as from 1858 form

Notes at the beginning described various terms:

I. By the term "a School" is meant a distinct group of scholars under the instruction of a head master or head mistress and not a separate school building.
II. If an Educational establishment consists of a boys' school, a girls' school, and an infants' school under three separate head teachers, a copy of this circular should be filled up by *each* head teacher.
III. The expression "belonging to the school" means all who are receiving instruction at the time the return is made, and all who are absent for a *limited period* in consequence of illness, bad weather, or other circumstances. . . .

Here is a summary of my responses to the questions asked on the form:

- Reading in the county of Berks had a population of nearly 23,000
- The British School had not been enlarged since 1851 and was calculated to accommodate 200
- It was situated in an agricultural rather than a mining or manufacturing district
- The average ages at which the children were admitted to the week-day school were 7 for Males and 6 for Females – there was no evening school
- The average age at which the children left the week-day school was 12 for both sexes but that was increasing
- The Boys' School had 152 boys (19 from three to six years, 44 six to nine years, 68 nine to twelve years, 13 twelve to thirteen years and 8 above thirteen but not more than fifteen years) attending 190 days. In 1857 there had been 111 of whom 54 had attended 176 whole days
- The Girls' School had 167 girls (3 under three years, 58 three to six years, 62 six to nine years, 27 nine to twelve years, 14 twelve to thirteen years and 3 above thirteen but not more than fifteen years). In 1853, there had been 157; in 1854 – 161; 1855 – 131; 1856 – 141; and 1857 – 180
- Under the Teachers section, I detailed The Master, The Mistress and two Assistants as paid employees. There were also two Pupil Teachers paid by the government but no monitors paid by the managers of the school
- Subjects taught in the school included: Reading, Writing, Arithmetic, Grammar, Geography, History, Algebra, Mensuration, Geometry, Natural Philosophy, Natural History, Drawing
- The total annual income of the school, other than that derived from Parliamentary grant, was £35. 12. 0 from school fees and £71. 0. 0 from voluntary subscriptions and other sources. The estimated annual expenditure on account of the school was £121. 1. 1½ with the deficiency being made up by subscription

114

- The fees had been raised from 1^d and 2^d to 2^d, 3^d, 4^d, 6^d but the increase had made very little difference to the attendance of the poorer class of scholars

Obviously I **signed** the form as follows:

For those of you who are not Quakers, perhaps I should explain that members of Society of Friends do not consider it appropriate to use the names of days (Sunday to Saturday) and the months of January to August as they derive from heathen gods or goddesses. Instead, we use numbers, Sunday being the First Day for us. We had no difficulty with the months of September to December prior to 1752 as they were literal translations from the Latin of the Seventh to Tenth Month. However, when the start of the year changed from March 25th (Lady Day) to January 1st, we referred to all months by their number, September becoming Ninth Month, using either Roman numerals (i – xii) or Arabic (1 – 12). The American practice of putting the month before the day, when giving a date in numerical form was also used by British and Irish Friends. Thus, my **12 mo 16 1858** means that I had recorded my responses on December 16th, 1858.

Elizabeth shared my interest in education. She had a persevering capacity for self-education, which made her fill whole notebooks with information about philosophy and natural history. She also tried to keep her well-stocked mind active even though much of her life was taken up with our large household and family and with such charitable works as taking round coal tickets to the poor. If I paid more tributes in my public speeches to my mother than to my wife, it was because I was exceedingly reticent over those matters about which I felt most strongly.

I was elected Alderman of the Borough in 1859 when the officers of the British School were listed in that year's *Macauley's Reading Directory,* as:

Mr. T. Gleave the Master, Mr. C. J. Andrewes the Treasurer and Mr. G. Palmer the Secretary of the Boys' School while Miss Thompson was the Mistress, Mrs. Boorne the Treasurer and Miss Champion and Mrs. Deane the Secretaries of the Girls' School.

We remained in those roles throughout the 1860s as *Macauley's Reading Directory 1865* gives the Master and Mistress of the British Schools,

115

Southampton-street, as Thomas Gleave and Catherine Thompson, and the *Guide for 1867* shows that the Treasurers and Secretaries of both schools were the same as they had been in 1859.

By 1860, the Huntley & Palmers factory, which covered an acre and a half of land and employed 500, was the largest biscuit firm in England, producing 3,200 tons of biscuits valued at £180,000 a year. In *Return of Owners of Land 1873*, I was recorded as owning just under 2,000 acres of land in Berkshire, Hampshire, Oxford and Surrey with a gross estimated rental of £2,360 a year.

In 1862, the Government had introduced a new, tougher set of rules. The Revised Code of 1862 gave schools 4/- for each pupil who attended school 250 times in the previous year; plus up to 8/- per pupil based on their results in the Inspector's examination in reading, writing and arithmetic. This new set of rules came to be known as Payment by Results.

Treats at The Acacias

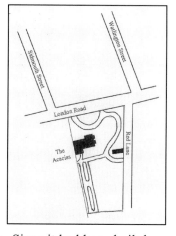

After several moves, Elizabeth and I settled in 1865 in *The Acacias* in London Road with our seven children. Miss Mary Weinholt had been living there (63 London rd in *1852/3 Slater's Directory of Berks etc*) previously when it and Sutton and Sons' nursery trial ground for testing new varieties of flowers and vegetables were the only landmarks between the Royal Berkshire Hospital and Kendrick Road and so it remained throughout my lifetime. Initially we leased the house from the Council before buying the freehold. Some people considered it to be a fairly modest villa but it suited us nicely. Since it had been built by a Reading coal and salt merchant in 1818, it was nicknamed "Salt Box Hall". Built of Portland stone, it was situated on the coaching London Road between Redlands Lane and Portland Place. From there, I was able to walk to the biscuit factory along Watlington Street, often encountering Martin Hope Sutton, whose transformation of the Reading seed business, Sutton & Sons, paralleled my own achievement. Between us, we provided two-thirds of the 3Bs for which Reading became known – Beer, Biscuits and Bulbs.

It was *The Acacias* that the British School children came to know and love as their annual treat took place in the grounds nearby. One such treat was described in *Saturday 2 July, 1869 Reading Mercury*:

TREAT TO BRITISH SCHOOL CHILDREN

One of the best and most successful of the many organisations for the care and education of the rising generation among us is the British Boys' and Girls' School, located in Southampton Street, formerly known as the Lancasterian. It was established half a century ago when such institutions as now abound among us were wholly unknown: and whilst these have sprung up around it in considerable numbers, the British School has not only held its own, but with little variation has gone on steadily increasing with the increase of similar establishments around it, supplying to successive generations of the little ones a thorough, useful and religious education. Indeed a visitor to the daily routine of the school, or its annual examination, would pronounce the secular education not only useful, but in the phraseology of the day "advanced"; whilst in the religious education they would find the theoretical difficulty solved of imparting scriptural knowledge and sound religious sentiments without a tinge of sectarian bias. The school is fortunate in having for its chief officer Mr. George Palmer, who has since the time of the late Mr. Thomas Letchworth, filled the office of secretary. Of late years Mr. Palmer has kindly invited all the children to a treat in a meadow contiguous to his own residence, also the Committee of the school and a large circle of friends to witness their enjoyments. On Wednesday last, being the eve of their Midsummer holidays, this annual treat, so long looked forward to by the children took place. When we give the numbers in the three departments into which the institution is divided, viz. boys 230, girls 160, infants 120, it will be seen that over 500 children were assembled; and some estimate may be formed of their enjoyments as well as the kind liberality of their host when we say that at half-past four these were all provided with an abundant tea, and subsequently, after indulging to their hearts content in swinging, racing and various games and contests, in which the victors were rewarded by a variety of toys, they were supplied with oranges, buns, nuts, biscuits etc. The lawn on which was stationed a band, was devoted to visitors, who were also liberally supplied with tea and refreshments. Probably 200 of these were present, among them the Revs. C. D. Duport, A. Clutterbuck, Aldis and Bulmer, Messrs. J. T. Morris, Andrewes, W. I. Palmer, Boorne, Thwaites, Bracher, Exall, Cooper, W. Slocombe, Joseph Morris, Catchpool, Minty, Isaac, Roaling, and many of the leading inhabitants, and a large company of ladies. Mr. and Mrs. Palmer were unintermittently engaged in catering to the enjoyments of the children; and when towards the close of the evening, at the suggestion of Alderman Andrewes, the children were called on to give "three cheers" for their kind host, they responded to it in a manner which proved that they understood what was meant and felt what was implied by that

117

proceedings. After singing the National Anthem, the company of children and friends dispersed at 9 p.m.

As usual I had been present at the examination at the Boys' British School earlier that year, as you can see from *27 March, 1869 Reading Mercury*:

Examination at BOYS' BRITISH SCHOOL

The annual examination of the boys attending this school took place in the presence of a large company of visitors on Tuesday evening, in the Schoolroom, under the presidency of the mayor (J.W. Hounslow esq.). Among those present were – The Revds. W. Legg, R. Bulmer, J. Foster and Lumb; and Messrs. G. Palmer, C. J. Andrewes, J. Boorne, J. O. Cooper, R. D. Catchpole, R. Bracher, Rolling and T. Gleave (Master of the School). The mayor briefly addressed the meeting, and the children having sung a hymn, the school-master examined the second-class boys in reading and spelling. Next followed the examination of the upper classes of the school in Geography. The answers on the whole were satisfactory. The first class boys were examined in reading, spelling and grammar, the Mayor remarking that the children had given very good evidence of proficiency. The boys generally were examined in mental arithmetic, Old Testament, history and chronology, several of the visitors taking part in the examination. The chairman here announced that the business of the annual meeting would then commence and called upon the Secretary (Alderman G. Palmer) to read the following report.

"Number of boys admitted since the report of 1867, 147, making a total of 6,437 since the commencement of the school: on the books at the commencement of the year 274; admitted during the year 147 – total, 421. Left the school during the year to work 70; other schools 41; removed 18; irregular 7; too far 7; sickness 6; pupil teacher 1 – total 150. For the year 1869, average number on books, 273; average weekly attendance, 339; average daily attendance, 213. The boys attend the following Sunday Schools or Places of Worship:- Attending the various Places of Worship connected with the Established Church, 91; Broad-street Chapel, 25; Castle-street Chapel, 35; Trinity Chapel, 23; Kings Road Chapel, 9; Wesleyan Chapel, 21; Wesleyan Reformers Chapel, 9; Primitive Methodist Chapel, 32; Oxford-street Chapel, 8; Shinfield Chapel, 3; Caversham Chapel, 4; West-street (Baptist) Chapel, 3; Peppard Chapel, 1; Queens-road (Baptist) Chapel, 2; Coley Street, 2; Friends Meeting House, 3; No Sunday-school, 3 – total 271. It has been the principle of the British and Foreign School Society from its establishment and constantly acted upon, that the single object of the Schools associated with the Society should be to educate the children in them in those subjects necessary for every educated person, the degree of advancement being only limited by the talent of the child, the regularity of attendances, and the time spent at School. The British Schools should, to be consistent therefore, have always before them a standard in advance of the public sentiment around them. Your committee rejoice in the fact that, Dr. Morell, the Inspector of British Schools for the district, at each visit adds by his tact and manner, a pleasant stimulus to the endeavour that the Reading Boys' School shall well represent the position that we thus claim for our Schools. The official summary of the Report of the Inspector just received from the Committee of Council on Education is very satisfactory. We are fortunate in our Master, Mr. Thomas Gleave, and the Pupil Teachers are doing well. Our numbers keep well up to the capacity of our accommodation, and the occasional written acknowledgements from parents of the success of their sons are very gratifying and encouraging. The financial circumstances of the School are satisfactory; but the Committee require the continued aid of its old friends, and will be glad of the help of others disposed to aid them in making the Institution still more useful. They will be glad to see their way to extend the upper classes, and to afford an opportunity for the sons of labouring men to pursue studies more advanced than were formerly considered necessary. Your committee believe the supporters of your School, in conjunction with the Teachers, are engaged in a good work, for which they earnestly desire the Divine help, and they asked for the hearty co-operation of all classes."

The Rev. R. Bulmer proposed the adoption of the report. He said that Mr. Palmer had bestowed such pains on the affairs of the school that no one could fail to feel a pleasure in assisting him in his efforts. Everyone must be very gratified with the whole character of the instruction given – Mr. James Boorne seconded the resolution, and complimented the children and the managers of the school. – The appointing of a committee for the ensuing year was moved by the Rev. Mr. Lumb in a humorous speech. The motion having been seconded by Mr. Catchpole. The Rev. W. Legg addressed a few words of congratulation and encouragement to the children and alluded to the state of education in Reading thirty-eight years ago when he first came to the town. Three cheers were then heartily given for the Mayor. Alderman Palmer, previous to calling on the Mayor to distribute the prizes, explained that the awards had been mainly given with the view of encouraging the regular attendance of the scholars. Numerous handsomely-bound books, writing desks etc. were then distributed by his Worship. The proceedings were brought to a close by votes of thanks and several hearty cheers.

Annual Examinations

Later in the year, I presided at the examination of British Girls' and Infants' Schools, as reported in *Saturday 13 November, 1869* edition of the *Mercury*:

BRITISH GIRLS' AND INFANTS' SCHOOLS

On Thursday the examination of the children of these schools took place in the School-room, Southampton-street. Ald. Palmer presided, and read the report,

119

which stated that the number of girls in the school is 213 and 179 infants, being a decrease on the numbers of previous years. The expenditure has been 190*l*, which is about 25*l* more than the income. The Rev. C. M. Longhurst addressed a few words of encouragement to the children, after which a number of prizes were distributed by the chairman. The children then sang the National Anthem, and the meeting terminated.

A week after that report appeared, I was also scheduled to chair a meeting in another Schoolroom – that of the Wesleyan Chapel. When I was delayed, it fell to the Methodist Minister, Revd. C. Hilliard, to take the chair until I arrived. It must be remembered that there were no telephones in those days (the first patent for one was in 1876) so there was no means of contacting to let people know if you had been held up. Here is the report of that meeting as it appeared in *Saturday, 20 November 1869 edition of the Mercury*:

NEW WESLEYAN CHAPEL – A social meeting was held at the Wesleyan Chapel Schoolroom on Monday evening, and a public meeting was also held. In the absence of Alderman Palmer, the Revd. C. Hilliard took the chair. He said that in Spring Gardens there was a population of 1,400 people, which was a large parish. Services had been held in a cottage in Spring Gardens for over 16 years and Wesleyans had had a Sunday School there. As many as 120 children attended the school. A church had been built in the neighbourhood, but he was not sure that a chapel was not more than ever desired. They had for some time rented two cottages which had been used for their meetings and the site had been offered to them for 200*l*, while 300*l* would be required for the new building – Alderman Palmer here entered and took the chair. – Mr. Bushell, the secretary, read a report, which stated that twelve months ago, it was resolved to build a new Chapel in Spring Gardens and the amount promised was 147*l* 17s, of which 68*l* 3s had been received. 50*l* more was required for the purchase of the site, besides the 300*l* for the building. The meeting was afterwards addressed by the Rev. S. M. Brough, Mr. Beecroft, and Mr. S. Whiting. – The chairman said that he should watch with more than passing interest the progress of the new chapel. – The sum collected in the room, and the promises made, amounted to 24*l* 5s.

It was around 1869 that I bought West Park in Horne, Surrey (near Felbridge) and had West Park House erected there that year. Like *The Acacias* in London Road, Reading, it was considered of moderate proportions and well

120

laid out with three reception rooms, ten bedrooms and two bathrooms with a large garage and stabling accommodation, a recreation room and servants'

West Park House

quarters. There was a large game larder near the kitchen as the shooting potential of the Estate was on average 800 pheasants per season.

On the night of the 1881 census, Elizabeth and I were there with our three youngest children. 21-year-old Alice Mary and her brother, Lewis (aged 20) were Undergraduate Students at London and Cambridge University respectively – but Lucy Elizabeth (18) was still at School. I was farming 225 acres with the help of ten men so described myself as "M.P., J.P. and Dales man Farmer, 225 acres 10 men". All our children had been born in Reading. Walter (23) was at *The Acacias* with our cook, Judith Clements (a 52-year-old widow) and housemaid, Mary Ann Hearn (23). Emily (25) and her husband, Edward Poulton, were on honeymoon at the Valley of Rocks Hotel in Lynton, Devon. Alfred (28), his wife, Alice and our first grandchildren, 2-year-old twins (Phyllis and Eustace), were living at 11 Victoria Square with four servants while George W. (29) and his wife Eleanor were staying with his cousin, Samuel Palmer and his wife, Amelia, in London. However, I am racing ahead and there is so much more I should have told you.

School Board elections

In 1867, George W. reached the age of 16 so he was introduced to the firm of Huntley and Palmers as an unpaid clerk. That year, my brothers and I provided £800 between us to support the reestablishment of Reading School – I gave £500 and my brothers gave the rest. The School had suffered from years of neglect after its peak in 1792 when there had been 119 pupils under Dr. Valpy. In 1866, a team of Inspectors had found only three pupils present so the School had been closed before the end of that year. However, new Trustees passed the **Reading School** Act, which laid out in 52 clauses how a

modern Grammar School should be administered and found a new site in Erleigh Road where a new school was opened on September 11th, 1871.

Nationally, the 1870 Education Act dealt with the provision of "elementary" education and established School Boards empowered to erect schools in areas where there wasn't already sufficient accommodation. [20] Following the Act, all children were to receive compulsory education and were not supposed to work at all under the age of ten. However, many of them were subjected to the "Half Time" system, whereby 10 – 14 year olds attended school for half the day and worked the other half, particularly within the textile trades.

It was William Edward Forster who had piloted through the 1870 Education Act in the House of Commons on February 17th, wanting to "fill up its gaps at least cost of public money". He had been appointed Vice-President of the Committee of Council on Education by William Gladstone following the 1868 General Election. He was a similar age to me, having been born in Bradpole, Dorset in 1819 and, like me, he was a member of the Liberal Party. He was also a Quaker until he was disowned for marrying Jane Arnold, a non-Quaker, the same year that Elizabeth and I married – 1850. Prior to 1870, many had thought that the teaching of children was a private parental responsibility and there had been terrific battles between High Churchmen and Dissenters on the issue. I was wholeheartedly behind William so proposed to Reading Council that the Act was an enabling one and should be put into operation here.

---

[20] *1945 – 1950 Reading Education Committee Report* states that there was only one place for every three to five children between five and ten years of age in private, endowed, church or ragged schools in the country as a whole at that time

The 1861 Census gave the population of Reading as 25,045 with an estimated projection of 31,125 for 1871. By then, the British School was the largest school in Reading, educating a seventh of the town's school population:

	School	On roll	Attendance
1	British School, Southampton St.	581	443
2	Greyfriars'	565	481
3	St. Mary's	521	411
4	St. John's	501	230
5	St. Giles'	349	243
6	St. Lawrence's	307	232
7	Christchurch	269	190
8	St. Mary's Episcopal Chapel	264	190
9	Ragged School, Silver St	190	143
10	British & Infant School, Hosier St	169	
11	New Town Infant School	130	130
12	All Saints'	67	48
13	Baptist Ragged School, Silver St	65	40
14	St. James Catholic	38	33
	Endowed Schools		
	Blue Coat School	44	44
	Industrial Protestant	25	21
	Green Girls' School	21	21
	Total	**4106**	**2900**

However, average attendance at the second-largest school, Greyfriars' (481) was slightly higher than our's (443). Those statistics were published in detail in *28th January, 1871 Berkshire Chronicle* under the title *The Education Returns relating to Reading*. There was also a section detailing *Names, Ages &c of Principal Teachers of all the schools in Reading*, even to the extent of their precise class of teaching qualifications! Statistics relating specifically to the British School (Southampton-street) were:

Dept.	Name	Age	How long teaching	Certificate
Boys	Thomas Gleave	36	Teacher since 1856	2nd division 2nd degree
Girls	Mary Ann Reay	33	Eight years	2nd division 2nd class
Infant	Fanny Anne Ace	21	10th January 1870	Second class cert.

The oldest Principal Teacher listed was Jane Leggat [21] of the Green Girls'

---

[21] Spelt Leggett in the 1881 census when she was still teaching aged 65

School, 55 Broad Street, who was 55 in 1871 and had been teaching for 46 years, 18 years as a Mistress. That would have made her nine when she became a monitress in 1825. Two other teachers had both taught from the age of thirteen – E. Hunt (aged 33) of St. John's Boys' School had taught for 20 years and C. H. Biggs (26) of St. Mary's Episcopal Boys for 13 years. Also of interest was:

> British & Infant school (Hosier–school). Harriet Leigh, age 30, a teacher 14 years, diploma from Homerton College, Cambridge.

On February 25th, 1871, the Mayor of Reading (Sir Peter Spokes) announced that an order had been received from the Education Department for a School Board to be set up in the town within 28 days of receipt of the order. As a result, much space in the local newspapers was devoted to the forth-coming election, especially since the artisans of the town had only been enfranchised in 1868 and were on the Burgesses' Roll along with other householders.

Exactly a month later, it was reported in *Berkshire Chronicle* that, on March 21st, the Mayor of Reading had declared the Board School election results:

1. Alfred Sutton (Seedman, Greenlands, Redlands Road)   3,642
2. William Payne (Vicar of St. John's, Reading)   3,521
3. George Palmer (Biscuit manufacturer, Acacias, London Road) 3,361
4. Joseph Henry Wilson (Gentleman, Whitley Hill, Whitley)   3,196
5. Rev. Arthur Percival Purey Cust (Vicar of St. Mary's)   2,750
6. Rev. J. Stevenson – Dissenting Minister, Clarendon Terrace, South St.) 2,607
7. Jesse Herbert (Boot maker, Horn St., St. Giles' Parish)   2,334
8. Ebenezer West – Headmaster, Amersham Hall School, Caversham 2,330
9. John Bligh Monck (Esquire & Magistrate, Coley Park)   2,231

The last-mentioned is the son of John Berkeley Monck who was named as one of the thirty who could act on the British School committee at its September 1st, 1809 meeting. Interestingly, it was pointed out that the five Church of England members elected (numbers 1, 2, 4, 5 and 9) gained 15,340 votes whereas the four Non-Conformists (numbers 3, 6, 7 and 8) gained 12,685 so our average was higher. Four others had not been elected but, of the nine that were, three of the six with the most votes were clergymen. [22]

---

[22] The others were later to have schools named after them, viz: Joseph Henry Wilson (1904), George Palmer (1907) and Alfred Sutton (1920, when Wokingham Road School (built 1902, was renamed)

At the first meeting of the Reading School Board, Joseph Henry Wilson was elected the chairman and I its vice chairman and leader of the nonconformists. We soon issued a circular to parents, dated 19th April, 1871, pointing out that:

> under the provisions of the Education Act of 1870, parents of every child between the ages of 5 and 13 years residing in the Borough should cause such child to attend school.

Education was not free then – in fact, fees were two pence a week for the first child in a family and one penny for each additional child. Children who appeared on a Monday without their money were refused admission. It wasn't until 1891 that 'free' education was introduced and pupils over 14 were exempt from compulsory school attendance.

By the time of the first Triennial Election on March 9th, 1874 when all the original members of the first Committee were re-elected and no others were nominated, three Board Schools had been established in Reading:

1. Silver Street erected and opened in July, 1873. Mixed & Infant – 252.
2. Coley Street commenced temporarily in hired rooms in January 1872 then moved in August 1874. Boys, Girls, Infants under three Principal Teachers. 490 at end of school year on 30 September 1876. Scarlet fever and measles had greatly interfered with attendance and progress.
3. Katesgrove commenced as a Mixed School of 678 pupils in a hired building in July 1872 and transferred to new buildings in August 1874.

The second Triennial Election was held on February 13th, 1877, and, by then, Rev. J. F. Stevenson, Archdeacon Purey-Cust and myself had resigned and been replaced by the Revs. John Wood and J. M. Guilding and Mr. Arthur Eisdell – the latter being a Master Miller, originally from Colchester. Mr. West had already replaced me as Vice Chairman when I resigned in October 1876 as, by then, I had so many outside calls on my time and I disapproved of taking on commitments which I could not really honour. I heard later that Rev. J. M. Guilding only lasted just over a year on the Board as it was reported in March 1879, that Rev. C. F. J Bourke had been elected on July 10th, 1878 to fill a vacancy occasioned by the disqualification of Rev. J. M. Guilding arising from his absence for six months from all meetings of the Board. In March that year, it was reported that the School Board Chairman was continuing something that had already proved popular at the British school:

School Treat

A treat to the elder of the Scholars (numbering about 1,100) was given in the grounds of the Chairman of the Board at Whitley Hill on the 9th August last, and the infants, numbering about 400, were feasted with cake and tea at their Schoolrooms on the following day. The cost (amounting to about £50) was defrayed by public subscription. There were also about 480 children belonging to Earley (scholars in the Combined School) who participated in the treat.

ELIZABETH SARAH PALMER
WIFE OF GEORGE PALMER OF THE ACACIAS, READING
BORN 1825. DIED 1894.
REPRESENTATIVE GOVERNOR
OF THE READING GIRLS' KENDRICK SCHOOL 1875-1894

Elizabeth, who shared my interest in education, was appointed Representative Governor of Reading Girls' Kendrick School in 1875 and remained such until her death in 1894. [23]

I had been elected to Parliament in 1878 and served until 1885 when the number of Reading seats was reduced to one and I stood down. Three years later, our eldest son, **George William**, followed in my footsteps by being elected Mayor of Reading for 1888 – 1889. During my time as M.P. there were two Elementary Education Acts – 1876 (Amendment) & 1879 (Industrial

Schools). Naturally, I was asked to preside over many local meetings at that time, one of them being the celebration in September 1880 of the 9th anniversary of the Cumberland Road Primitive Methodist Chapel, being supported on the platform by the Revs. M. Simmonds (the new minister), G. S. Reaney, J. P. Langham and T. Penrose. Mr. D. Berry of London had preached both sermons on Sunday and the Monday meeting was preceded by a public tea.

By 1894, the School Boards had done their work sufficiently well for the age of exemption from compulsory school attendance to be raised from ten to eleven years. It was in March that year that Elizabeth died of bronchitis. The

---

[23] In the upstairs' Palmer Library at the present day Kendrick Girls' School, London Road, Reading (built in 1927), this photo & plaque of Elizabeth Palmer can be found

report in *7th April, 1894 Reading Mercury* under the title *Funeral of Mrs. George Palmer* described how the previous Monday the sad procession of eighteen carriages left The Acacias shortly before 3 o'clock. That was about a year after my younger brother, **William Isaac Palmer**'s sudden death. For Elizabeth's funeral, I was in the first carriage with our eldest daughter, Emily and our eldest son, George William and his wife. Arriving at the Friends Meeting House in Church-street, Reading, the coffin, which was covered with lovely flowers, was at once borne to the  newly-made brick grave in the burial ground, the ground being lined with moss, studded with arum lilies, hyacinths, azaleas, tulips, narcissi and so on. When the coffin had been lowered, simple but earnest prayers were said by John Albright of Witney and Mr. John T. Dorland of London. The wreaths sent by our children and grandchildren were interred with the coffin, on which was the inscription:

ELIZABETH SARAH PALMER
Born 11th mo. 16th, 1825
Died 3rd mo. 30th, 1894

As soon as the ceremony at the grave was over, a service was held in the Meeting House when addresses were delivered by Mr. James Boorne and Mr. Dorland, each of whom spoke in eulogistic terms of Elizabeth while Mrs. Allport offered prayer. A large number of people had attended to pay their last mark of respect to Elizabeth's memory, including the Mayor (Mr. C. G. Field) and Deputy Mayor (Mr. J. H. Martin) and nine complimentary carriages were sent by, amongst others, Mr. M. H. Sutton and Mr. Alfred Sutton. There were also many manifestations of sorrow by the poor especially at losing by death a kind and generous friend. Elizabeth had played her unassuming part as governor of the British Schools and of the Kendrick Schools and regularly attended their annual outings. She was a true blend of the great lady and the intellectual woman so now is probably a good time to give further details about our children as Elizabeth and I had ten, of whom four sons and three daughters survived infancy. Three of our sons entered Huntley and Palmers as Biscuit Manufacturers but here is a summary of the family in order of birth:

1. **GEORGE WILLIAM**, born May 23rd, 1851; married Eleanor Barrett at Croydon in 1879. He became M. P. for Reading 1892 – 1895. [24]
2. **ALFRED** born 1852; married Alice Maria Exall 1877. Their twins Eustace Exall & Phyllis Maude were born 1878, the year Alfred became a Director.
3. **EMILY**, born 1856; married in St. George, Hanover Square, early in 1881, Edward Bagnall Poulton, Professor of Zoology at Oxford. [25]
4. **WALTER**, born early in 1858; married Jane Craig in Pancras in 1882. [26]
5. **ALICE MARY**, born 1859, London University graduate, married (Dr.) Augustus Desiré Waller in Reading early in 1885.
6. **LEWIS**, born 1860, was a Cambridge Graduate and became a solicitor.
7. **LUCY ELIZABETH**, born 1862, married Lewis Anstruther Hope in Marylebone 1887.

Less than two years after Elizabeth's death, I proposed to retire at the end of the financial year (March 31st, 1896). However, my remaining brother, Samuel, whose health had not been good since 1887, would not hear of it so I remained on the Board, despite suffering a severe stroke in June. My robust constitution did seem to help me to rally and I was able to go out again for short periods. In recognition of Queen Victoria's Diamond Jubilee on June 20th, 1897, the biscuit factory gave £7,000 to the Royal Berkshire Hospital to endow a special ward. All employees were given a day's pay, and fifty guineas

Myself, George Palmer

were presented to the Town towards the civic festivities. In the Southampton Street Schools, Thomas Gleave had retired December 23rd, 1896 after 39 years of service and Edwin Thomas Caton B.A., previously Head Master of Redlands Boys' School, had been appointed from January 11th, 1897.

---

[24] & 1898 – 1904; Huntley & Palmers Chairman 1904 – 1906; Privy Councillor 1906

[25] Lady Emily Poulton from 1935. Son, Ronald Poulton Palmer (born September 12th, 1889) captained England Rugby before being killed in WWI. She died in 1939 and her 1886 – 1934 diaries were presented to the Bodleian Library in 1990

[26] He became a Director 1898 – 1910, M.P. for Salisbury 1900 – 1906 and died 1910

V.Committee Lady's Tale: ELIZA BARCHAM 1860–1889

I was born Eliza Goddard in Knodeshall, Suffolk in 1819 and was 27 when I married Thomas Barcham in Reading towards the end of 1846. Thomas was two years younger than me and had been born in Tunbridge, Kent. He was a Bookseller and had taken over an existing business at 89 Broad Street from William Thomas, who was termed "Bookseller, Stationer, Printer, Bookbinder & Engraver" [27] at the time of the 1842 Directory, when there was a Plumber, Glazier and Painter at no. 88 and, opposite the entrance to the Independent Chapel, at no. 90, a Milliner and Dressmaker. We started our married life at **89 Broad Street** and, by 1851, Thomas employed two men and we had two

daughters – Julia, born in 1848, and Ellen in 1850 – although our first-born, Maria, born a year after our marriage, had died mid-1849. Alice was born later in 1851 then Augusta in 1853 and Arthur three years later. Unfortunately he was to die before his second birthday so we also named our next child, born early in 1859, Arthur. However, both he and Augusta died towards the end of 1861.

Thomas had been elected onto the Boys' British School Committee and was mentioned as such in its 1860 and subsequent reports. By the time of the 1861 census, I was in Plomesgate, Saxmundham, Suffolk with Julia. Thomas' mother Maria had been born there in 1792 but was living in Tunbridge by 1851. Thomas had gone into partnership with Joseph John Beecroft (who had been living in Reading from 1861) by 1865. Joseph had been born in Lowestoft, Suffolk in 1839 and married Sarah Ann Lawrence of Retford, Nottingham towards the end of 1862. The sketch of **Barcham & Beecroft PRINTING OFFICE** was done by their son, Lawrence Herbert Beecroft who was born in 1865 and was a bookseller's apprentice by 1881.

---

[27] In 2011, Waterstone's Bookshop occupies the "United Reform Building, 89a Broad Street", although no. 89 housed a fruiterer and florist in the 1880s prior to demolition in 1892 when a separate frontage building was built for the Chapel

Two new Mistresses – Mary Ann Reay and Fanny Ace – in 1870

Thomas was part of the Committee which agreed to the lighting of the School Rooms with Gas. Since Mr. Gleave had informed them that he would keep the School open during the winter months the same hours as the rest of the year if Gas lighting was installed, they resolved on 24th October 1867, when R. D. Catchpool was Secretary, to light the School with Gas. Soon after the Reading British School was accepted as a Government School, and therefore placed under Government Inspection, I was part of the Committee which appointed the 33-year-old teacher of eight year's standing, Mary Ann Reay, as Mistress of the Girls' School and Fanny A. Ace as Mistress of the Infants' School. They took up those offices on 10th and 11th January 1870.

Miss Ace had come straight from Stockwell Training College and was ill and unable to attend to school duties on 13th and 14th so Miss Sweetzer conducted school in her absence. When Miss Furnell (Elizabeth, born 1799 in Middlesex) and I visited on Tuesday 18th, we found attendance good and discovered that there had been 85 present on Miss Ace's first day when she had taken the first class for reading, writing and arithmetic, finding them backward in writing. She felt that the order had improved by 12th when Revd. Chapman had visited though the children were not very punctual when she returned on 17th.

I had also looked in on the Girls' School on 18th and found the attendances the previous day had been 114 and 115 whereas there had been 104 on Miss Reay's first day. She had previously taught at the Girls' British School, Tottenham, London. Mr. Worsley and Miss Cooper visited on the 20th, when I did also, the latter bringing some needlework. My daughter had visited the Infant School the morning of 19th, when ordinary progress was reported following the tea-treat given by King's Road Baptist Chapel the previous afternoon. Following my visit to both schools on 21st, when I found order and attendance good in the Infant School, I didn't return until 22nd February, when we had a Committee meeting, the School year having commenced on 1st, so the Infants had been dismissed at 11 o'clock in order that we might meet in the School room at 11.30 as we had on 25th January.

In March, I visited on the 15th, the day after the children of Trinity Sunday School had their portraits taken. Just over a week later, Miss Smith, who had been Assistant Teacher in the Girls' School for nearly seven years, left after being presented with a handsome Bible and Inkstand by the Teachers and children. The next occasion I carried out my duties as a Visitor was on 28th – the day the Report had been received following H.M. Inspector J. Morrell Esq.'s visit to the Schools on 22nd March:

> The Infants Room is a very good one, and the school is orderly and duly taught.
> C. Seward P. T. passed her examination successfully

That for the Girls' School was similarly good:

> "This has for many years past been a very good Girls' School: and the children have now every appearance of having been carefully taught. Proper registers have not been kept till the commencement of this year so that no standards have been made out. But above 20 I should suppose would pass well in the fourth standard; and as many in the third and second standards."
> The candidates have been accepted.

On the 31st, the Girls of the upper class went to the Examination of the Infant School, Hosier Street, at 11 a.m. There was no school during the afternoons of 8th and 14th April on account of a Public Examination in the boys' School-room and the commencement of the Easter Holiday. Miss Wood, who had been ill since the 5th, returned when School recommenced on the 19th. The following Tuesday was Committee Day, so I attended with several of the other Lady members, then, a month later on 25th May, I was pleased with the order of the Infant School and the good number present, when I visited with a friend, especially since fellow Committee member, Mrs. Long, had complained that the school looked dirty and more untidy than she had ever seen it previously when she and a friend had visited on 13th. She had also disagreed with keeping the Assistants employed in needlework when the children were grouped together for collective work under the management of the Teacher. Miss Furnell had called at the Girls' School the previous day with a present of 1000 needles. The May Committee meeting was held in the Infant schoolroom on 31st, the children having been dismissed at 11 o'clock.

School attendance was only 60 at the time of the next Committee meeting on Monday, 27th June, probably on account of Tuesday being the Anniversary of Queen Victoria's Coronation and Friday the visit of the Prince of Wales. Miss Champion and several of us ladies went into the school afterwards. There was no Committee meeting in July as school broke up at 12 o'clock on 8th for three weeks. Julia Walker left that day to go to a private school for one

131

year to finish her education and Fanny Kendal left Reading while Rose Willis had left the previous day, her education being finished. However, we were back to the usual routine for Tuesdays 30th August and 27th September. On the latter occasion, we heard that the mother of Amelia George, a girl in the third class, had come to complain of Miss Sweetzer on 26th and used abusive language so Miss Reay had sent her daughter away with her when she left.

Following the Committee meeting on 25th October, I visited Tuesday and Thursday, 1st and 3rd November, when Miss Reay removed several girls from each of the classes into a higher class. I also visited the Infants on the 9th. At our Meeting on 29th, Miss Sweetzer sent in notice that she would leave at Christmas. Final Committee meeting that year was held 20th December before school broke up on 22nd for a Christmas vacation of a fortnight.

I remained as a member of the Committee for a further 19 years, following a similar routine of monthly meetings as for 1870, and visiting on other random occasions to check that all was progressing as expected. I shall not bore you with all the details. However, I should like to share some highlights with you.

When the Girls' School reopened after the Xmas vacation on 9th January 1871, only 25 pupils attended as it was very snowy and cold. By the time I visited on Tuesday 17th, numbers had increased to 100 (although they had only been 80 the previous day) but the average for the Infants had only been 32.8 the previous week. The Secretary, Miss Helen Williams, accompanied me when I visited again Friday of that week and we found that the Pupil Teachers had visited Girls' School absentees during the week and gone to find out the reason for their absence the previous day so the average had more than doubled from 42.8 during the first week of term to 93.5. Our next Committee meeting was held on 31st, the day before the commencement of the school year whereas the February one was on 28th after Inspector J. D. Morrell had examined the Standards in writing and the Pupil Teachers on 20th. My daughter visited the first week of March as did Miss Collier and Miss Page, the former taking the 1st Class in the Infants' for Mental Arithmetic. In May, Helen recorded the Infants' School 1871 report as:

Summary of **Inspector's Report of the Reading Infants' School 1871**
"The Infants School is managed with a good deal of care and much spirit. The efficiency with which it is taught is commendable."
Copied from Inspectors Report by Helen Williams, Sec.

132

By 1871, Julia, Alice, Thomas and myself were living in the St. Giles area of Reading. Our daughters visited the School on Tuesday, 12th September, and Mr. Barcham and I on 14th, the average attendance for that week being 120.

Bank Holidays introduced

Bank holidays were first introduced by the Bank Holidays Act of 1871, which designated four such holidays in England, Wales and Northern Ireland, and five in Scotland. The only holiday common to both lists was the first Monday in August. The others for England, Wales and Northern Ireland were: Easter Monday, 26th December and Whit Monday as both Christmas Day and Good Friday were traditional days of rest and Christian worship (as were Sundays) in those countries so did not need to be included in the Act. New Year's Day, Good Friday, the first Monday in May and Christmas Day were the other days for Scotland. Prior to 1834, the Bank of England had observed about 33 Saints' Days and religious festivals as holidays, but, that year, the number was drastically reduced to just four: Good Friday, 1st May, 1st November, and Christmas Day. The 1871 Act had been introduced by Sir John Lubbock, the 1st Lord and Baron Avebury [28]. He was the first President of the Institute of Bankers and, in 1865, published what was probably the most influential archaeological text book of the nineteenth Century – *Pre-historic Times, as Illustrated by Ancient Remains, and the Manners and Customs of Modern Savages*, and was responsible for inventing the names Palaeolithic and Neolithic to denote the Old and New Stone Ages respectively.

The result of H.M. Inspector's Examination of the Infants' School came on Monday, 22nd April 1872:

Inspectors Report April 6th 1872
Infants School. Unquestionably with such cramped space and with no kind of separate room for them, the admission of more babies has greatly increased the Mistress' difficulties & lowered her results for I am convinced that her teaching power is equal to producing much more than the fair School results of this year." The superficial area of the Infant School room is not sufficient to admit the number in average attendance & must be enlarged to the required proportions Article 17(c) under the number in average attendance is limited to that allowed by that article. Miss Ace will shortly receive her certificate.

---

[28] 30th April 1834 – 28th May 1913, banker, politician, naturalist and archaeologist

I visited the Infant School twice during the first week of December and Mrs. Jas. Boorne did twice during the second week. Children had to be refused admittance around that time because there was just no accommodation for a larger number and we had had a steady stream of new admittances. On 18th January 1873, two children left for Christ Church School (which had been built in 1868) and ten others were refused admittance that year.

However, when the new Mistress, M. J. Stephens, took charge on 3rd March, she admitted new scholars – two that day, two the next and eight more by the end of that week. In fact, 23 had been admitted by the time I visited on Wednesday 19th March; a further seven by the time of my next visit on 10th April and ten more by 2nd May. Receipt of the Copy of the Infant School Report towards the end of that month though changed that:

> **Infant School**. The whole work of the Infants' school is progressing very satisfactorily, a great advance in thoroughness having been made since last year. One or two short Sewing Lessons weekly should be introduced into, at any rate, the First and Second Divisions.
>
> I am directed to state that my Lords will be unable to make any Grant to the Infants' School next year, if the Average Attendance exceeds the limits prescribed by Article 17 (c).

> Present Mistress of School   M. J. Stephens
>
> Teachers
>
> Elizabeth Seward   4th Year
>
> Ellen Martha Maggs   1st Year
>
>   S. M. Long pro Miss Isall

as on 9th June, she admitted in the Log Book:

> Large no. present. Refused admittance to 5 children today, the room being too small to admit more than are already on the books.

With the consent of parents, she allowed the first and second division children to go on the 11th to the funeral of a little girl who used to attend the school, sending the two Pupil Teachers to take care of them. A holiday was given on 23rd in order to decorate the room for the public examination held that evening prior to four weeks' midsummer holiday from 27th June to 28th July.

Zilpah Waite had commenced duties as a Monitor at the beginning of August in place of L. Ellis and it was at the end of that month that admittance was refused to five more children. On 15th, Mrs. Long complained of the noise in the school but it seems that that was because the second class were reading simultaneously. The average had increased to 102 that week.

When I visited on the morning of 27th October, I was pleased with the neat appearance of the room. Seven children had been refused admittance that week and Mrs. Boorne had visited the previous week when the Infant School had been left in the charge of the Pupil Teachers.

By 5th November, a large number of children were absent with Whooping Cough and only 61 were present on 6th on account of the weather. The fireplace was repaired on the 19th. Two new scholars were admitted on 13th December prior to breaking up for Xmas holidays on 19th.

New Schoolroom for Infant School

School reopened after the Xmas holiday on 5th January 1874. When I visited the Infants on the 13th, I was very pleased with the order. I discovered that Zilpah Waite was to be recognised as a paid monitor from 23rd. On 4th and 5th of February, School was left in the charge of Lizzie Seward, the eldest Pupil Teacher, as the Principal Teacher was not well, then, on the 16th, the Infants were given a holiday as the Pupil Teachers were to be examined at Maidenhead. The Government Examination took place on 24th so school was dismissed at 11.30 a.m. that day and the children had a half holiday.

The 1st Class was sent into the Boys' and Girls' Schools and fourteen new scholars admitted on 2nd March but two had to be refused admittance, as there was no room, on the 3rd. Mid-March, the Infant School had again to be left in the charge of E. Seward, as the Principal Teacher was absent three times on account of sickness and death at her home. She was also absent the following week for the funeral of her mother, 71-year-old Elizabeth Mills Stephens, who had been born in Devon.

I was present with six other ladies and thirteen gentlemen at a Special United Committee Meeting at Mr. Palmer's on 30th April held to determine:

> in what way the schools should be enlarged, the time having arrived when the demand for accommodation considerably surpassed supply. After a great deal of deliberation on the probable states of the school in the future it was unanimously resolved that the schools should both continue on the same site, instead of being separated as was at first proposed & that the best possible outcome should be

135

taken for enlarging & improving the present premises. A sub committee consisting of Mr. Palmer, Mr. Exall, Mr. Bracher & Mr. Andrewes was appointed to examine the places and decide upon the best means of accomplishing this object.

At a further Special Ladies' Committee meeting held at Lady Spokes' on 12th June when nine of us were present, the secretary read a Government Paper which stated that the Annual Inspection would in future take place in October instead of February. Mr. Boorne attended part of the meeting and stated the different courses which might in the future be pursued with respect to the school. The deliberation which followed his leaving was unanimously in favour of retaining the Infant School but raising the fees to 4d. for juniors and 6d. for the elder girls, by which increase the number of really small children might be largely decreased and, as a result, the school should be able to reach the standard of the Board Schools and the ordinary Middle Class Schools.

At the United Committee Meeting the following day, Mrs. Boorne relayed our conclusion to the assembled gathering under the chairmanship of Mr. Exall. They approved it with the exception of raising the fees to 4d. as they thought it unwise to reduce the number of younger children so proposed that fees for them should be 3d. The resolution proposed by Mrs. Boorne, seconded by Mrs. Bracher and carried unanimously then, was:

> The secretary having laid before us some places for the improvement of these premises involving an expenditure of about £1000, it is the opinion of this committee that the same should be carried out. This meeting pledges itself in connection with their secretary to exert themselves to raising the required amount.

We also decided that the school vacation should commence on 6th July instead of the date previously fixed (26th June – only decided on 9th – when £9 was allocated to prizes) in order that it might take place at the same time as the Board Schools. Mrs. Colebrook proposed a vote of thanks (which was heartedly carried) to Mr. Palmer for his generous offer of £500 to the Gallery Seats Fund. Three days later at the Special Committee meeting held 16th June, we unanimously decided that the raising of the fees of the Infant School to 3d. and of the Girls' school to 4d. & 6d. should commence in October after the Government Inspector's visit and be charged to the whole schools – to old scholars as to new. A rise of £12 was voted to raise Miss Stephens' salary to £75, it not having been definitely settled when she had thought of leaving. It was again stated that the examination would be held on Friday 19th.

136

Mary Ann Hunt, Pupil Teacher in her 5th year in the Girls' School, died on 2nd July 1874, just prior to the vacation. The knowledge of that sad event made the breaking up very mournful for everyone.

When School reopened on Monday 10th, Mr. Palmer visited that day and Miss Exall during the week. It was conducted in the old Wesleyan Schoolroom, **Church Street** [modern day view shown here looking from Southampton Street towards St. Giles' Church]. Attendance was small but was much increased the following week, several new scholars having been admitted.

Annie Williams and Annie Spencer were both absent on account of illness during parts of that week and Mr. Minty had visited just before I did.

Inspection of the Girls' School took place Tuesday 13th October commencing at ¼ to 10 a.m. and finishing 2 p.m. and, the following week, ten girls were promoted from the Infants. That all happened while we were in the temporary accommodation and Miss Reay kept an eye on progress with the new school-room, popping along when she gave a half holiday on 3rd November to see if it was being dried sufficiently by large fires. The school furniture was removed to the new schoolroom morning of 13th and another holiday was given that afternoon.

On Monday, 16th November, school removed to the new Schoolroom so fees were raised from 2d., 3d. & 4d. to 4d. & 6d. Those of the old scholars whose parents could not afford to pay when fees were raised were allowed to attend at the same fees and a great many availed themselves of that privilege. Mr. Palmer visited school Monday morning; Miss Barcham and I on Wednesday afternoon and Mrs. Boorne on Thursday. The following week, the gentlemen's Committee visited the Girls' School on Tuesday morning and the report came the same day:

Report for October 1874

"Specially when the distraction of changed School Premises is remembered, the Standard results and discipline are highly creditable. Needlework is good throughout. Grammar Paper work seems rather beyond the Girls' present powers. Geography too has been rather thrown out by this year's distractions."

Mary Ann Reay	Principal Teacher.
Lydia Stevens	Passed 5th year
Emily Lawrence	Passed 4th year
Annie Spencer	Passed 3rd "
Annie Williams	2nd year
Rhoda Pilgrim	1st "
Florence Shepherd	" "

Eliza I Eisdell

Mr. Palmer and Mr. G. W. Palmer visited the school on Friday. A beautiful table had been sent on Wednesday afternoon.

When Mrs. Eisdell, Mrs. Gostage and myself visited in January 1875, we found that Miss Reay had admitted four scholars on the reopening of school on 11th. Attendance had been good for the first week, averaging 140 and increased to 160 the following week when another scholar had been admitted. Mrs. Gostage Senior again visited School on 4th February when a special Committee meeting was held. Miss Reay examined 1st, 2nd and 3rd Classes the following week and promoted six girls from 2nd to 1st, and seven from 3rd to 2nd Class. Mrs. Boorne and friend visited Friday morning then Lady Stokes morning of 15th and on Thursday afternoon in company with her daughter. Averages had been around 160 until the last week when it was 144.4 as weather was very cold and snowy. H.M.I. C. Du Port Esq. and J. Herbert Esq. barrister visited afternoon of Wednesday 24th. The former, Charles D. Du Port, was H.M. Inspector of Schools for Berkshire and was living at 35 London Road – very close to George and Elizabeth Palmer and their family at The Acacias (designated no. 34). In fact, Charles Du Port was across Redlands (or Red) Lane, next door but one to the Royal Berkshire Hospital.

In March, I again visited with my daughter, as did Mr. Boorne, soon after Miss C. White of Wandsworth Road British School commenced her duties as

Assistant Mistress on 15th. The whole school had worked for that week by a new time table made to suit the requirements of the Code of 1875. On the morning of Tuesday 23rd, school was visited by Mrs. Eisdell and her daughter then immediately afterwards by myself, Mrs. Tinling and Mrs. G. Gilligan, average attendance having dropped from 172 to 159. Miss White left on 30th, it being her Father's wish that she should have a situation in or near London. There had been no school on 29th, it being the Bank Holiday. There had been a Committee Meeting on Tuesday morning and School was visited that day by Miss Potter, Principal of the Girls' Practising School, Stockwell. Miss Reay was absent Tuesday afternoon, all day Wednesday and Friday morning with a bad foot. During April, there were two Committee meetings – both being held on Tuesday mornings – the usual one on 12th and a special one on 26th.

I found that several children were absent morning of Wednesday 18th August because the United Sunday School Treat was being held so Miss Reay gave a holiday that afternoon. Several children and two teachers – E. Lawrence and R. Pilgrim – had also been absent on the 16th owing to the excursion to Portsmouth so average was 165. On 20th, notification of the Inspector's visit on 19th October was received. Following Mr. Du Port's inspection, we had the usual Committee meeting on Tuesday and an examination was held before the Ladies' Committee on the morning of Friday 12th November, when prizes were distributed. Carrie Smith obtained first prize and there was no school that afternoon. The average attendance for the Girls' School for the preceding year had been 166.97 and 156 were on the schedule for the examination.

Miss Newman, the Certificated Assistant, had commenced duties when the Girls' School recommenced on Monday 10th January 1876 but that afternoon there'd been a half-day as the repairs had not been completed. When visiting on the morning of Tuesday, 14th March, I found Miss Reay had given a further half holiday on the afternoon of 10th in recognition of the increase in the weekly average to 187.7. My visit to the school in August was soon after the Bank Holiday on Monday 7th, so the average then was small – 143. However, it was good to see Miss C. Herbert and Miss L. Stevens, formerly Pupil Teachers in this school, visiting as well.

The Drawing Examination was in progress when I visited the Girls' School on Monday, 12th March 1877. 75 girls presented in Freehand in addition to eight Pupil Teachers and paid Monitors. When I visited the Infants' School on 14th,

I found that four new scholars had been admitted at the end of February when S. Haslam was appointed as paid monitor. In the Log Book was a copy of:

Report for 1876

"Very Fair Order, method and general results."

Myra Janet Stephens	Principal Teacher
E. M. Maggs	passed 4th Year.
Annie Henderson	passed 1st Year.

The latter resigned her monitorship and left 23rd March, as she'd been obliged to leave the town. However, it was not till the Committee meeting on the last Tuesday of April that her resignation was received and her indentures cancelled. By then, the weekly average had increased from 98.5 to 115 as fresh scholars were being admitted each week.

On morning of 10th May, C. Smith and S. Haslam were late and E. M. Maggs did not bring the children in punctually when she was in charge of the school during the dinner hour. However, C. Smith's class had made good progress during the preceding fortnight and, the following week, E. M. Maggs was absent by permission as she was taking charge of the Caversham British School. Mrs. Byrt and Revd. G. S. Reaney's visits on Tuesday and Thursday afternoons respectively preceded my next visit to the Girls' School at the end of May. Miss Fenner commenced her duties on 4th June. She had been used to Infants, and was not equal to the 1st Class, therefore she took the 3rd and Annie Spencer, 5th Year Pupil Teacher, took the 1st till Miss Newman's return.

Infant School Deaths

Henry Wiggins died from Scarlet Fever so his name had to be crossed off the Infant School register at the beginning of August. A Bank Holiday on 6th meant there was no school that day but both myself and Mrs. Boorne visited later that week with our daughters and also a friend in the case of the Boornes. Attendance remained good and 206 girls and 142 infants attended the School Treat given by Mr. G. Palmer in Mr. Young's field on Tuesday 14th. The following afternoon, buns were distributed to the Infants at close of school.

At the beginning of September, C. Smith told us that she wished to give up teaching after the next Government Inspection on account of ill health so she left the Infants on 9th November. Visiting that School on Monday 12th, I found that the classes were being reorganised and four girls were being trialled as monitors – L. Griffin, P. Barker, S. Fabry and C. Hensler. The following week, 14 Girls were removed into the Girls' school and the week after that, when Mr. G. Palmer and three other gentlemen visited the Infant School, 24 Boys over seven years of age were removed to the Boys' School.

C. D. Du Port had written the following in each School Log Book in October:

Registers   Circular Memorandum

1. Always mark Registers at exact time appointed, however small the nos.
2. Never leave a blank whether for presence or absence.
3. Never make a knife erasure.
4. Always enter in ink at the time of calling Registers in each Register the nos. present.
5. Always cancel in ink the mark for any child who may leave before the two hours are up, altering the ink totals accordingly.
6. Always note on an attendance slate hung on the wall the No. present finding this No. by yourself counting heads.
7. Always compare the totals shewn by the Registers with this slate total.

Eliza Eisdell copied the latest Government Report into the Log Book:

Government Report
Nov. 1877

"The first class is poorly taught all round. In other classes there has been very fair work & progress."

Present Mistress of School	M. J. Stephens
Pupil Teachers	
E. M. Maggs	passed 5th Year
S. Haslam	passed Candidate 1st Year

Eliza Eisdell

Mr. Bourne of Borough Road College visited during February 1878. Miss Stephens was ill and unable to attend to duty from 17th May until after the Summer vacation so Miss Reay had to keep a watchful eye on both schools, especially on the new Infant School monitors. Fortunately, we did manage to get Carrie Smith, a former Pupil teacher, to lead the Infant School from 5th June until the Principal Teacher returned.

I found a small Girls' School owing to the Children's Flower Show when I visited on Wednesday, 28th August but A. Spencer, formerly a Pupil Teacher

141

at the school, was also visiting. Average that week was 173.5. Following the 1878 Inspection, when Mr. Du Port saw Pupil Teachers at work afternoon of Tuesday, 29th October; examined and passed the whole school in Needlework afternoon of 1st November and he and Mr. Pearce inspected School the morning of 4th; a holiday was given Wednesday evening till Monday morning, Mr. Pearce having finished afternoon of 5th. By 11th November, when Lady Spokes visited, many girls from the 1st Class had left and sixteen new scholars had been admitted. On receiving the Schedule Thursday evening, Miss Reay had re-organised the classes Friday morning. It had been very wet that week and numbers had been small in consequence. However, I was pleased to see that attendance had improved from 170 to 181 by the time I visited later that month. Around that time, we heard that Miss H. S. Newman, who had been absent since 26th September, had ceased to be Assistant Mistress in the Girls' School owing to her delicate health.

When work commenced on 6th January 1879 after the Xmas holidays, a copy of **H. M. I.'s Report for 1878 (Oct.)** was received, and we were told that:

"This Infants' School has made great advances this year. The order and results are both thoroughly good".

Head Mistress	M. J. Stephens
Pupil Teacher	S. A. Haslam passed 2nd year.
Paid Monitors	Mary Jane Barker & S. A. H. Fabry

That week, Annie Victoria Pattie Atwood was recognised as a paid monitress.

My daughter visited the Girls' School following Miss Reay's week of absence 17th – 21st February. The weather had been very bad and average dropped to 149 during her week of indisposition when school was visited by Mrs. Boorne and Miss H. Ridley. A. Gleave returned along with Miss Reay on 24th but Kate Chandler was ill that day and Tuesday and E. Hensler was too ill to have lessons for some weeks. As well as my daughter, Mrs. Eisdell, Lady Spokes, Miss Davis and Miss Collier visited that week when the weather was still very wet and dirty, so average only rose to 154.9. However, it had risen to 169 the following week and all Teachers were present although Miss Reay was absent on 7th March on account of a bad cold. On the afternoon of Wednesday 12th, my daughter again visited, as did Miss Nield and Miss Williams. Following the custom of some years past, there had been a half holiday afternoon of 10th for the Boys' Drawing Examination. Attendance had been good, average 181, and there had been several new scholars that week. Lady Spokes had visited morning of 18th and afternoon of 21st and I had visited Wednesday morning with my elder daughter. Emma Hensler had been ill Tuesday morning, and Miss Spencer, Assistant Mistress, on Thursday and Friday.

During the winter months, the Infant School Pupil Teachers had had to remain each evening for their lessons. However, from 5th May, Miss Stephens commenced teaching them from 8 a.m. to 9 a.m. and an hour on one evening each week. Five fresh scholars had been admitted that week and average was 117.1. The following week, four boys were transferred to the Boys' School.

The School year ended 30th September. Rhoda Pilgrim's apprenticeship actually expired on the Tuesday of the Committee meeting (3rd October) but we asked her to remain till after children's examination, which she did. At the next Committee meeting on Friday 17th October, Registers were examined and found right, averaging 186.2. 22nd – 24th inclusive were the days set apart for the inspection, but Mr. Du Port did not examine girls till Thursday and Friday. He expressed himself as very pleased with the school altogether and also Pupil Teachers. Mrs. Boorne, Lady Spokes and myself all visited afterwards.

I was very sad to hear of the deaths of two Infants when I visited that school on the 12th December. The names of Annie Harper and Jessie Reid had to be cancelled from the Registers. Jessie had died of Diphtheria.

The Infant School was much depleted in numbers when I visited towards the end of January 1880. It had been closed after a snow storm and, even when it reopened, the weather was too stormy for the little ones to venture out. Consequently the average attendance was only 41.1 by 28th. Miss Reay was absent the first two weeks of February (when averages for Girls' School improved to 161 and 168.4) so I visited Girls' and Infants' School twice during that first week – on Monday and Friday – and the Girls' School the week following her return. Mrs. Eisdell also visited during the second week and Mrs. Boorne during Miss Reay's first week back. She felt quite recovered when she returned on Wednesday, 18th and found everything to her satisfaction, much to the credit of the Teachers, especially of the Assistant Mistress. That week was very wet so average dropped back to 158.5.

I had visited the Infants' School on morning of 22nd September prior to the completion of the School Year. The following week, Miss Stephens sent to us Committee Ladies her notice of resignation of the headmistress-ship at Xmas

143

next. M. J. Barker and A. Fabry had also sent in, on 29th, their notice to leave at Xmas and we accepted their resignations at our Committee meeting on 12th October. New School Registers had been commenced on Friday, 1st. Average attendance had dropped from 138.7 at the completion of the school year to 131.3 by mid-October but 139 children were present on Monday, 25th when H. M. Inspector visited to inspect them. Since the inspection of all three schools was over by 27th, Thursday and Friday were granted as holiday.

Miss Reay had a week's absence with the Committee's sanction in November so I made a point of visiting the Girls' School then and found all going on right. Attendance was small, averaging 156, as many had left after the Exam. However, fourteen children were admitted from the Infant School on the 8th so average increased to 163, and reached 166 the following week when Annie Gleave was absent from a severe cold. Miss Reay began selling needlework on Thursday and Friday. When I visited the Infants' School on the morning of Tuesday, 30th, I found that Miss Stephens was absent with a cold and the average attendance was down to 95.3.

Emma Ryder succeeds Myra Stephens as Principal Infants Teacher

At the close of term on 22nd December, the Committee ladies and friends presented Miss Stephens with a handsome marble timepiece, a pair of candle-sticks and urn to match on resigning the charge of the Infant School. The Teachers and Scholars of the Girls' and Infant Schools presented her with a beautiful work-box well fitted up. Myra Janet Stephens had been the Infant School's principal teacher from 3rd March 1873 and was to be replaced by 39-year-old Emma Ryder when School recommenced Monday 10th January 1881.

Miss Ryder had visited the Girls' School on Friday, 26th November 1880 and spoken with that School's Mistress, 43-year-old Mary Ann Reay. Being a Londoner (born Islington, Middlesex), she had asked about accommodation in Reading and so ended up boarding with Miss Reay at 2 Shepton Villas next to 52 South Street, in Reading St. Giles area, living in an all-female household. Another Public Elementary Teacher, 36-year-old Ann E. Rivers, from Dover, Kent, also boarded there and a friend of Mary Ann's, Ellen Cooper, aged 41 (born in Midgham, Berkshire) acted as their Domestic Housekeeper providing them and a lodger, Mary Tutty (Age 34, who had been born in Reading and had income from dividends) with meals. None of them had married.

Mrs. Eisdell had visited the Infant School during the last half of Miss Ryder's first week and found attendance much thinned to 118 on account of snow and severe frost, and that dropped to 89.3 the following week. School had had to be closed after Tuesday morning as the children were not able to come on account of a very heavy snow storm. When it reopened following the snow storm, I visited and found the position even worse, average attendance being only 41.1, as weather was still too stormy for the little ones to venture out.

In fact, it wasn't until March that the average attendance exceeded that at the start of Miss Ryder's headship (120.2). Boys', Girls' and Infant Schools had a half holiday on Monday 7th, in consequence of the Drawing Examination that afternoon. Edith Smith, who had been engaged as a paid monitor in the Infants during the week ending 4th February, was due to leave at the end of the quarter not being strong enough for the work after absence. However, the Committee considered her case under Mrs. Eisdell's guidance and decided to give her a further trial till midsummer. Mrs. Eisdell, Mrs. Davis and Mrs. Song had visited, and the most forward pupils were removed to a higher class after the quarterly examination.

Thomas had retired by the time of the 1881 census and we had moved to 26 Eldon Road. We had our unmarried daughters, 31-year-old Ellen and 29-year-old Alice, still living with us. They naturally did not have an occupation and we had a general servant, 25-year-old Sarah Searle, who had been born in Yateley, Hampshire. When Thomas retired, his partner, Joseph John Beecroft had decided to go into business by himself as a printer and stationer so moved his family to 24 Market Place, close to the junction of The Forbury with Friar Street. By 1881, he was a Master Printer employing six men and three boys and his son, Lawrence Herbert Beecroft, who had been born in 1865, was a bookseller's apprentice. His wife, Sarah, had her mother (Hester Lawrence, aged 71) and two younger unmarried sisters – Ellen and Hettie Lawrence (aged 36 and 32) – staying with them. Their daughter, Hettie Roberta Beecroft (born 1868) and niece, 9-year-old Edith Mary Ghey were scholars.

When I visited the Girls' School during the afternoon of Monday, 27th June, I found a very small School, owing to the Factory Excursion; a trip to Brighton and a Fete at Mortimer all happening on the same day. There were also two Sunday School treats that week so the average dropped to 162.8. The teachers and children presented Emma Hensler, an ex Pupil Teacher, with a handsome work-box as a token of their affection and esteem on her leaving. Similarly, in the Infants' School, the average dropped to 129.4 during first week in July on account of the summer treats held by various Sunday Schools in the town.

Infant School overfull

When School reassembled the week ending 12th August after four weeks' summer vacation, the average weekly attendance in the Infants' School was 162.2, which meant that it was overfull so no more scholars could be admitted 'til November. Although the monitor Edith Sutton gave a week's notice to leave the following week, as her parents were leaving Reading for Croydon, Miss Reay sent Beatrice Coxhead from the Girls' School, on trial by the next week and she was doing very nicely in the Babies' Class by 9th September.

The Ladies Committee met a week Tuesday after the end of the school year to test the accuracy of the Registers and to pass the year's accounts. The separate urinal for the Infant Boys and improvement in the closet accommodation for them was completed just a week before Her Majesty's Inspectors inspected the children on 28th October. Of the 175 Infants present, 109 had made 250 attendances (which was up from 86 the previous year) but all were pleased when the inspection was over, that the schools were closed on Thursday and Friday. The following week, 47 children moved from the Infants' School to the other schools on the site – 24 to the Boys' School and 23 to the Girls'.

My next visit on Wednesday, 14th December – the day after the Committee meeting was held – coincided with the arrival of the **Report for 1881**:

"The tone of steadiness and attention and quiet is much below par. Hence the first Standard Reading is but poor very often. There is very fair progress being made in some respects however."
The discipline of the Infants' School should improve or payment under Article 19 (a) 3 will have to be refused.
The average attendance in the Infants' School must not be allowed to exceed the number suited to the accommodation (i.e. 126) otherwise the whole grant will be liable to forfeiture. Article 17 (c).

Head Mistress   Emma Ryder
Assistant under Article 32 (c).3.   Mary Jane Barker
Pupil Teacher   Patti Victoria Attwood end of 2nd Year

Signed on behalf of the Managers *S. A. Long*

Infant School is enlarged

Apart from the previous move after the Inspection and the one at the end of March 1882 of 31 Standard 1 girls into the Girls' School, there was very little that could be done about the overcrowding of the Infant School until 1st June when Mrs. Song, Mrs. Davies, Mr. Andrewes and Mr. Bracher looked at the rooms to see how more accommodation could be provided. Mrs. Andrewes visited the following day then, a fortnight after the annual treat at G. Palmer Esq. M.P.'s home "Acacias", on the afternoon of Friday 23rd, 132 children were given a five week holiday to enable the Infant School to be enlarged. When it recommenced on 14th August, it had **two additional classrooms** and Mrs. Andrewes, G. Palmer Esq. M.P. and Mr. Andrewes all visited during the following week.

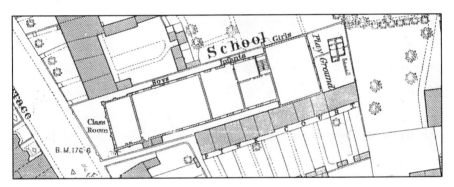

Pollie Barker, an assistant under article 32 (c), had left to become a forewoman in the Factory. Her departure was unexpected so the Principal teacher, Emma Ryder, had to take her Standard I class until the time of the inspection. Mary Jane Barker (born March 1863) was a 19-year-old School Teacher and her father, Joseph, was a 48-year-old Journeyman Biscuit Baker at that time, so she would no doubt have known about Huntley and Palmers Factory and any vacancies from him.

The following week, fifteen new dual desks and one large mounted slate were received for school furniture and, a fortnight after that, the Gentlemen's Committee inspected the new rooms. Despite new class rooms and furniture, life was no easier for Miss Ryder because, as well as the timetable in classes I and IV having to be reversed on Tuesday and Thursday afternoons while she was having to teach Standard I, all needlework classes had had to be omitted for the first week in September on account of Beatrice Coxhead's illness.

Mrs. Eisdell, Mr. Boorne and I visited the Girls' School week ending 13th October to see about fixing new **fireplaces**. The Committee examined the Infants' School registers for the year and found them correct on the 21st prior to the Annual Inspection on Wednesday 25th to Monday 31st! [29] The Infants' School was inspected on the morning of the 25th then given holiday that afternoon whereas the Girls' School was inspected on 26th and 27th when weekly average was 232 (Tuesday having been very wet) but results weren't known for certain by the end of the week.

I visited the Infants' School with a friend during the first week of December when Mrs. Davis and Dr. Shea also visited. The latter stated that there were fewer absent from measles in our schools than in others in the town, so we were left for the present. Mr. Gleave had brought the Report in on Friday morning so we knew that the Grant earnt was £190. 2. 0.

Government Report for 1882

"This shows great improvement as regards working, discipline, and results. This is now a good Infants' School."
S.A. Fabry is recognized qualified to serve under Article 84. Code of 1882.

Head Mistress	Emma Ryder
Assistant under Article 32.c.3.	Sarah Ann Fabry
Pupil Teacher	Patti V. Attwood end of 3rd Year

We were pleased to see that Thomas' former partner, Joseph Beecroft, had described Reading British Schools as follows in his *Guide to Reading 1882*:

Much of the work of elementary education in the town has been carried on by these useful schools. The buildings, which are in Southampton Street, are very centrally situated as far as the working population of a large neighbourhood is concerned.

---

[29] as quoted from the log book

148

Since the opening of the Boys' School, no less than 8,918 scholars have passed through it and the Reports of H. M. Inspectors have invariably been encouraging. The present Master, Mr. Gleave, has occupied the post for many years and probably few schools of anything like the number of scholars which this contains have been effectively conducted with so small a staff of assistants.

The Girls' School, although not so strong numerically, has been remarkably successful and many of its former scholars are now occupying respectable and responsible posts.

These schools are in receipt of Government Grants, which being made upon the percentage of passes are in themselves criterions of success. Private subscriptions are also raised to meet the expenses and George Palmer Esq. MP, who has always manifested a warm interest in the Schools, annually invites the scholars to a Tea in his grounds at **The Acacias.**

When our daughter visited the Girls' School with Mrs. Eisdell in December 1883, the latter realised that she had not recorded the School staff below the Inspectors' report so added:

Head Mistress	Mary Ann Reay
Assistant Mistress	Marian Walters
Ex: Pupil Teachers	Emily Annie Gleave (leaving Xmas for Stockwell College)
	Ellen Murton
Pupil Teachers.	Effie Helen Walker, Florence Huggins
Monitresses	Susan Warwick, Kate Wicks, Kate Gough

All teachers were present for the last fortnight of term and the start of the next 'though School was very small indeed (averages being 190, then 162) owing to measles, and was only 178 during week ending 11th January 1884. At the Committee meeting on 18th December, it had been decided not to give prizes till after Xmas holiday so, on morning of Friday, 18th January, Revd. J. Oates distributed Prizes, with Committee Ladies and friends present and a half holiday was given that afternoon. It was the week ending 25th before children come to school in greater numbers (average 203). Annie Emily Gleave, formerly Pupil Teacher here, had taken leave of the teachers and children on Wednesday afternoon as she was entering Stockwell College as a First Class Queen's Scholar. Friday morning she was presented with a very nice work box, the gift of the teachers and children. She and Kate Chandler visited School on 21st and 22nd April during their College holiday and the latter gave a Criticism Lesson to Standard II on the Adjective on Thursday afternoon, 14th August. On the 18th, Effie Walker returned to school having been absent, ill, from the 4th February. **A door was put up at the top of the steps –** finished 11th December, just a week before school broke up at noon on Thursday, 18th for the Xmas vacation.

We reopened on Monday, 5th January 1885 – a week before the other Schools in the town. As a result, all teachers were in their places but School was not large (average 206). No visitors or other officers came that week but five ladies and two of Mrs. Gostage's children attended the Prize Giving by Revd. W. Anderson on the morning of the 16th. Certificates were given for the first time to those who passed in three subjects, but had not attended 300 times. The teachers were presented with very nice books, and there were three attendance prizes given to F. Miles, E. Sheppard, and L. Dorchester.

I realised that the staff has not been settled in consequence of an omission in the report so rectified that as follows:

Head Mistress	Mary A. Reay
Certificated Assistant	Marian H. Walters
Uncertificated Assistant	Ellen Murton
Pupil Teacher 3rd Year	Florence Huggins
Pupil Teacher 3rd Year	Effie Walker
” ” ” ”	Susan Warwick
Pupil Teacher 2nd Year	Kate Wicks
Monitress	Kate Gough

Mrs. Barcham.

In July, 1886, the Scholars and teachers went for their annual treat to the "Acacias" on Wednesday afternoon by the kind invitation of G. Palmer Esqr. just a week before School closed for the summer holidays at noon on Thursday. During the holidays the cloak room and closets were painted and coloured and some of the paint repainted in the main room and class rooms.

When School recommenced on Monday, 9th August, it was visited by G. Palmer Esqr. and the date of the Pupil Teachers' examination was fixed for 30th April 1887. When I visited the Infants' School on 21st, I found that the average weekly attendance had risen to 147.7 and Edith Wheeler's Class had obtained the highest percentage in the weekly examination.

Each year there was a Government Inspection and so it was on Tuesday, 26th October 1886 that S. Tremenheere Esq. H.M.I. visited the British School to examine the Infants' Department. Miss Ryder gave the children a holiday that afternoon. On Wednesday morning, he took the Class Subjects in the Girls' School and Miss Reay then gave the girls a holiday that afternoon. Pupils of both schools were also given a holiday Friday afternoon. The average weekly attendance was 170.6 in the Infants' School and 246 in the Girls' School that week and Mrs. Eisdell, G. Palmer Esq. and myself visited the former during it. Mr. Pearce, who had given information of the new Inspector's modes of inspection to a Committee meeting of Teachers at the beginning of June that year, took the Reading etc. on Thursday. He had also taken the Music Exam in both Schools the day the school year ended – Thursday, 30th September. Both schools had been notified on the 24th that the Government Inspection would take place October 26th – 29th.

Seymour Greig Tremenheere had been born in Penzance, Cornwall in 1848 – the fourth child of Charles William Tremenheere and Camilla Eliza Greig. He obtained a B.A. from New College, Oxford and was Master at Wellington College, Sandhurst, Berkshire (where the teachers were known as Ushers) 1874 – 1875. By 1881, he was H. M. Inspector of Schools (C5) and staying at En Yeat, Preston Richard, Westmoreland with a gunpowder manufacturer. [30]

53 children were absent when I chose a very wet morning to visit the Girls' School in August 1887 – Wednesday, 17th. All teachers had returned when school reopened after the summer holiday on Monday, 8th but the average had only been 196.5 for the first two weeks as a great many children were still absent. The monitress, Bertha Bowman, was ill on 19th. Mr. Tremenheere inspected School again in 1887 when he failed M. Hardie and C. C. Witham.

When I visited the school with my daughter on 27th April 1888, I found that Standards IV – VII had nearly all finished their Exam knitting at the proper

---

[30] He died aged 93 in Kensington in the first quarter of 1942, according to BMD site

151

time on Friday afternoons so were keeping on with the Exam garments. We heard in June that year that the long-standing Secretary of the Girls' School, Miss Susan Champion, had died in Hastings, aged 78.

Canon Routledge [31] and his assistant Mr. Rapson, inspected both the Girls' and Infants' Schools on the afternoon of 24th October and morning of 25th. Miss Reay gave the rest of the week holiday after the inspection finished Thursday at noon. Average of 228 dropped to 178 the following week when several girls left and Infants were not put up. Miss Murton was absent, ill for four weeks and during the third **Her Majesty's Inspector's Report for 1888** was received:

> The discipline of the girls is excellent, and I consider their needlework to be unusually good. Poetry is also very well repeated, and Grammar creditable. Reading, Handwriting and Spelling deserve great praise, Arithmetic, with the exception of the Fourth Standard, is generally accurate.

School Staff 1888

Head Mistress.	Mary Ann Reay
Assistant (Certificated).	Ellen Eliz: Murton
Assistant Uncertificated	Lilian Gertrude Marsh
Assistant Uncertificated	Susan Amelia Warwick
Assistant Uncertificated	Kate Florence Gough
Pupil Teacher.	Bertha Bowman
Candidate.	Annie Pocock

Eliza C. Eisdell

On Thursday, 23rd May 1889, I bade the children "Good bye" as I was leaving Reading to reside in Tunbridge Wells. Miss Reay described me as "one of the Ladies who has been longest on the Committee". Our daughters, Ellen and Alice, moved with Thomas and myself. Thomas, who was returning to his roots as he was born in Tonbridge, died there, aged 77, in 1897.

---

31 Spelt Routelage in Girls' School Log Book

VI. Infant Teacher's Tale: ANNIE FABRY 1877 – 1924

From scholar to trial monitor

Having been a pupil at the Reading Girls' British School, I was asked in 1877 if I would like to become a trial monitor in the Infant School, where I had started my own education. I was 13 at the time, having been born towards the end of 1863. Although my parents, William and Emma Fabry, had had me christened Sarah Ann Holt Fabry on 14th February 1864 in the St. Giles area of Reading, I had always been known as Annie. They had married in Reading in 1859 although Dad had been born in Stratfield Saye, Hampshire in 1834 and Mum, Emma Holt, in Swallowfield, Berkshire the previous year. My brother William had, like me, been christened in the St. Giles area of Reading on 8th January 1860 but, by the time our sister, Clara Priscilla, had been born – 2nd September 1865 – the family had moved to the St. Mary's area of town.

I had always enjoyed school so was thrilled to be given the opportunity to become a monitor. When the classes were reorganized on 16th November 1877, following the Government Inspection by C. D. Du Port in October, I became a trial monitor in the Infants' School along with L. Griffin, Pollie Barker and Clara Hensler. At that time the average weekly attendance of the Infants' School was 119.8. 14 of the 1st Standard Girls were removed into the Girls' School during the following week and 24 Boys over seven years of age were removed to the Boys' School during the last week in November.

The Mistress of the Infants' School, Miss Stephens, continued calling me by the name Annie and Mary Jane Barker, Pollie as she had when we were pupils. There were two Pupil Teachers in the Infants' – Sarah Haslam had passed Candidate 1st Year (having been appointed as a paid monitor on 2nd March that year) and Ellen Martha Maggs had passed her 5th year (having completed her 1st Year under Miss Ace in 1873) so she left for Kates Grove School on 15th February 1878 – the week I was absent from school, ill. Several children were absent around that time with Ringworm and Whooping Cough and there were even one or two cases of Scarlet Fever. L. Griffin had been ill when I was but for a longer period and she left for good on April 26th when the average attendance was only 84.5 and four more children were sent home with ringworm. Sarah Haslam's brother had Scarlet Fever in March so she was absent then.

Miss Stephens was then ill from 17th May until after the Summer Vacation, so Miss Reay, Principal Teacher of the Girls' School, kept a watchful eye on both schools, until Carrie Smith, a former Pupil Teacher in the Infants', took over that Department from Wednesday, 5th June.

In October, Pollie was very upset and absent from Tuesday 15th for the remainder of the week on account of the death of her sister. I had a day's absence through illness on Monday, 9th December. School that week was small (average 81.9) on account of snowy weather.

I was ill several times during February 1879, needing the second week of the month off then 27th and 28th. Similarly, in May, I was ill on Thursday 1st then, from 15th – 19th inclusive, with a bad foot, and again from 27th – 29th. In June, I was absent by permission on the afternoon of Friday 13th. Eight fresh scholars had been admitted that week.

On Saturday, 30th September, four of us had to attend St. Giles' School-room for the Pupil Teachers' Examination. Sarah was sitting for the end of 3rd Year, Pollie for the end of 1st and Patti and myself were Candidates. We

 had some early snow that year – attendance was small on the afternoon of Friday, 21st November on account of snow falling. The following week, attendance dropped even further from 114.8 to 103.4 and, that Friday afternoon, School was closed to have a **new stove** put up in the school room. On 8th and 9th December, I was absent with a sore throat then, on my return, was very sad to learn that two Infants had died – Jessie Reid from Diphtheria, and Annie Harper.

I had a bad cold the first week in February 1880, so was absent until the afternoon of Wednesday 4th. Sarah had also been ill on the Monday.

Just prior to the end of the School Year, Pollie and I sent in notice to leave at Xmas. We had done that on 29th September and found that our resignations were accepted by the Ladies at the Committee Meeting on 12th October. Miss Stephens had sent to the Committee Ladies her notice of resignation of the head-mistress-ship of the School from Xmas on 30th.

I was ill on Thursday, 2nd December and Miss Stephens had been absent earlier that week with a cold. When school broke up for Xmas vacation on 22nd, Miss Stephens left. She was presented with a beautiful workbox, well fitted up, by the Teachers and Scholars of the Girls' and Infants' Schools. The average was only 91.6, having been 95.3 the previous week.

Porter and Portress at the Union Workhouse in Oxford Road

When school recommenced after the Christmas Holidays, Emma Ryder took over as Principal Teacher and Pollie and I had been persuaded to continue as Pupil Teachers. My class obtained the highest percentage in the weekly examination of the school during weeks ending 18th February, 25th March and 1st April while Pollie's class obtained highest percentage for the week ending 29th – I was absent from illness on Wednesday that week. The weekly average attendance had increased from 110.9 to 141.5 during that time.

At the time of the 1881 census – 3rd April – my sister, Clara, and I were lodging at 4 Battle Terrace, Oxford Road, Tilehurst with Miss Mary Hunt; her 27-year-old niece, Elizabeth Banks (both of whom had been born in Reading) and Elizabeth's children – 2-year-old Charles & 7-month-old Annie, who had been born in Wokingham. Our parents were working at the **Union Workhouse in Oxford Road** as Porter and Portress at that time. The Master of the Workhouse was 47-year-old Joseph Pope and his wife, Eliza Jane (42), was Matron. Their 6-year-old daughter, Ella, lived with them but, as you can see from the following 1873 advertisement for a Porter and Labour Master at the Oxford Workhouse, the Porter and his wife were to be "without family" and the Labour Master single so our parents had arranged for Clara and I to lodge with Miss Hunt:

Oxford Incorporation
Wanted, at the Workhouse of the above Incorporation, a man and his wife, without family, to fill the offices of Porter and Tramps' Attendant; and a single

155

man to fill the office of Labour Master. The duties of the Porter will be to keep the door, to attend to the cutting up and serving the meals, the bathing of the male tramps, the fumigation of their clothes, and the cleanliness of the male inmates generally; he will also have to perform all the duties prescribed for him by the Orders of the Local Government Board, and also any the Guardians may from time to time think reasonable.

The duties of the Tramps' Attendant will be to assist the Porter to keep the door, to superintend the bathing of the female tramps and the fumigation of their clothes; she will also have to perform any duties which the Guardians may from time to time think reasonable.

The duties of the Labour Master will be to superintend the labour of the male inmates in the Workhouse.

All of the above-named officers will be expected to make themselves generally useful under the direction of the Master and Matron.

The Salary of the Porter will be £20 per annum; that of the Tramps' attendant £10; and that of the Labour Master £20 per annum, together with board, lodging and washing in the establishment.

The Reading Union Workhouse, which had admitted its first inmates in August 1867, also employed a Cook – Edward Smith (43); two nurses (29-year-old Susannah Pinington and 43-year-old Thomas Marchant) and a Baker – Thomas Absolom (62) – to look after the 234 inmates in 1881.

When School reassembled the week ending 12th August, after four weeks' summer vacation, the average weekly attendance in the Infants' School was 162.2 which meant that it was overfull so no more scholars could be admitted till November. The following week, the monitor Edith Sutton gave a week's notice to leave as her parents were leaving Reading for Croydon. However, Miss Reay sent Beatrice Coxhead from the Girls' School on trial by the next week and she was doing very nicely in the Babies' Class by 9th September. Us pupil teachers worked very hard the following week to prepare our classes for the Government examination then, before the official close of the school year at the end of September, we were each given two days' absence to study for our own examination which took place on 1st October.

The Infant boys were more interested in the separate Urinal and the improvement in the closet accommodation that had been provided for them. They were completed just a week before Her Majesty's Inspectors visited for the inspection of the children on 28th October. Of 175 children present, 109 had made 250 attendances – up from 86 the previous year. We were pleased that, the inspection being over, the schools were then closed on Thursday and Friday. I was ill Thursday, 17th November. Mrs. Reaney presented the prizes just before school broke up for the Christmas holidays on 22nd December.

When it reconvened after a two week holiday, there was further training for us teaching staff. A singing class commenced on 13th January 1882 and was scheduled to take place each Friday afternoon after school so that we might be instructed in the New Notation (Tonic Sol-fa) by Mr. Moss.

Sometimes, the activities of the older children impacted on those of the younger, as of course the latter often relied on the former to take them to and from school. One such instance occurred on 9th June when afternoon school was closed on account of a meeting for children in the New Town Hall to which the elder children were going. Attendance books were closed 9.10 a.m. and were marked for a second time at ¼11 a.m. for all children under 7 years in order not to lose the second attendance and school closed at 12¼ p.m.

A fortnight after G. Palmer Esq. M.P.'s treat to the Boys', Girls' and Infants' Schools at the **"Acacias"** on the afternoon of Friday, 23rd June, the Schools closed for five weeks in order that the buildings might be enlarged and more classrooms provided for the Infants' School.

Pollie Barker had decided to take the plunge and leave quite suddenly around the time of our five week summer holiday. Her father was a Journeyman Biscuit Baker so she had heard about vacancies at Huntley and Palmers Factory from him and left to become a forewoman there. She had been considering doing this ever since Miss Stephens left. At that time, she'd tried to persuade me to do similar and I was very tempted then but this time I was enjoying the teaching too much, especially with the new classrooms. As Pollie's departure was unexpected, Miss Ryder had to take her Standard I class until the inspection of the school.

The Pupil Teachers' examination was held on 30th September, at which date the school year closed. The Inspection occurred just before a spate of childhood illnesses took hold for the winter in the Infants' School as, by 3rd November, attendance was thin, many children being ill with whooping cough, measles and fever. 30 boys and 12 girls passed into the other schools following the usual holiday given after the government inspection took place from Wednesday morning for the rest of the week. By the 24th, nearly half the school was away through measles or whooping cough and average attendance was down from 130 to 67. The following week, Dr. Shea ordered the school to be closed as measles was epidemic in the neighbourhood.

Even when school reopened five weeks later on 8th January 1883, the average weekly attendance had only increased to 77.7 as many children were still poorly. Several of the Committee were present on 19th January when prizes were distributed by Rev. C. Gullan. By then, the following had been received:

Government Report for 1882

This shows great improvement as regards working, discipline and results. This is now a good Infants' School.
S.A. Fabry is recognized qualified to serve under Article 84. Code of 1882.

Headmistress:	EMMA RYDER
Assistant under Article 32 c 3:	SARAH ANN FABRY
Pupil Teacher:	PATTI V. ATTWOOD end of 3rd year

Attendances remained low – rain, then intense cold and windy weather, as well as sickness, kept many children away from school. The monitress, Beatrice Coxhead, left in consequence of continued ill health. Even by 18th May, there was still concern about numbers being thin as average attendance was only 107.2. Each teacher was therefore allowed one further day's holiday in addition to Whit Monday. Miss Ryder attended the Conference of Teachers and Managers. There was a dramatic increase in average attendance to 142.4 on 1st June, the day Miss Ryder punished two boys for indecent conduct in the playground and my class obtained highest percentage in the weekly exam. On the morning of Wednesday 13th, the children and teachers were photographed in six groups. A fortnight later, term finished for four weeks.

By 6th April, Miss Ryder had compiled a list of Criticism Lessons for Friday mornings with us teachers taking the lesson in turn, and the others criticising:

April 13:	A Feather	Patti
April 20:	Brushes	Florrie
April 27:	Things used in building a house	Bessie
May 4:	Colour (red)	Edith
May 11:	Sponge	Annie

158

May 18:	Fishes	Patti
May 25:	The Whale	Florrie
June 1:	The Duck	Bessie
June 8:	Four sided figures	Edith
June 15:	Birds	Annie
June 22:	The Ostrich	Patti
June 29:	Dogs	Florrie
July 6:	Sugar Cane	Bessie
July 13:	The Cat	Edith

However, the closure of school on 29th June for four weeks until 30th July (followed by a Bank Holiday on 10th August) meant that the last two items on the list were transferred to the list for week ending 31st August:

Teacher	Class			Subjects		
Annie	I	The Hare	A Brick	Windows	Uses of Water
Patti	II	The Reindeer	Needles	Rice	Frogs & Toads
Florrie	III	The Bee	Pins	Lighting a fire	A Tree
Bessie	IV	The Owl	A Bird's Egg	Things made of stone	The Street
Edith	V	The Cat	A Thimble	A Baker's Shop	The Tea Table

Criticism lesson: The Sugar Cane by Bessie

During that year's inspection, Mr. Tremenheere left lists of work that he expected from the different Classes of the Infant Department, Poetry of which he approved, and Object lessons that should be conducted during the following year. They were recorded in the Log Book and, since they give you an idea of the work that was expected of the children as they progressed through the school, I am reproducing them here:

Work expected by S. Tremenheere Esq HMI in the Infant Department

1st Class   Reading from books of monosyllables,
Capital and small letters from dictation and figures up to 20,
Add any two units mentally,
Subtract any unit from any number not exceeding 18.

2nd Class   Reading from Sheets,
Writing as 1st Class from blackboard,
Arithmetic as in 1st Class but up to 10 from ball frame.

3rd Class   Reading from Sheets,
Writing small letters from Blackboard,
Arithmetic. Count objects.

159

Poetry approved by S. Tremenheere Esq. HMI

For Pupil Teachers   Shakespeare's "Merchant of Venice"

For Standard I   "The first Grief"

List of Object Lessons for 1886 and 1887

Standard I   Geography. River, Mountain, Island, Lake, The Sea, Cardinal Points
              Animal Physiology. Parts of the body generally. Head, face, nose,
              eyes, ears, mouth, teeth, breath, voice, hand, arms, legs, bones.

General.   Silkworm, Birds, Fishes, Money, Glass, Soap, Iron, Coal, Division of
              Time, things used for writing.

1st   Natural History. Eagle, Beaver, Squirrel, Camel, Elephant, Lion,
Division   Spider, Bees, Birds.
              Objects. Ink, Needles, Pins, Cotton, Candles, Boots and Shoes, Chair,
              Water, Chalk, Silver, Bread making, A Letter, The Railway, Biscuits.

2nd   Natural History. Black beetle, Butterfly, Sparrow, Reindeer, Goat,
Division   Frogs and Toads, Ostrich, Fowls, Tiger, Bear, Monkey, Worm.
              Objects. Leather Brushes, Books, **Slates**, Trees, Cup and Saucer, Cork,

              Salt, Leaves, Lighting a Fire, an Egg, the Farm, a Pen. Colour & Form.

Babies.   Natural History. The Cat, Mouse, Dog, Cow, Horse, Sheep, Donkey, a
              Fish, Lion, Birds.
              Objects. Knife, Fork, Spoon, Setting table for tea, Comb and Brush,
              Butter, Cheese, a Ship, Apples, Pears, Oranges.   Colour and Form.

2nd November, the Tuesday following Mr Tremenheere's visit, the Committee determined that Standard I should be resumed in the Infants' School. The schools then received his Government Report on 25th. 7 girls and 21 boys had by then passed from the Infants' School into the Senior Schools and six Dozen Boxes of Blocks had been bought for Kinder Garten as a Gift. The amount of Grant for Infants' School was £106 " 17 " 0 and the Report stated:

Government Report 1886 (S. Tremenheere Esq. HMI)

Infants School. The children are in good order on the whole and have been very successfully taught in the elements. Object Lessons, Needlework and other occupations are also satisfactory, though more stress might well be laid on these essential characteristics of sound Infant training. Attention is directed to Article 107 (c). The classification is in much need of amendment. The same Merit Grant as was awarded last year is recommended in the conviction that these points will receive attention. The Note Singing should also improve.

F. A. Chandler and E. A. Wheeler have passed fairly but Wheeler should attend to arithmetic and method.

E. M. Hayter. Arithmetic. Now qualified under Article 50 but can only qualify under Article 52 by passing satisfactorily examination specified under Article 46.

S. J. Ford. Reading and History.

Teaching Staff 1886 and 1887

Emma Ryder	Principal Teacher
Florence Annie Chandler	{Pupil Teachers
Edith Annie Wheeler	{End of 3rd Year
Sarah Jane Ford	Pupil Teacher end of 1st Year
Sarah Ann Fabry	Assistant under Article 84

Marks obtained by Teachers for School Work for year 1886

Edith Annie Wheeler	5775
Florence Annie Chandler	5665
Sarah Ann Fabry	5487
Elizth Mary Hayter	5346
Sarah Jane Ford	4926

It will be recognised from this list that the Florrie referred to in 1883 had been christened Florence Annie Chandler whereas Bessie was Elizabeth Mary Hayter and Edith was Edith Annie Wheeler whereas you will recall that I (Annie) was christened Sarah Ann Holt Fabry.

New heads for all three Schools during 1890s

'Free' education was introduced in 1891 and, on 31st August that year, there was a holiday to commemorate its introduction. The following March, Mary Ann Reay retired after 22 years' service as headmistress of the Girls' School and the newly-qualified Catherine Pierpoint was appointed. Catherine had only just become certificated at the time of her appointment and it was to be her only Headship as she was still in post when she committed suicide in December 1916. [32] Thomas Gleave retired after 40 years' service as Head of

---

[32] See pages 58 – 60 of *So many hearts make a school* (Daphne Barnes-Phillips, 2007)

Reading Boys' British School in December 1896 and Edwin Thomas Caton B.A. was appointed to replace him from 14th January 1897. The Voluntary Schools Act that year provided special grants for such Schools. On 1st February 1899, Emma Ryder was the last of the three Heads to retire, having been Infants' School Mistress for 18 years. Edith Varley replaced her from 6th.

The Elementary Education (School Attendance) Act of 1893 had raised the minimum age for working from 10 to 11 years and in 1899 to 12 years, which particularly angered the Textile Unions. It must be said that there was also some opposition from parents towards the new exemptions as their children's wages were an integral part of the family income whether they worked in the textile industry; in coal mines; engineering trades; 'in service', working as servants of all descriptions; or on farms, as bird scarers, picking stones out of fields, and suchlike. Half-timers started work at 6 a.m. and attended school in the afternoon. The following week they went to school in the morning and worked from 1 to 5.30 p.m., with a Saturday morning shift as well. Thus two children shared one job. The following year saw the 1894 Prevention of Cruelty to Children Act but it was not until the Fisher Act of 1918, when exemption from fulltime education was banned, that the little half-timers were finally released from their bondage.

A half-holiday for George Palmer's Funeral

However I am racing ahead and have forgotten to tell you that George Palmer died in 1897 before the change of Infants' School headteacher. When School re-opened on 23rd August, following the mid-summer break, a Half holiday was given that Afternoon on account of his funeral. The *21st August* edition of *Reading Mercury and Reading Observer* reported his death as follows:

Death of Mr. George Palmer

The sad event took place at his residence The Acacias shortly before ten o'clock on Thursday morning (i.e. August 19, 1897). His four score years had been well nigh reached ere the head of the famous firm (Huntley & Palmer biscuit manufacturers of Reading) was gathered to his fathers and entered into his rest.

162

Immediately on the information of the death of Mr. Palmer, the flags on the Biscuit Factory, the Municipal Building and the Royal Berkshire Hospital were lowered to half-mast and, at one p.m., the great tenor bell of St. Lawrence (the municipal Church) was tolled.

The funeral will take place at the Cemetery behind the Friends Meeting House at noon on Monday and will be officially attended by the Mayor (Mr. W. Ferguson) and the Town Clerk. The Memorial Service at St. Lawrence will be attended by the Deputy Mayor.

On Monday, the day of the funeral, the Biscuit Factory will be closed entirely and the Mayor has issued an appeal to the tradespeople of the town to close their business establishments from noon until 2 p.m.

In the *Saturday, August 28* edition under *The Funeral of Mr George Palmer of Reading*, it was reported that the Funeral procession was probably the largest ever seen in Reading, including as it did nearly 70 carriages. George was buried in the simple grave which had been prepared for his wife, Elizabeth, when she predeceased him in March, 1894. This was in the Friends' Burial Ground in Church Street, Reading (just off London Street), only a few feet from where his mother, sister and younger brother lay as well as Thomas Huntley and his wife.

With George's death, the surviving partners of Huntley and Palmers immediately went ahead with preparations for creating a limited company. Those preparations did not take long for, on 29th March 1898, Huntley and Palmers Ltd. was formally incorporated. Later that year, Barnum & Bailey's *Greatest Show on Earth*, came to Reading as part of its tour on 28th October, having visited Aldershot on the 27th and was travelling on to Swindon for the 29th. Similarly, it returned to Reading the following year on 28th April 1899, following a performance in Swindon on the 27th and moving on to Oxford for the 29th. Naturally, attendance was low in all three schools while the circus was in town.

My mother died in Reading during the third quarter of 1900, aged 67, and my father therefore had to look for another job. I was settled in mine and did not want to move but Clara was prepared to move with him to Thanet after the 1901 census. Huntley & Palmers was still the biggest employer in Reading as it had been 50 years earlier though, by then, the workforce numbered 5,000. Huntley, Boorne and Stevens (founded 1832) was next highest with 850.

163

Name changed from "British" to "Southampton Street" School

Soon after the Reading School Board celebrated its 30 year existence on 20th March 1901 and the tenth triennial election had taken place on the 12th, the British School joined the ten Board Schools – Coley Street, Katesgrove, Silver Street, Oxford Road, Newtown, Grovelands, Redlands, Central Boys', Battle and Swansea Road. Previous to that, the School, which could accommodate 801, had been termed a Voluntary School, along with St. Giles', Christ Church, St. John's, St. Stephen's, St. Lawrence's, Greyfriars', St. Mary's, St. Mary's Episcopal, Holy Trinity, All Saints and Lower Whitley. Out of a total 13,511 children being educated in Reading Schools, 5,259 were in the twelve Voluntary Schools and 8,252 in the ten Board Schools.

READING SOUTHAMPTON STREET BOARD SCHOOL

On 1st October 1901, our School was renamed Southampton Street Board School – Infants. The transfer to the Reading Board of Education had been reported in *Reading School Board's Report for year ending 31 December 1901* as follows:

TRANSFER OF THE BRITISH SCHOOL TO THE BOARD

The British School was transferred to the Board on 1st October last and has since been carried on as a Board School. The Board took over the entire Teaching Staff of the late school and no material alteration has been made in the manner of conducting it. The name, however, has been changed from the "British" to "Southampton Street" School.

However, it soon became apparent that the Board of Education was not happy with our premises. In its *Year ended 31st December 1902 Report* was written:

SOUTHAMPTON STREET SCHOOL (late the British School)

One other important matter will require the attention of the new Education Authority. It is the following –

164

On 2 March last, a communication was received from the Board of Education, stating that they understood from H. M. Inspector that the premises of this School were not such as could be permanently recognised for a Board School and that the Board of Education would be glad in due course to receive the School Board's proposals "for the reconstruction or replacement of them, and that additional playground should at the same time be provided."

The School Board devoted much time and attention to this matter with the view of sending proposals to the Board of Education in accordance with their request; but after negotiating with the owners of several of the properties adjoining or near to the School, they came to the conclusion that the "reconstruction or replacement of the School premises and the addition of more playground" on the present site and in connection with it was out of the question and that the most practicable course to pursue would be to purchase a new site as conveniently near as possible and to erect a new School upon it to take the place of the present school and to supply additional accommodation for the neighbourhood, to continue the present school until the new one could be provided and then to sell or otherwise dispose of the old School premises. After considerable negociation, the offer of a suitable site was obtained and a proposal to the above effect was sent to the Board of Education who expressed their wish that the matter might be left to be taken up and dealt with by the New Education Authority. So it remains.

The need for secondary education had became apparent after the raising of the compulsory school attendance age to eleven in 1894 but the School Boards were not deemed to be appropriate bodies to make that provision. [33] They were therefore abolished by the Education Act of 1902, which placed the duty of providing elementary education on County and County Borough Councils and on the Councils of certain non-County Boroughs and Urban Districts while the power of providing secondary and technical education was given to the County and County Borough Councils alone. As a result, Southampton Street Board School was renamed yet again and became:

SOUTHAMPTON STREET
COUNCIL SCHOOL

Balfour's Act, as the 1902 Act was known, placed all Elementary Schools on the Rates, except for those in London. It was to make quite a difference to the Rates as can be seen from the following extract from the *Finance* section of the *Education Committee Report for the year ended 31 March 1905*:

---

[33] According to the *1945 – 1950 Reading Education Committee Report*

The cost of education still shows a steady increase. In 1902, the cost per child in the Board Schools was £3 11s. 0¾d; for last year the cost was £3 14s. 4½d. The actual cost per scholar to the Rates was in 1902 £1 19s. 7d. and last year £1 13s. 9½d. The difference is due to the Special Aid grant provided by the Education Act 1902.

Alice E. Osman replaced Miss Varley as headmistress on 25th April 1902. She had been a certificated teacher for seven years prior to that and was thirty years of age, having been born in Reading about 1872 and living with her parents and two younger brothers – Arthur and Francis – at 50 Kennetside in the St. Giles' district at the time of the 1881 census when her father was a Carpenter Journeyman. Her parents had both been born about 1844 – Arthur Roland in Chiseldon, Wiltshire and Sarah in Kings Clere, Hampshire.

The following tables show the transfer from Miss Varley to Miss Osman:

Stock & Stores Accounts

Page 2   *Reading* **School Board**   **Half-year Ending at** <u>March 1902</u>
<u>E. M. Varley</u>   Schoolmistress of the <u>Southampton Street School</u>

Articles	Stock brought forward	New stock	No. of Invoice or Name of Tradesman supplying	Totals of stock b. f. & New Stock	Taken out of store — For Sale to children	For use in school
Needlework & Apparatus						
Scissors	1	5	Nicolle *11*			
Sewing Needles	14 pkts.	12 pkts	Heelas *7*			
Knitting Needles	112 pairs	12 sets	Heelas *8*	136		
Thimbles	21 doz.	3 doz.	Long *9*	24		
Needle threaders	190	-		190		
Sewing Cotton	20 reels	-		20		
Knitting Cotton	-	1 lb.	Heelas *1*	1		¼ lb.
Berlin Wool	-	½ lb.	Long *3*	½ lb.		1 oz.
Calico	8 yds.	6 yds.	Wellstead *2*	14		5
Print (material)	-	2 yds.	Long *5 & 9*	2 yds.		2
Handkerchiefs		3 doz.	Heelas *6*	3 doz.	3 doz.	-
Apron Check		15 yds.	Wellstead *10*	15 yds.	15 yds.	-
Check Material	4 yds.	2 yds.	Long *3 & 4*	6 yds.		2 ½ yd.
Crash		6 yds.	Long *3*	6 yds.	6 yds.	-
Hem demonstrator	3			3		
Tape Measure	1			1		

I have omitted any totally blank columns from that and the following table:

Page 12   *Reading* **School Board   Half-year Ending at** September 29th, 1902
A. E. Osman   Schoolmistress of the Southampton Street School

Articles Teachers Reference	New stock	Invoice no. or Name of Tradesman supplying	Totals of stock b.f. and New Stock	Remain in Store	Totals taken out of Store & remaining in Store
Master of Ballantree	2	Golder *14*	2	2	2
P. T.'s Note Book	2	Golder	2	2	2
Historical Atlas	2	Golder *23*	2	2	2
Christian's Arith.	1	Golder *23*	1	1	1
Lymes Historical	2	Golder *25*	2	2	2
Nesfield's Grammar	1	Golder *25*	1	1	1
Gregory's Science	2	Golder *25*	2	2	2
Infant Drill Wilsons	1	Golder *28*	1	1	1
Paper-Ball Making	1	Golder *29*	1	1	1
Nelson's Knitting	1	Golder *30*	1	1	1
Bible	1	Golder *30*	1	1	1
Guide Drawing Book	1	Golder *32*	1	1	1

The School became known as Southampton Street Council School – Infants – from April 1903. Around that time, we had ten staff and 195 pupils in the Infants' School, a similar number to the Girls' ten staff and 186 pupils. However, our school really only had accommodation for 181 whereas their's could accommodate 280 as can be seen from the table recorded in *Report of the Reading Education Committee for the 11 months ended 31st March 1904*:

Southampton Street School	Boys	Girls	Infants	Total
Number on Register	194	186	195	**575**
Total accommodation	340	280	181	**801**

The organisation of the Southampton Street Schools was also given as:

	Head Teach	1st Assist	Cert	Article 50	Article 68	Pupil Teach	Monitor	Total
Boys	1	1	5			1		**8**
Girls	1	1	4	1		2	1	**10**
Infants	1		2	2	1	2	2	**10**

Thus, it can be seen that, although the Boys' School has the least staff, it has more of the higher-qualified ones and also the most generous accommodation.

167

Richard Williams appointed Principal Teacher of Boys' School

Eighteen months after Alice Osman's appointment as Headmistress of the Infants' department of the Reading Southampton Street Board School, Richard Williams was appointed Principal Teacher of the Boys' Department of Southampton Street Council School as from 1st October 1903. His remuneration was to be at the rate of £160 per annum for the first year of service, rising by £10 per annum at the end of the first, second and third years of service respectively to a maximum of £190 per annum. The appointment had been resolved on the motion of Chairman, Alderman William Berkeley Monck, and seconded by Mr. Councillor Parfitt at 16th July meeting of Reading Education Committee. It was terminable by three months' notice in writing given either by it or by Richard Williams. Also at that same meeting, the Sub Committee had reported on the dangerous condition of playground so the Committee had recommended that the tar paving of the Southampton Street School be repaired during the Summer holidays at a cost of about £10.

Three weeks after Mr. Williams had taken over as Principal Teacher, boys from Southampton Street Council School, were recorded as present when H.M.I. P. L. Gray Esq. visited the Manual Instruction class at the Central Continuation/Industrial School. However, the Instructor had a severe attack of Rheumatic Fever from 28th October to 5th December so classes did not operate. During the ensuing Christmas holidays, the interior walls and ceilings of the Boys' Department were cleansed and coloured, such work having been termed urgent by Mr. Councillor Parfitt at 17th December Education Committee meeting.

Training of Pupil Teachers

Also from the 1904 Report, we gain some idea of how teachers were trained at that time, rather different to my training over quarter of a century earlier. A new scheme had been introduced for which candidates had to be not less than 14 years of age on 1st August following the examination which was to be conducted in November each year. Pupil Teacher scholars would then receive instruction for two years from 1st January in an approved Secondary School. Instruction, books and stationery would be provided free but no salary would be paid to them. They would then serve for seven months as Probationers (1st January to 1st August), during which time they would be engaged for half of each school day in the practice of teaching in the Elementary School to which they were attached. Their salary would be four shillings a week for girls and five shillings for boys and they would then enter a Training College. There were also to be Scholarships for two years of secondary school education, which could be extended to four years for those who were younger than 12. Boys over 14 years of age were to be given maintenance money. That same report gave the holidays of the Pupil Teachers Centre as three weeks each for Christmas and Easter but six weeks for the Summer, and the salaries of the Pupil Teachers were:

Pupil Teachers	1st year	2nd Year
Girls	£18	£24
Boys	£25	£30

By the following year, we knew that the Board of Education had passed plans for a school for about 1,200 children to be erected at Whitley for the accommodation of the Southampton Street School and for the needs of a growing district and that it should be ready for occupation early in 1907, £2 8s. 0d. having been expended towards it that year when the grant for the Southampton Street School was:

Southampton Street School	Attend	Annual	Fee	Aid	Total
	474	£498 17s.	£172 5s.	£214 4s. 6d.	£885 6s. 6d.

General Grants and those for special subjects were also then, per pupil:

	Standard	No	Cookery	No	Laundry	No	Manual Instruct
Boys	22/-					20	6/- or 7/-
Girls	22/-	26	4/-	0	2/-		
Infants	17/-						

Shillings were often denoted by /- so 22/- was 22 shillings or £1 2s.

Joshua Swallow becomes Head of Boys' School

In his 40th year, Joshua Swallow took up position as Head of the Southampton Street Council Boys' School on 3rd April 1905, having previously been Head Teacher of Coley Street School since 26th December 1898. We discovered later that his dates of recognition as an Uncertified Teacher at Leeds Darley Street Wesleyan Boys' School were from 2nd April 1883 until 15th January 1886 when he trained at Borough Road College until December 1887. As a certificated teacher, he was first employed by Reading Education Authority at

169

Oxford Road Boys' School from 26th January 1888 to 25th December 1898.

He had been born in Leeds, Yorkshire about 1865, the youngest child of Edward and Harriet Swallow, who were both Stay Makers and their other children – Jane, Polly and Alfred – had all followed them into the family business as "Stay Maker (Assistant)". However, Joshua became a "Pupil Teacher (School)". He had married Emily, who had also been born in Leeds, Yorkshire, and they had a daughter, May, in 1893.

Joshua replaced Richard Williams, who had been Head Master of the Boys' School until 30th March 1905. The epidemic of measles which had broken out at the beginning of that year continued until June and was responsible for a serious drop in the average attendance of the schools, especially the Infants'. The afternoon of 7th June, school was closed so that us teachers might have the opportunity of attending the ceremony of laying the foundation stone of Reading University College by **Lord Goschen**. We heard on 19th  July that in future all Head and Assistant Teachers were expected to be present at 8.50 o'clock in the mornings and at 1.50 o'clock in the afternoons. A poor attendance was registered on 22nd September as many children were either absent or late, watching troops of soldiers pass through the town. Towards the end of 1905, tar paving was again needed and, at the 16th November meeting of Reading Education Committee, the tenders of Mr. F. Talbot of Caversham Road were laid before the meeting and accepted:

For Katesgrove School £10: 2: 8. For Southampton Street School £5: 0: 0.

On a Sunday in the middle of February 1906, four boys broke into the School and stole 30 tubes of water colour and other property therefrom. Despite the dilapidated condition of the School's buildings, the Sub Committee ordered the prosecution of the offenders. By then, the buildings of George Palmer School were in the course of erection and they were expected to be ready for occupation early in the autumn of the following year. However, other works on the Southampton Street Schools were still being carried out in June for the better ventilating, trapping and flushing of the sewer drain at a cost of £50. By then, the scheme of Scholarships tenable at Secondary Schools, adopted in 1903 was in full operation and the number of Scholars who were in enjoyment of the opportunities provided were:

Council Scholarships: Corpus Christi College, Cambridge – 1; Reading School –7
Kendrick School Boys – 12; Kendrick School Girls – 9.
Pupil Teacher Scholarships: Kendrick School Boys – 18;
Kendrick School Girls – 47.   Total: 94.

In April 1907, the Southampton Street Schools took part as usual in the Children's Concerts, as reported in the *4th May Reading Standard*:

> Miss Bennett played the piano and Miss Hutchings arranged the piece while those performing in *Go Away Mr Crocodile* were:
> Misses D. Baker, D. Tennant, J. Hamblin, D. Kent, O. Brooks, S. Paget,
> V. Goodship, L. Herke, L. Fuce, M. Burt, W. Findlay
> Masters F. Goddard, G. Webb, V. Burrows, E. Golby, F. Gordon, W. Barkus,
> H. Moore, L. Goddard, C. Morris, W. Pocock, A. Smith

Mr. Swallow later became very involved with the organisation of the annual Children's Concerts as the following summing up of the 1911 Concert in the *Reading Standard of 25th February* shows:

> Taken altogether, the acting was good and the music pleasing. As there was fresh audience each evening, nearly four thousand persons have the elementary teachers of the town to thank for a thoroughly bright and happy entertainment. The organisation of the concerts was undertaken by a committee of which Mr. C. G. H. Smith of St. Mary's School was the chairman, Mr. F. G. Sheldon of George Palmer School was the vice-chairman and Mr. J. Swallow of George Palmer School, the honorary secretary.

I was absent owing to sickness on 26th June and not fit to return to school until 3rd July. That was the day the children were photographed so work had to be suspended for a time that morning. A half holiday was given that afternoon

171

and on the 10th for local Sunday School treats. Since that was also the time of the terminal examinations, the Time Table was not strictly adhered to then.

When school reassembled on 27th August, all members of staff were present. On the 29th, the Head Teachers of all departments left school at 9.45 a.m. to accompany the Clerk of Works to the George Palmer School to give necessary instructions for the fixing of cupboards and desks preparatory to removal there. The following afternoon, school was closed so that the staff might attend the garden party by kind invitation of Mr. and Mrs. Sutton. Our Head Teacher left school at 11.40 a.m. on the 18th September to meet W. H. J. Pugh by appointment regarding the removal to George Palmer School.

GEORGE PALMER SCHOOLS

1907 sees completion

Friday, 27th September 1907, was a momentous day for us all as that was the final day in the Southampton Street buildings before our transfer to the new School in Basingstoke Road. The final entry in the *Infants' School Log Book* was:

> Ordinary work was suspended after 3 o'clock this afternoon & children had games etc. in the playground. This school will be closed from today & staff & children transferred to the George Palmer School. Alice Tucker P. T. completes her apprenticeship this week & in consequence resigns duty today.

Miss Ryder, Infants' Mistress from the 1880s, had visited us and the Boys' and Girls' Schools as Mr. Swallow recorded in the *Boys' School Log Book*:

> The Southampton St. Schools, formerly the British, established in 1810, were finally closed on the afternoon of Friday of the appended date. Several old boys came to see the school before its transfer to the new buildings. Miss Ryder, a former Infants' Mistress, was a welcome visitor.

Jos. I. Ridley found the registers marked correctly and 138 Scholars present that day. On 3rd October, 145 Infant School children transferred to George Palmer Council School and 47 were admitted from other schools, thus making 192 total on the books for the first week, during which two Education Committee members – Miss E. Sutton and Mr. W. Thatcher – visited the

School. There was only one new teacher: Miss E. Davis   (Certificated)
joining Southampton Street Council Infant School staff: –

PALMER SCHOOLS, WHITLEY.

Miss A. E. Osman –
Head Teacher
Miss F. E. Gibbs –
Certificated
Miss S. A. H. Fabry –
Supplementary
Miss S. J. Killford –
uncertificated
Miss C. E. E. West –
uncertificated
Miss M. Wellman –
(Mabel) Nurse Girl

It was recommended that any of the old furniture from the Southampton Street School that was capable of repair was remodelled in the Clerk of Works Department for use in the Schools and any desks beyond repair were taken to pieces and the ironwork sold as scrap iron. A wheelbarrow and Extension Ladder were also to be supplied for the use of the Caretaker of George Palmer Council School. [34]

Despite those changes, the plans for the George Palmer School Opening were reported in 21st September 1907 *report of Reading Education Committee*:

The Latest Addition to
Reading's Splendid Elementary Schools

It was resolved that the Southampton-street School should be closed on Friday, the 27th inst., that Monday the 30th inst. and the two following days should be given to transferring the furniture, apparatus etc. to the George Palmer School, which should be opened for the admission of scholars on Thursday, 3rd October.

As was the custom at the time, a two-page spread appeared in the Saturday, 26th October 1907 edition of the *Reading Standard* under the title:

The George Palmer Schools [35]

---

[34] *Monthly report of Clerk of Works* to Reading Education Committee – 17th October

[35] See pages 27 to 30 inclusive of *So many hearts make a school* by Daphne Barnes-Phillips (published 2007) for full details of this report

[Editorial note: One photograph of Infant School pupils taken around the time of the transfer was later found by Sidney Gold among his mother's possessions. He stated:

> My mother went to George Palmer as it was opening whereas her older sister went to the British School. I would say it is one of these two schools. My mother's maiden name was Muriel Pullen. I should say step mother as my own mother died in 1950 and my father remarried in 1952. Muriel died in 2002 aged 98 and started at George Palmer Infants, she used to say, aged 3 and a half, which would have been in 1907 making her amongst the very first intake, I suspect.

The *George Palmer Infants Admissions Registers of 1907 – 1920* confirms Sidney's mother's recollections. As well as details of five-year-old Iris Pullen being admitted on 11th March 1907 (admission number 216) to the British School and then transferred to George Palmer School on 3rd October that year, three-year-old Muriel Pullen's name appears a few pages later where her admission number is given as 313 on 7th October 1907. However, four pages further on, her name appears again under RA403 as she was readmitted on 4th May 1908, aged four and a half. The cause of her leaving on 25th October 1907 is the best in the whole register – *Left till older!* However, she was obviously ready for school when readmitted as Sidney also found photographs of her performing in the 1911 Children's Concert as she did not leave until 4th September of that year, when she was promoted to the Girls' Department.]

174

In 1908 it was reported that:

the buildings of the George Palmer School were completed in September last and were at once occupied by the scholars of the Southampton Street School which was condemned in 1901 by the Board of Education. On 31st March last there were 693 scholars on the school registers.

I had stayed in Reading and continued teaching at George Palmer Infants' School [36] where the staff remained the same until September 1909 when Miss E. C. E. West was transferred by the committee to the Silver Street Council School. That meant that the classes were then reorganised as follows:

Class I	Miss Fabry
Class II	Miss Davis
Class III	Miss Gibbs
Babies Class	Miss Killford

Towards the end of 1910, we heard that Eliza Barcham had died aged 92, in Eastbourne. By the time of the 1911 census, I was an Assistant Teacher and had a friend, Miss Annie Drury (who had been born 1878 in Burton-on-Trent Staffordshire) living with me. We had a lot in common as she was a 33-year-old Head Teacher, and, like me, was employed by Reading Borough Education Committee. I was Head of Household at **12 Christ Church Road** but, by the time of the *1914*

Kelly's Directory of Reading, we had moved to 77 Whitley Street (on the east side) and she was listed as the Mistress of St. Giles' Church Girls' School in London Road, which had been built for 201 girls and had an average attendance of 175. That school had been partly rebuilt in 1885 at the time the slightly smaller Boys' School was entirely rebuilt when Albert Smith was its Master. George Palmer School, Basingstoke Road, having been built for 1,248 children in 1907 had average attendances in 1914 of 249 boys, 245 girls and 187 infants. The years of service as a certificated teacher of the George

---

[36] For further details of George Palmer Infants' School see pages 31 – 37 of "So many hearts make a school" (Daphne Barnes-Phillips, 2007)

175

Palmer Schools head teachers were given that year as:

Department	Name	Years of service as certificated teacher	George Palmer School Start Date
Trade (Mixed)	Mr. W. D. Williams	18	16 April 1912
Boys	Mr. Joshua Swallow	26	3 October 1907
Girls	Miss Kate Pierpoint	22	3 October 1907
Infants	Miss Alice Osman	19	3 October 1907

Joshua Swallow can be seen in this photograph with Standard 4 of the Boys' School. It was taken just prior to his retirement at the end of 1929 and shows a tiered classroom which enabled the teacher to see everyone in the class.

My sister Clara had stayed on in Thanet after our father died in 1910 and had married there four years later. Her husband, William Rasdill, had been born in Gautly, Lincolnshire but was living in Canterbury, Kent (formerly St. Mary Northgate) in 1901 and died at Thanet, aged 78, in 1920. Interestingly, there had been very little change in Infant School staff during that time as this table

1909	September	1920	16th April	1923	10th April
Class I	Miss Fabry	Class I (a)	Miss Fabry	St. I	Miss West
		Class I (b)	Miss West	Cl. I	Miss Fabry
Class II	Miss Davis	Class II	Miss Gibbs	Cl. II	Miss Gibbs
Class III	Miss Gibbs	Class III	Miss Harding	Cl. III	Miss Capell
		Class IV	Miss Manning		
Babies class	Miss Killford	Class V	Miss Killford	Cl. IV	Miss Killford

176

shows that Misses Gibbs, Killford and myself were teaching throughout that period and beyond. Miss Manning went on to become Head Teacher of St. Giles' Infant School.

My doctor ordered me out of Reading for at least a month in 1921 when I was ill from the 10th October. A Student Teacher, Miss Cooper commenced supply duty from the 24th and remained until I resumed duty on Monday, 28th November. In February 1922, I was ill on the 20th and had to have the day off school at a time when the illness of Misses Gibbs and Harding for longer periods caused the school to be badly disorganised. I was ill again from 13th March and Classes I, II and III worked in two divisions during my absence. I resumed duty when School reassembled on Tuesday, 29th August, it having closed on 28th July for the Summer Vacation.

All lessons were abandoned during the afternoon of 20th December and the children were favoured with a visit from Santa Claus. He drove up in his car and gained entrance through an open window, laden with a sack of oranges and toys, and, amid intense excitement, he was greeted with surprise and delight at such a welcome, though unexpected, guest. The children sang and danced to him and had the greatest fun. Several visitors accompanied him and one and all had a delightful afternoon.

I was ill on the 26th January 1923 and again on the 29th. Thomas Gleave, who had been Master at the Boy's School on the British System from 1857 until just before Christmas 1896, died in Reading early that year and a former pupil of both him and myself, Stanley Jackson Coleman, then a Barrister-at-Law, organised a reunion of staff and pupils of the Boys', Girls' and Infants' British Schools.

I had, of course, always known Mr. Gleave as Master of the Boys' School as he started teaching there before I was born. By the time of the 1881 census, he and his wife were in their 40s and living at Sankey House, Earley with their three-month-old daughter Ethel, who had been born there. I knew the older children better as Frederick (then 18) and Emily Annie (17) were both Pupil Teachers at the Boys' and Girls' British School and Evelyn (11) was a Scholar at the latter. Mr. Gleave had been born in Warrington, Lancashire and Emily was to marry one of the Boys' School teachers, Arthur William Moss, in 1889.

177

Expectations Largely Exceeded at BRITISH SCHOOL RE-UNION

Naturally Mr. Gleave's death and the subsequent reunion provoked many articles in local newspapers and one, in *9th February 1923 Reading Observer*, even mentioned myself as having taught Stanley Coleman:

TO-MORROW'S BRITISH SCHOOL RE-UNION

Expectations Largely Exceeded

Anecdotes about the old British Schools are legion and many of the stories to be told to-morrow (Saturday) on the occasion of the British School Reunion – or "British School Flag Day," as it is being more familiarly called – would undoubtedly provide an opportunity for the compilation of another volume of "Tom Brown's Schooldays." Miss S. Fabry, who was formerly a mistress at the Infants' School, is going and she may have even something to say about the troublesome disposition of Mr. S. Jackson Coleman, Barrister-at-Law, the honorary organiser, who was in her class over 30 years ago. It is seldom indeed that an institution grows so rich in affectionate legend, so endowed with personality, as did the old British Schools, and the "Old Scholars" will certainly be pardoned for recalling the proud line of Reading's leading professional and commercial men who were educated within those time-honoured walls and being perhaps a little sore that these historic buildings should now be used merely for the undignified purpose of a soup kitchen. Wouldn't the "Kendricks" have kicked up a noise if their buildings in the Queens-road had been utilised for a similar purpose? . . . .

Although that particular article continued, it is probably a good idea at this point to give you some further information about the use to which the Southampton Street School buildings had been put when we moved to the new George Palmer School in Basingstoke Road, since there is mention in there of them having been "used merely for the undignified purpose of a soup kitchen".

In the *Wednesday, 15th February 1911 Reading Standard*, mention was made of the fact that the Local Authority had converted the old British School on Southampton-street into a kitchen as a result of *The Education (Provision of Meals) Act, 1906*. The number of children fed during the year ended March 1909 was 721, which was 5.5% of the 13,219 children on the registers of the local schools. As a result of that Act and the subsequent one of 1914, James Piper, who was the Superintendent of the Centre, wrote on 30th June 1915:

Southampton Street Feeding Centre

The year ended March 31st, 1915 made greater demands on the accommodation of the above centre than any previous year. Subsequent to the outbreak of war and especially during the month of October 1914, the number of children presenting themselves at one sitting for dinners on more than one occasion exceeded 300. Yet in spite of numbers the actual distribution of meals proceeded as smoothly, and I venture to remark as satisfactorily as ever; and this result is very largely due to the children themselves. The system of "Monitresses" besides proving efficient in meeting actual working demands has a wholesome disciplinary effect in two respects, it encourages emulation among the girls, and the monitresses themselves exert quite a valuable influence with rarely an attempt at being officious. Besides, their training in "Service for others" is an item of educational importance.

The object of the general discipline of the centre is to approach the standard of a well regulated family. Punctuality, cleanliness, the singing of grace, carefulness and table manners are insisted upon. Conversation is not forbidden but the children are well acquainted with the limits permitted by the Superintendent. Aesthetic training has also been possible, gifts of flowers having been occasionally provided by various ladies; the children also are encouraged to bring wild flowers for table decoration.

With very rare exceptions the varieties of meals are appreciated by all; and as a consequence it does not require a very keen observer to note the marked difference in the appearance of the children at the start and end of the session.

In conclusion I would like to direct attention to the fact that of the many hundreds of children provided with meals during the year none have been reported to me for improper behaviour in the street on their way to, or from the centre; and I am delighted to report that although the **tramways** are perilously near the centre exit, and  traffic is particularly brisk in Southampton Street at noon, there has been no accident of any kind.

The photograph, which shows The Carpenter's Arms Beer House on the corner of 55 Crown Street and 65 Southampton Street around 1910, was taken at a much quieter time of day! The School Medical Officer for the Borough, John A.P. Price, M.D. went on to report that the highest number of children fed on one day was 1,238 on 16th October and the lowest was 75 on

17th August 1914. The number of children being fed daily increased so rapidly that it was found by the end of September that the Authority's Kitchen in Southampton Street was not large enough or sufficiently equipped to cater for more than 1,000 children each day and steps were taken to open a relief kitchen in a convenient part of the Borough.

By the kindness of Mr. Councillor A.W.A. Webb, his premises in Tudor Road, once used as a Soup Kitchen, were placed at the disposal of the Authority at a nominal charge for rental. They were equipped and the kitchen opened on 28th September 1914. The Borough was then divided into Districts and arrangements were made for Southampton Street Kitchen to supply food for East and West and Tudor Road Kitchen for Central and Caversham Districts. Food for children of the Tilehurst District was prepared at their own Centre. Meals were only provided six days a week – Monday to Saturday, with less being fed on Saturdays.

Menus were typically:

DINNERS

Menu 1D (Winter Menu)		
Monday	Lentil Soup	Boiled Rice & Currants
Tuesday	Irish Stew	Baked Jam Tarts
Wednesday	Green Pea & Vegetable Soup	Boiled Currant Pudding
Thursday	Lentil Soup	Boiled Rice with Sugar
Friday	Haricot Bean Soup	Boiled Ginger Pudding
Saturday	Meat & Potato Hash	Baked Jam Tarts

Menu 3D (Summer Menu)		
Monday	Bread & Cheese	Boiled Rice & Currants
Tuesday	Hashed Meat, Gravy & Potatoes	Baked Jam Tarts
Wednesday	Bananas & Bread & Butter	Macaroni boiled in Milk
Thursday	Irish Stew	Boiled Currant Pudding
Friday	Tomato Hash & Beans	Boiled Jam Roly Poly Pudding
Saturday	Hashed Meat, Gravy & Potatoes	Baked Jam Tarts

They were continued during the School Christmas Holidays with the Authority providing food for 25th and 26th December in bags that were given to the children on Christmas day morning.

180

A bag of food valued at 6d. contained:

2 cooked sausages	2 oranges
1 banana	1 slice of "Rugby" cake
2 apples	2 packets of "Popular" biscuits

During the time that the 7th & 8th Battalions of the Royal Berkshire Regiment were stationed in Reading, the Officers Commanding kindly offered the raw bones to the Authority for use at the Kitchen. The six tons collected from the Military Kitchens provided large quantities of stock for soups and in addition 13 cwt. of meat and 42 cwt. of dripping, all of which was used in the feeding of the children. After all the nutrition had been extracted, the waste bones were sold for £9. 15s. 10d. The value of the material constituted a donation to the Funds of about £180 for which the Authority was extremely grateful.

As you can imagine, we were all looking forward to seeing inside the original buildings to see what memories they held for us and how they had changed in the ensuing years. *9th February Berkshire Chronicle* described it on page 11:

BRITISH SCHOOLS "AT HOME"

TO-MORROW'S GATHERING

Old scholars of the British Schools in all conditions of life are meeting together to-morrow (Saturday) on social equality in the hope of seeing their old-time "pals" once more. Several old scholars are coming in their "cars," while one of the "old girls" is even shutting up her little shop that afternoon to meet the "Britishers" at the Cemetery Gates at 3.30 so as to pay her last respects to "dear old Daddy Gleave," and probably many another old scholar who has been precluded from attending the reunion dinner on account of the last-minute rush for seats will be in evidence at the remarkable graveside service to be conducted by the Rev. R. G. Fairbairn.

At 4.30 fresh recruits will gather outside the historic schools in Southampton Street to pay a visit to the scenes of so many happy memories. It will be a Britishers "At Home" – the refreshments alone will be absent! Mrs. Smith will be able to point out the place where she used to sit in bygone days, while Bob Brown, who has perhaps now blossomed out as Mr. Robert E. Duckers Brown, will show with some glee the place where "Daddy" whacked him in the pleasant time of long ago.

Seats for the reunion dinner have for some considerable time all been allocated, and amongst those present will be old-time masters and mistresses of all the departments of the school of which Reading was once so proud. The Deputy Mayor of Reading and Alderman Eighteen propose attending the dinner as well as prominent members of the Greenwich and Windsor Borough Councils. The dinner will represent the well-known hymn-book insomuch as the "Ancients" — those before 1890 — will sit upstairs, while the "Moderns" those after 1890 — will be accommodated in the smoking room. Any old Britisher — lad or lass — may take light refreshments in the commercial room of the Hotel Co-op after 8.15 even though not otherwise participating in the reunion, and join in the conversazione which will take place informally amongst those who cannot find room in the concert room. This concession was granted by the manageress, owing to the large number who would otherwise be prevented from joining in the reunion celebrations. Miss Helen Tocock, of Beech Hill, who was twice encored at the Central last Saturday evening, will without doubt secure an ovation for her rendering of "The British School Song" and "The Lankee Doodle Chorus" both of which compositions have been written and set to music by Mr. S. Jackson Coleman, barrister-at-law, especially for the occasion.

So enthusiastic are the old-time scholars of the British Schools that there is a disposition not to allow the "question" of forming an association to arise on Saturday's reunion. They are forwarding their shilling subscription to Mr. Coleman, at 54, Catherine Street, and are asking him to consider them as being desirous of being members.

A **Centre for the training of Pupil Teachers** from the age of 16 was attached to Palmer Central School from September 1922 to 1925. This photo of Pupil Teachers was taken in Miss Talbot's Needlework Room in November 1923 with head master, Mr. E. J. Andrews standing in the back row. At the far right of that row is Sidney Lodge. [Sidney's sister, Muriel Nutt (née Lodge), recalled in 2008 that Mr. Andrews was "a true gentleman".]

On 28th March 1923, the children had been promoted to their new classes, and School closed at noon so that Stock taking could be effected as usual that afternoon. The new Educational Year commenced at the re-opening of school on 10th April. At that time many of the children were ill with chicken pox and whooping cough. 42 girls were promoted to Standard I in the senior department but the boys were retained in the Infants in accordance with the Committee's instructions as they considered the present staff sufficient to meet this increase in the number of scholars, there having been 18 fresh admissions. We had an extra day's holiday that year on the 26th in honour of the Wedding of His Royal Highness the Duke of York. It had been granted by the Board of Education in accordance with the wish of His Majesty The King. During May, there was the usual holiday for Ascension Day, two days for Whitsuntide and the half holiday for Empire Day after the children had assembled in the Hall to receive the special message from the King and Queen by Gramophone.

I had a day's illness in September – on the 20th. School was closed on the 28th for the 5th Annual Conference of Teachers then from 31st October – 2nd November inclusive for half-term holiday and on 6th December for the Parliamentary Election as it was required for a Polling Station. On the 10th, H.M.I. Mr. W. Spikes visited this school and on the afternoon of Wednesday the 19th, ordinary work was suspended when the Infant children had a right royal time once again, drawing for tiny gifts from a beautiful Xmas tree, the latter being the gift of Mrs. Alfred Palmer. Unfortunately about 100 were forced to be absent from school, owing to an outbreak of measles which had been slowly spreading during the preceding month, and had apparently reached its climax – 55% only of attendances were registered that week.

Xmas vacation was from 21st but things were not that much better when school reopened on Tuesday, 8th January 1924 as only 156 scholars registered out of a possible 251 and I found myself ill from 14th – 18th inclusive. Miss Eva Thatcher, Head Mistress of Grovelands School, died around that time. School was closed for the matinee of the Children's Concert on the afternoon of 6th February. I was ill for three days from Monday, 25th February and, since Miss Gibbs had also been absent from Thursday 21st and did not return until 17th March, Miss Lewis, a Student Teacher from the Girls' Department, had been on supply.

Parents were invited to an "Open Day" in March. On Wednesday 19th, Classes Standard I and 1st class were visited, then, on Thursday 20th, Classes II, III and IV. A very large number responded to the invitation and expressed great satisfaction in the methods both of training and instructing throughout. Children and parents alike spent a very enjoyable time. School was closed on the afternoon of Monday the 31st for the annual stock taking. The children were promoted to their new classes during that morning, in readiness for the new educational year, which commenced the following day. 79 were transferred in total – 27 boys to the Boys' Department and 52 girls to Girls' as Standard I boys were again retained in this department. The arrangements of classes and teachers in charge were as before with one exception as Miss Capell and Miss Killford exchanged classes, the latter having Class III and Miss Capell the Babies.

School was closed on Monday, 7th April as the building was required for use as a Polling Station for the Guardians Election. Easter holidays were from mid-day on 16th April until Tuesday 29th and we had the usual Empire Day celebrations 23rd May followed by half holiday that afternoon; the Ascension Day holiday on 29th; Whitsuntide on 9th and 10th; and Annual Sports closure on 24th along with afternoon closure on 23rd July for the Annual Swimming Gala prior to a month's Summer holiday from 25th.

From 30th June, the School was granted the services of a Nurse Girl again, since a large number of children under five years of age were in attendance, so Evelyn Andrews, of 40 Surrey Road, commenced a month on trial then was appointed as from 26th August – the start of the new term. I had a day and a half's illness on the 11th and 12th September and school was closed on 26th for the Teachers' Annual Conference.

I resigned duty on 30th September 1924 "after 47 years of most valuable service", according to Miss Osman. Alice had shared 22 of those years with me, being the fourth headmistress under whom I had served. Miss D. A. Capell was my successor and she commenced duty on 1st October.

VII. Tales of the Master: THOMAS GLEAVE 1857–1897

1923 Reunion of old Britishers

Naturally, both before and after the 1923 reunion, photographs, letters and memories appeared in the local papers. Among them, in *27th January Reading Standard*, was the following article but without the photo referred to therein:

At the British Schools Fifty Years Ago

I am forwarding you a photograph (which perhaps you might reproduce) of the boys taken in the playground of the school 50 years ago – 1873. The elder boys in the group were in the first and second classes, but the revered headmaster (Mr. Gleave), who laboured so assiduously for so many years, gave permission for the younger brothers of the first class boys to be included in the group, which accounts for so many younger boys. The teaching staff then consisted of Mr. Gleave (headmaster), Mr. Jesse Herbert (afterwards Sir Jesse Herbert [37]), Messrs. Joseph Lane, Thomas Legg, William Waite and William Cook. It was, I think, about 1873 that Mr. Moss joined the staff and is seen on the right of the photo, while on the left stands the beloved and honoured, Mr. Gleave, and near him (third row, left side) his son, Mr. Fredk. Gleave, then a boy. The teaching staff about that period in the Girls' School consisted of Miss Thompson, Miss Ray and Miss Clara Herbert, as far as memory goes. Many of the boys have passed to their rest, but one can still see several who are holding honourable positions in the town and elsewhere.

Another of that era, Sam W. Gyngell [38], wrote on 3rd February 1923, from his home in Erleigh Road, Reading:

..Yes, I am an Old British School Boy & it is over fifty years since I first started at the school. The teachers then were Jesse Herbert, Lane, Legg, Waite, Cook & Williamson. The latter I well remember throwing a book at Gaffer Gleave's head and running out of school to the Mill Lane barracks & enlisting…

---

[37] Knighted in 1911

[38] Samuel Whiting Gyngell born in 1862

Word of the Reunion even reached Canada as Arthur Brown's letter of 21st April from Brampton, Canada testifies:

> I was one of the best-known boys at the British School for five years and attended there from the spring of 1872 to Christmas 1876. During the whole of that time Mr. Gleave was never absent except for a few days after his second marriage and an occasional day or half-day when he indulged in his great pastime, skating. I have frequently seen him on the ice in the Bulmershe Park Lake, which, under the ownership of Squire Wheble, was made a welcome meeting place for a delightful time.
>
> The late Mr. Geo. Palmer was secretary of the School and to name the visitors at the annual prize-giving and school treat would be to name all the principle heads of industry in Reading. Perhaps the best remembered would be the Mayor Mr. Catchpole, Mr. Andrews, Mr. Exall and Mr. W. G. Colebrook, not forgetting the speech of Mr. Soper, the gun maker (Friar Street).

Arthur's mention of Mr. Gleave's second marriage led me to discover that he married Emily Swain in 1861 and their children Frederick John, Emily Annie and Evelyn Maud were born in Reading in 1862, 1864 and 1869. In the *1865 Macauley's Reading Directory*, Thomas is shown as living at 63 Southampton Street, just eleven houses away from the British Schools at No. 52. Emily died aged 37 in the Wokingham area in 1874 so it is possible that the family moved to Earley in the early 1870s. Less than two years after her death, Thomas married Sarah Ann Marris, which ties in beautifully with Arthur's recollections of his dates at the school. Their daughter, Ethel, was born in Earley in 1881. Sarah also predeceased Thomas as she died in 1910, aged 71.

As well as the publishing of individual memories, the personal recollections of several former pupils was pieced together by *The Berkshire Chronicle* Reporter, James Jarche, for his article of 16th February, placing emphasis on the Cage as news of its existence had had quite an impact on him:

The Cage Cure for Naughty Boys

Ex-Pupils Who Went Through It Weep Over Their Teacher's Grave

> I wonder if they will call it the Reading Cage Club!
>
> A month ago, old "Daddy" Gleave, aged ninety, died in Reading. He arrived from Warrington sixty years before, and became headmaster of the British School, until it closed, after more than a century's existence, twenty years ago. And "Daddy" Gleave or "Gaffer", as some of them called him, became the best-known citizen of the town.

I am not surprised, for it was his habit, when boys and girls in the school had broken any of the rules, to put them in a small wooden cage, which he had specially made, and to haul them up to the ceiling of the class-room, nearly thirty feet high up. Naturally not one of his scholars forgot him. In later years, when education authorities grew over-paternal, the cage was abolished; but it lived in the memory of the town. And now scholars would be shown where it used to hang.

And so it happened that S. Jackson Coleman, once one of the boys put in the cage, but now a serious barrister-at-law, advertised, the other day, for former scholars, and last Saturday they met at the old man's grave, placed a wreath upon the mound, wept, many of them, at the memories conjured up, and then dined together in state, after deciding to subscribe for a tombstone to mark their respect for their old schoolmaster, and to form a club in memory of the old cage days.

It was pathetically funny to see grown men, some of them now grey with age, meet each other after all these years.

Old Boys Recall the Past

"I'm Cusden," would say one, now the head of a large printing works in Reading. "Do you remember when Gaffer put me in the cage twice in one morning!"

"But I was in three times in one day," would reply somebody else. And there he would be left while the other boys were playing, their shouts coming in the window and through the hateful, mocking bars.

A PEEP INTO THE PAST.

Sometimes a boy was left there for hours, passing his time by writing the word "Duty" on a sheet of paper, until there was so much "Duty" on the paper he couldn't write any more. Yes, and the girls too. They are grandmothers, now, some of them; and when their grandchildren are naughty they think, "Now if I had a cage __ !"

The old man would cane his pupils on the left hand, leaving the right one still well for writing purposes. But he also had "a cage look" as they call it. He was a long-bearded man, with a clean-shaven upper lip, and there would come a *look* into his eyes, sometimes.

187

His lips would shut firmly, this making the beard go up a little. Then the boys knew that somebody was due for the cage.

The cage would come down from the ceiling, and, when the boy was in – or the girl it was, sometimes – the master would pull the cage up to the ceiling, sometimes calling on Dick Atkins, the good boy who never went in the cage, to help him. Dick Atkins, now Richard Atkins Esq., was there on Saturday with all sorts of cage stories.

It was hard work, and old Mr. Atkins, as he is now, said on Saturday that he would just as soon have gone in the cage himself as pull someone else up. The boys liked being pulled up; but the being-left-there part was boring.

Yes, this story of the cage has gone all over England, for former pupils went to live at Warrington and Preston, and other towns far away. One, Sir Jesse Herbert, even became a judge in China. And with him to China went the story of the cage – to China, where criminals are often put in cages and left there for days at a time.

The caged boys all looked very respectable on Saturday. One is now Deputy-Mayor of Reading; he said that the cage had done him "a world of good."

"Spare the cage and spoil the child," was the old schoolmaster's motto. But, so much did his high character remain in the memory of his former pupils, that when, one by one, they were called on to say a few words at the graveside, most of them could only stammer, ending in unblushing tears. It is not nice to be old and to remember the days of childhood.

The Cage Has Gone Now

From the grave the procession of old people, men and women, went along to what was their old school, to look at the ceiling from which they had hung. But now it is a soup kitchen for the unemployed, and the cage has gone, and the hook also.

It seems that the idea of the cage came from the fact that there was a big hook in the high ceiling of the school, and its emptiness worried the schoolmaster, who finally found some useful way of employing it.

His thoughts wandered around naughty children, I suppose, a good deal, and thus the idea of the cage was born.

So, if you are a schoolmaster, or, perhaps, a parent with two naughty boys and you see a hook anywhere about, buy a cage as quickly as you can. . . .

The ordinary rabbit size won't do; but one of the unused ones from Cruft's Dog Show might come in handy. It is sure to do good and to turn out well, because the most casual glance at the former scholars on Saturday showed that, thanks more, perhaps, to the cage than to the other things they learned about, they are all now useful, respectable citizens, with a pride in their work, and a pride in their old school, and with an abiding affection, more than that, for the earnest, ingenious old man who found a new use for cages.

Although James' interpretation of the Cage was somewhat different to Joseph Lancaster's concept of it – see page 23 – we realise that his embellishment was based on hearsay. It seems more likely that Henry Allen's letter sent from his home at Loosley Row, Near Princes Risborough, Bucks on 12th February and published in the *24th February Reading Standard* gives a truer picture of the status quo during much, if not all, of Thomas Gleave's headship. Henry mentions that the preferred Quaker form of punishment had changed to the more traditional caning by his day:

OLD BRITISH SCHOOL

Re your very interesting notes on the old British School in "Current Topics", one remembers Mr Caton as a French scholar in his talk with the Breton onion sellers, who used to be such picturesque sights in the streets of Reading. "Everything" and "cough" strips, apples, marbles and the host of other things which used to delight the hearts of the old British boys (and girls) were sold by an extremely nice kind old couple named Shepherd in Southampton Street, near the bottom of Alpine Street. Beside the school fights, sometimes pleasant, sometimes otherwise (the Britishers always won), one remembers some old Reading characters – "Old Bozzill" and "Old Moey" and a number of others, whom at times the boys used to "rag". Our's was a caning school; we deserved it; and no doubt we are better for it. The present generation misses much. We "got the stick" if we waited outside the Girls' entrance. We were not allowed to see the ladies home in those days. The playground, although small, was the scene of many boxing and sparring matches, in which numerous friendships were firmly cemented.

Certainly, the *16th February 1923 Reading Mercury* quoted an interview that a representative of that paper had obtained with Mr. H. T. Pugh, Clerk to the Reading Education Committee, concerning the actual facts about the cage:

The cage at the Old British School

Not used in Mr. Thomas Gleave's time

Mr. Pugh said that the cage fell into disuse about 1840, and it had never been used in Mr. Gleave's time. He thought that there was no one living to-day who had seen it. He went on to say that a certain Joseph Lancaster, who was the pioneer of popular education, was very much averse to corporal punishment. He started the original British School in Borough-road in the South of London, and he put a notice on the door to say that boys who went there would be taught to read for nothing, although they could pay if they liked. After a year had passed he had 1.000 scholars under him. Joseph Lancaster had a means of punishing a boy without resorting to corporal punishment. A boy was tied up with ropes by the schoolmaster before the other boys. He was, in fact, something like a

189

Christian martyr. This man, Lancaster died in 1838, but the school was started in 1810. The British School in Reading was founded by a committee in this town after the idea of Joseph Lancaster, who had their plans submitted to him, which he himself altered.

It is practically certain that the cage was used, but not in the late "Daddy" Gleave's time.

"The same idea of the use of the cage," said Mr. Pugh, "seems to have prevailed in some of the old schools, for at the school which I attended in 1880, they had a similar device called the rostrum, a pulpit-like structure with stone steps leading to it, and which was surrounded by lattice work, from which the culprit's head only was visible and in which they were made to stand."

Mr. Pugh thinks that what really has happened was that some of the old boys must have heard tales of the cage when they were boys from their parents, and have enlarged upon it.

We also understand that the Education Committee are investigating the matter.

Other newspaper reports are reproduced here as they give interesting insights into the pupils' perceptions of Mr. Gleave and of the Infants' and Boys' Schools at the time. "Lankee Doodle"'s was particularly relevant to Annie Fabry's teaching career in the 1890s:

Memories of a "Lankee Doodle"

MEMORIES OF THE BRITISH SCHOOL
By A "LANKEE DOODLE" OF FORMER DAYS
"Reading Observer" Exclusive – 9th February 1923

Happy are the reflections that one gets in quiet moments of the Old British School with which so many have been proud to be associated. Those grimy walls and well worn floors could tell many a merry story, indeed, if only they had tongues to tell and lips to speak. To relate my own experiences I must go back to about 1892 or 1893, when I entered the Infants' School, which was at that time under the care of Miss Ryder, a lady that memory seems to picture as of matronly build and bearing. In 1895 I was transferred to the first standard classroom of the "Big Boys" and came at once under the influence of dear old "Daddy" Gleave, who has recently passed to his well-earned reward. In that class we had a number of interesting lads including Cherry Cripps, Cyril Lovegrove, Joey Moore, Horace Coleridge, Stan Coleman, Sid Brown, Perce Scrutton, Fred Broughton, Len Moss and Ernie Rivers, with only a few of whom I am to-day conversant. We were nevertheless a genial throng and not the least memorable privilege which we had in that class was to see "Gaffer" spanking the other "kids." Little did we envy the recalcitrants! Neither did we believe poor old "Gaffer" who was never weary of telling us that it hurt him much more than it did the lad he whacked! Certainly we would have preferred to have been the spanker than the spanked!!! One day is vivid in my memory. "Gaffer" went out of the class, and, upon returning, asked who had spoken during his absence. Voluntarily or involuntarily the whole class – with one or two exceptions – strolled out and corporal punishment having been administered with due form and ceremony, we returned somewhat sadly to our well-worn and well-chiselled desks.

Transferred in 1896 to the second standard my records bear witness that I was awarded for regular attendance and progress the fourth prize. It consisted of a book, "Birds, Beasts and Fishes." Before this time, on 14th January, Mr. Edwin Thomas Caton had come amongst us. Mr. Caton – whose Mephistophelian nickname will be at once apparent – thereupon became our headmaster. A log book then brings to mind that I had two years under Mr. Arthroll as teacher of the 3rd and 4th standards. Mr Arthroll was a teacher who would stand no foolery and I must confess that I was by no means sorry to leave his class! Our boys at that time consisted of such old-time footballers as Billie Deadman and Bob Coath. Among the others I recall Wallie Bradford, the popular secretary of Simonds Club, Len Fellows, Edgar Thornberry, Bertie Corp and Billie Dunton.

In 1899 I was a scholar in the 5th standard classroom, which contained a mysterious cupboard which to my mind seemed peculiarly cadaverous. The only two things in that cupboard which I can distinctly call to mind at this present day is a quaint collection of bones, which were used for physiology lessons, and a number of paper sheets containing the song "O what can the matter be?" Mr. W. A. Saunders whom for some inconceivable reason was nicknamed "Sausage", was our teacher in this class, and I was so sorely grieved at being robbed of the weekly physiological lessons – French being substituted therefor – that I joined the evening Temperance Science Class in the Palmer Hall and obtained for my pains the first prize in the Junior Division – a book entitled "Old England at Sea." I slipped through the 5th standard in due course and heard to my surprise that I had obtained the second prize for regular attendance and progress. I did one better in the sixth standard and came off with the first place, being awarded Pitman's Shorthand Dictionary and a couple of French Dictionaries. The former has become a bit out-of-date with the 1913 revisions in the Pitmanic art but the latter are well-worn and in almost daily use.

Poor Frank Sherwood, who was our teacher, did not appeal to me so much as Mr. Saunders. Mr. Sherwood, who met so untimely an end however, knew the way to interest us lads. He spake of the Starry heavens, gave us an insight into Greek and Roman mythology, and taught a number of subjects which were not included in the curriculum. Mr. Saunders, nevertheless, always appealed to me for his outstanding courtesy. He realised to the full that the "British" was a superior school, renowned for many an age, and he treated us all as the sons of old country gentlemen rather than the "little devils" we undoubtedly were.

Mr. Sherwood had certainly a number of good qualities, and I well remember his kindly good wishes when I only too soon had to wish him adieu. He had a certain specific against all ills. If he wanted to do anything – such as a count of pence which were regularly brought Monday by Monday or to fill up any schedules – he would give us some job to do in which he could see an immediate result. The whole book of Psalms, I should consider, was transcribed into Pitman's phonography. For this task was equally appropriate for both Scripture and Shorthand Lessons.

Our interest in this class – apart from the pat-ball [39] that we exercised during our play-time hours – was the points which our never-failing football team were getting. Charlie Robbins, Harold Duguid, Will Deadman, Bacon and Williams were names inscribed on our hearts as heroes of many a fight. Of that class Leo Twiney has become a priest in the Catholic Church, Frank Freeman has entered the Civil Service, Arthur Drury and Len Harris have become teachers, Stan Coleman has entered the ranks of the lawyers, Frank Weeks and Reg Winning have obtained official positions in our civic life, while others have joined the clerical staffs of Messrs. Huntley and Palmer, Sutton and Sons, and H. and G. Simonds. A number, too, have opened up business for themselves in this and other towns, and, judging from outside appearances, seem to be doing fairly well.

S Jackson Coleman is to the right of the swimming trophy. Mr E.T. Caton BA (Head) is on the left of the photo and the other teacher is Mr. Frank Sherwood

Just before I left there was some excitement over the swimming championship. Bob Coath, who appeared to be champion in all sports and is now doing well in

---

[39] A small ball had to be hit with the hand so that it bounced on the ground before hitting a wall. The opponent then had to hit it on the volley or after only one bounce.

America, had left the school and gone into the offices of Wallis, Son and Wells. There was therefore a keen competition for the swimming trophies. Drury, who was at that time plying his hand to teaching work in anticipation of the forthcoming pupil teacher's examination and Coleman came first and second respectively in this event and I know the latter always contested the eligibility of the former, whom I believe beat him for supremacy by a narrow margin.

These reflections are perhaps a little at random, but they may assist others to try their hand in this direction. If not, they will without doubt bring to mind a host of jolly experiences to tell at the forthcoming Reunion of Old Boys and Old Girls on Saturday, February the 10th. That the old school will ring with merry laughter on the occasion of the ramble through the buildings in the afternoon goes without saying. That the "Old Girls" may have many an interesting tale to tell of childhood's days is also certain. That some have risen who are too proud to recognise the school which gave them their start in the world is no less a fact. For if an organisation of old Britonians were formed and properly supported it could outnumber all other similar local associations, and the Town Hall would not suffice for a future Reunion. A Century in a school of such a character is not to be found in every town.

The movement initiated in Reading has, however, inspired "British" boys elsewhere to similar activities. Nevertheless, what a pity it is that nothing was done in the lifetime of Mr. Thomas Gleeve! That the heart of this "dear old man" was not cheered in his declining years and his funeral lacked any really representative attendance of his "Old Boys" is, perhaps, a sad commentary on the seeming ingratitude of the present generation. It may be, however, but a symptom that leadership is the only thing needful. The forthcoming Reunion will without doubt indicate which analysis is the more correct. In any case it will cement the Old Scholars in brotherly fellowship once more and form a never-failing memory to them of the life's work of one who was not disrespectfully known throughout his early existence by all – and will still be remembered in death – as "Dear Daddy Gleave." Of him at least there may be applied from the wisdom of Ecclesiasticus [40] in some measure the inspired words:- "Let us now praise famous men, and our fathers that begat us. The Lord had wrought great glory by them through His great power from the beginning. Such as did bear rule in their kingdoms, men renowned for their power, giving counsel by their understanding, and declaring prophecies; leaders of the people by their counsels, and with their knowledge of learning meet for the people, wise and eloquent in their instruction. Rich men furnished with ability, living peaceably in their habitations; All these were honoured in their generations, and were the glory of their times." *(Eccles 44)*

---

[40] 5th book in the *Apocrypha*

193

Other snippets appeared in the *10th February 1923 Reading Standard*:

Bell-ringing Escapades of the "British" Boys

British school boys are welcoming the opportunity of gathering together and chatting about old school days and of all their juvenile escapades. One of the "Old Boys" recalls the glorious fights which took place against the Christchurch boys and Crowny Bobs with sticks and stones and rolled up mufflers, etc., and how Mr. Gleave would try, ineffectually, to make them keep in front of him on their way home. Not only that, they can also tell of climbing the trees opposite Sidmouth House or "following my leader" round Albion Place and ringing all the area bells! They have also some recollections at a later date of St. Giles' Sisters. How they did delight in annoying the Crowny Bobs' Sisterhood! But Sister Mary would come sweetly to the door – and, well, the Britishers were gone! After all, Britishers could not help forgiving a lad of to-day for being up to similar mischief; in this, like other things, their accomplishments were well known. And who, with memories dating back over half-a-century, cannot recall the school cage, wherein the refractory were placed and hauled up to the ceiling?

The British School "Dinner" Boys

The superior type of boy that the British Schools attracted often came from a very long distance. For this reason many of them stayed in school during the luncheon interval. As might be imagined, many a harmless prank was played during this period. One day, when returning for their afternoon 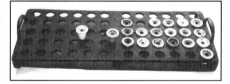 school, the lads found the **ink wells** duly supplied with aqua pura, whilst "daddy" often tried in vain to find culprits who were in the habit of making mysterious signs on the blackboard during this appropriate two hours. The lads were wont to have some sumptuous repasts in those days. The old school was heated by stoves, and to provide a moist atmosphere there was a small utensil attached to each of them which was regularly supplied with water. In this water the boys were accustomed to boil their eggs. One lad had tried, somewhat ineffectually, to boil a plum pudding in the water, while another tried to make Bovril! A fried fish restaurant next door was the favourite rendezvous on Fridays, and many a lad got a good "tanning" for leaving the remains of the noon-day feast upon the dusty school floor. And what British boy has not pleasant memories of Mrs. Cottrell's farthing "Everything" strips?

A photograph, thought to have been taken in 1892 or 1893, was produced at the time of the 1923 Reunion. It shows some of the boys with bearded **Thomas Gleave** sitting to the left.

In the *2nd February edition of The Chronicle*, a "younger" old boy recalled the transfer of the Mastership from Thomas Gleave to Edwin Caton:

THE OLD BRITISH SCHOOL

SOME REMINISCENCES

BY AN OLD BOY

No question has probably been asked more frequently of late than one concerning the location of the old British School. For almost twenty years the name of this highly successful institution has been hidden under the proverbial bushel, and very few who did not live in the town in olden days are aware of this establishment, which, in its day and generation, was often preferred by parents to the secondary schools which at that time were perhaps less known. Bearing a date, however, showing that it is more than a century old, there still stands in Southampton Street the quaint building, whose structure certainly lends no suggestion to-day of the commanding positions held by its old-time scholars, and the remarkable success for which it has been responsible. These in particular were in no small measure due to the late Mr. Thomas Gleave, who known affectionately to his scholars as "Gaffer" or "Daddy" Gleave, recently passed away, at a ripe old age, and concerning whom an appreciation was published in last week's "Chronicle."

Throughout the town, practically in every sphere, the "British" ranked supreme right to the days the school was fast nearing its "allotted span." Coath, Bacon, Robins and others, clad in the claret and amber colours of the school, led the football eleven to victory again and again; Cocks was a specialist in all things scientific; Drury and Coleman were foremost at the swimming bath; while H —
— was regarded with a certain amount of lofty pride owing to the celerity with which he was capable of doing his homework. Then it was that one of its scholars, Sir Jesse Herbert, was shedding the full lustre of his office upon the school in representing the Crown in a legal capacity in China, Mr. Samuel John Vinden was presiding over the guardians; Mr. Arthur Wheeler sitting as the Town Clerk at Bury St. Edmunds; while many of her sons were deliberating upon our

local bodies as the accredited representatives of the rate payers. Even now it is a well-known fact that some of our finest business men in Reading had at least the grounding of their education at the British Schools, while not a few have distinguished themselves in other ways. "Loo" has budded forth as the Rev. Father Twiney and has charge of a R.C. mission in Staffordshire, "Stan" Coleman called to the Bar about two years ago, two or three have become medical men, one or two Nonconformist ministers, and a few accountants and solicitors. So complete is the circle of interests, indeed, that a person in Reading could spend his whole life dealing alone for his food and other needs from those who were educated at Reading British School.

With the installation of the late Mr. E. T. Caton B.A. to this position a change took place. An innovation in the nature of a roll-top desk one day made its appearance in the sixth standard classroom, and French began to be taught. Mr. Gleave's services however, were retained for a while, probably in a consultative capacity, and I well remember forming one of the boys who sang on the occasion of his farewell presentation a simple French melody — "Dans les bois j'etends le coucou." In yet another way the "British" led the way — and that was in the teaching of Pitmans shorthand. [41]

When one considers that I am speaking of something like 25 years ago it will be quite understood that this introduction effected in the standing of the school in local circles, especially when coupled with the influence which French was exerting on our grasp of the King's English. Indeed, I am not exaggerating matters by saying that the "British" lad, if he so wished, could withstand the opposition of the boys from any other school. I once remember the occasion, in fact, when I ran against an old "Grammar School" boy and an old "Kendrick" and overheard them say with an air of solemn awe; "But he's one of the Britishers!"

Although we had conduct cards and so forth, I must confess that we were not always kept within bounds. There were, in fact, various categories of punishments to the refractory — the "capital punishment" consisted in my day of being led to the cloakroom, there to be beaten with considerable force on a certain part of the anatomy adaptable for the purpose. For the minor failings, which were far more numerous, the popular sanction in Sherwood's days was to be detained in school after the normal period to work out a particular "tot." There were perhaps 200 tots in the book, and, although we had necessarily to do different tots on each occasion, it was obviously in keeping with the ingenuity of youth to exercise a little assiduity in the direction of compiling a complete key. Once this had been formulated the terrors of staying overtime were considerably minimised.

One sad day, however, we met in the school and the news was suddenly broken to us that the schools were to pass over into the hands of the old Reading School Board. Foreseeing a passing away of all the splendid traditions a number

---

[41] Sir Isaac Pitman's shorthand for the English language, first presented in 1837

of us lost no opportunity for seeking pastures new, and, with the opening of the George Palmer Schools, its portals as an educational institution were finally closed. Its scholars were scattered to all four corners of the globe — some have emigrated to the Colonies, others have made a fortune in the States. Of those who remain in Reading a number perhaps do not care nowadays to be associated with a school building that has fallen into such desolate a condition. Others pass one another each day without recognition. The impending re-union on 10th February is forming a welcome opportunity for those who care, to renew many of the friendships which have temporarily been shattered. May it prove in every way successful!

The reference to Mr. Gleave's services being "retained for a while, probably in a consultative capacity" following the installation of Mr. Caton as Head Master is interesting as very few people will have known that the School was visited without notice by an Inspector on 3rd September 1896. The following letters give some idea of what transpired and how the managers dealt with it:

November 24th, 1896
Sir
    In reference to your letter of November 17th the Managers beg to reply that when they received the Inspector's Report they inquired into the reason of the absence of the Head Master. He stated that on the afternoon in question he left school at 3.5 pm on account of the ill health of his wife. Taking into consideration the nature of the reason that influenced him and the fact that for years past he has never once been away from his post during school hours, the managers accepted his application but instructed him for the future to enter in the Log Book the fact and reason for his absence at any time in the same way that the absence of other members of staff is notified.
    With regard to the other irregularities the managers believe that all is complained of by the Inspector arose from departures of the Time Table and that the Teachers who were "chatting at the School door" considered themselves off duty at the time, their classes being in recess.
    At their meeting on 26th January 1897, it was agreed to insert in the Minute Book "Our head master, Mr. Thomas Gleave after holding that post for thirty nine yeas finds it desirable to seek some relief from the onerous responsible duties it involves. We have therefore appointed our senior assistant Master, Mr. E. T. Caton B A as Head Master whilst retaining the services of Mr. Gleave as an assistant Master.

We feel that it is our duty as well as our hearty desire to place on record in our minute book our high appreciation of the long and valuable
. . . .

Wm Armstrong (Correspondent)

A week after the *Berkshire Chronicle* had published "Some Reminiscences by an Old Boy" we learn the names of some of the boys who were at the School at that time:

The British School Reunion

The British School Reunion to take place to-morrow, was undoubtedly the "Talk of Reading" during the week-end, by reason of the splendid photographs reproduced in our columns last week. The reference by "An Old Boy" to the punishments meted out 25 years ago led one of our readers to say that the 18 stripes on each hand which he received from "Daddy Gleave" for playing truant was thoroughly deserved, while several told how a prominent local person had been placed in the curious cage, which was in the school some 50 years ago, but was afterwards abolished. One reader observed that as two local pawn brokers attended the British School there was always an opportunity for a Britonian to be particularly friendly with "uncle" without causing undue alarm. All the colours — grey, brown, white and green — were represented at the old schools, while at one period "East" sat next to "West," and the "Baker" in Wokingham Road certainly attended the historic institution before he knew anything about "boots." Not only had the British School an undertaker's son as a scholar, but it had what perhaps no other school in Reading could claim; it was actually attended by a "Deadman," and, more wonderful still, he lives even now and proposes attending the reunion. Ornithology will also be in evidence, for whereas there will only be one "Swallow", there will be present several "Robins" but no "Wrens." No one will object to having "Bacon" with "Salt" and "Sage," at the dinner. Not only is there more than one "Coleman" going to the reunion, but there is also a "Shepherd," a "Cooper," a "Tanner" and a "Carter," who propose sitting beside the "Beaches" near the "Mills" and the "Barley."

In the following day's *Reading Standard* on Page 12 appeared:

British School Reunion

No tickets available now – cemetery 3.30pm. – Daddy Gleave.

One old boy recalls how one of his scholars one day got his own back. He threw a book at the head of the late respected headmaster and then ran out of school to the Mill Lane Barracks and enlisted! A good number are trying to recall the ascending cage into which Mr Gleave was wont, about half a century ago, to place the naughty ones, indeed the cage is a mystic expression by which a very

198

old Britisher may always be known. Those who take the opportunity of joining in the ramble over the old buildings in Southampton Street at 4.30 will without doubt be shown by some of the ancients where the cage stood in bygone times.

It is understood that the old Boys department will be represented by Mr. A. W. Moss F.R.C.O, L.R.C.M, who left 1887, Mr. Herman, Mr. Swallow and other teachers; the old Girls' department by Miss Clara Bloomfield [42] and the old Infants' by Miss S. Fabry, Mrs Priest and Mrs. M. A. Leighfield of Isleworth (Mistress about 60 years ago). Among other old Britishers attending will be the deputy mayor of Reading, Mr. Councillor Roland Howell F.R.I.B.A., Mr. Alderman Eighteen, Mr. Councillor Gill (Windsor) and possibly a prominent member of a London Borough Council. Mr. F. B. Gleave B.A. will bring back memories of the late Mr. Thos. Gleave while the late School Managers will be represented by Mr. Harrison H. Jones.

Being known by his pupils as "Daddy" or "Gaffer", Thomas Gleave remained as the school's headmaster for 40 years. He would ride to and from the school on his tricycle and introduced new systems of punishment. The least severe was cleaning his tricycle whereas the most severe involved use of the cane. Despite that, the pupils had great respect for him and many of his pupils went on to achieve great things in later life. One of those, S. Jackson Coleman, became a successful barrister and felt that the British School had provided him with the education he needed for his legal position. While searching for old pupils for a reunion, he came across the deputy mayor of Reading, councillors, clergymen, diplomats and leaders of industry and, as the *Reading Standard* commented in its full page report on *17th February 1923*:

> The dinner began with the singing of "Be present at our table, Lord," in accordance with the practice at the school treats at The Acacias 25 or 30 years ago, which was the last occasion when the old scholars had feasted together.

Britisher's Barrister and Durham's Dean

> In proposing the toast of "The continued success of the old British Scholars," Mr. S. Jackson Coleman said that nothing had surprised him more during that British School whirlwind than the startling number of prominent men and women in Reading, both in professional and mercantile life, and often directing the largest commercial concerns, who were educated in some measure at the Old British Schools. It was true, of course, that a number of old scholars who had achieved distinction in Reading, had soared so high that they would nowadays

---

[42] Commenced as Assistant 15th October, 1894, left after 16 years' service on 28 July, 1911 to take up "Special First Assistantship" at Battle School

only be observed in the clouds through the closer telescopic examination of which a movement like the present had brought into play. (Laughter). They all hoped, however, that if the smell of the soup at the Old British Schools had not brought them down to that year's dinner they would at least be in time for the next. (Hear, hear). They were old elementary school boys possibly of the best elementary school which Great Britain had ever produced. (Hear, hear). It bore the title of "British," of which all of them were so proud. Many of those present had achieved some distinction as a result of primary education, a fact of which they need scarcely be ashamed. It would not surprise him in the least if an old Britisher was even now a Member of the House of Commons – if that were any distinction – (Laughter) – and one result of their Reunion and of the prospective Britishers' Association would be to discover some of their old scholars who had succeeded not merely in getting civic honours but also in obtaining in the legislature of some of His Majesty's dominions. Several, he already knew, had held very high office in the Colonies. All that was the result of that elementary education which had been decried of late by the Dean of Durham a worthy bishop who had come to the conclusion that the Commandments as well as elementary education needed some revision to bring them into harmony with present requirements. "If you want your child well educated," Lord Beaverbrook said some time ago, "send him to an elementary school." That greatly emphasised and strengthened Lord Beaverbrook's statement.

Also from that newspaper, we learn that one of those who sent a telegram of apology for 10th February was H. F. Foster of Streatley. He was formerly a scholar under the late Mr. Gleave at Heath Side School, Warrington. We know from the censuses that Thomas Gleave was born in Warrington around 1835. However, there were two of that name baptised at St. Elphin Church, Warrington in 1834 – one on 6th July and the other on 7th December – so we know that his father was a shoemaker named John (because they both were!) but we cannot be sure of his mother's name or their address.

Warrington, Lancashire is on the Liverpool and Manchester line of the London and North Western Railway – the first passenger line in England, which was opened in 1830 – being about equidistant from Liverpool and Manchester. The Temperance Movement also began there in 1830 instigated by a Quaker merchant, George Harrison Birkett of Dublin and it is interesting to read in a report of the Reading Temperance and General Philanthropic Society in *13th November 1880 Reading Mercury* that T. Gleave seconded the approval of its financial statement at the Lodge Hotel, Kings Road.

From the 1841 and 1851 censuses, we can see that Thomas was still living in Warrington and, in the latter, his place of birth is given as Sankey. Since, in the 1881 census, we see that our Thomas Gleave is shown as living in Sankey House, Earley, Berkshire, that would seem to confirm that it is he. It was not until the 1850s that he moved to Reading where he met Emily Swain and they married there in September 1861, she having been born in Reading.

Back to *The Reading Standard of Saturday, February 17*, we learn that:

The crowds that assembled last Saturday at **the cemetery**, the British School buildings and the Hotel Co-op in honour of a late school master and in memory of an historic educational institution – an institution to which so many of Reading's most successful men owe their start in life – are without parallel in local and possibly English history.

The day had started at the graveside of "Daddy" Gleave at 3.30 pm before moving on to the **British School** an hour later for a ramble over the old buildings in Southampton Street. Later there was a dinner at the Hotel Co-op where speeches were made praising the old British School. Jackson Coleman summed up the importance of the British School by saying: "Through the foresight and the wisdom and generosity of many men who were revered, the Old British School was launched and sailed a good course until, by the passage of time, others took its place."

As you have read in *This is our School*, by the time of the 1923 Reunion instigated by Stanley Jackson Coleman following Thomas Gleave's death, the Reading British School name had already been superceded by the Southampton Street Board School in October 1901 then the Southampton Street Council School two years later, prior to its move to the Basingstoke Road/Northumberland Avenue site as George Palmer Council School four years after that, in October 1907. However it is interesting to observe that,

 despite, the name changes imposed upon it, the words **"BRITISH SCHOOLS"** were still retained on both the main building and the archway in front as can be seen in this photograph, of a gathering of Old Britishers taken at the time of the 1923 reunion. The shape of those words were still visible on the building into the 21st century.

Stanley's words continue to have significance today in that the schools have sailed a good course until, by the passage of time, others have taken their place and will no doubt continue to do so as the process of educating the young evolves. The history of the replacement school and its subsequent changes of name is revealed in *So many hearts make a school (Daphne Barnes-Phillips, 2007)* and its photographic record in *George Palmer School in photographs (Daphne & Jim Barnes-Phillips, 2004).* (See page 208 at the back of this book for details of how to obtain copies)

Reading should be proud of the part it played in providing free education to those whose parents could not afford it for them eighty years before the State began providing it for all children. It was thanks to the comparatively small Quaker meeting in the town that a school providing such an education was founded on the principles of the Quaker, Joseph Lancaster.

In the early nineteenth century, access to the professions such as Medicine, the Law and Teaching was denied to those who were not members of the Church of England so many Quakers and other Non Conformists like George Palmer and James Boorne became industrialists and very successful ones they were. With their accumulated wealth and philanthropic ideals, they founded a non-Denominational school that did not require its pupils to be, or become, Quakers. The only related requirement was that they should attend a place of Christian worship on a Sunday.

List of Principal Sources

<u>Primary Sources</u> (Including Berkshire Record Office References)

Admissions Registers – handwritten
1887 – 1907   :   Reading Girls' British School, later Southampton Street Board then Council School
1905 – 1907   :   Southampton Street Infants' School

Reading Lancasterian School Minute Book – handwritten
R/vol 1868   :   27 July 1810 – March 1820

Reading Free School on The British System – handwritten
R/vol 1869   :   April 1820 – 1843

British Boys' School Visitors' Book – handwritten
R/vol 1876   :   18 April 1822 – March 1852

British Boys' School Trustees Minutes – handwritten
R/vol 1871   :   1 July 1858 – 16 March 1868
R/vol 1872   :   14 March 1868 – 16 June 1879
R/vol 1874   :   12 February 1890 – 30 May 1901

British Girls' School Trustees Minutes – handwritten
R/vol 1877   :   31 May 1822 – 29 September 1835
R/vol 1878   :   27 October 1835 – 27 November 1849
R/vol 1879   :   18 December 1849 – 30 November 1850

British Girls' & Infants' School Trustees Minutes – handwritten
R/vol 1880   :   7 May 1872 – 22 April 1898

Central and Katesgrove School Records – handwritten
1893 – 1923   :   *Manual Instruction classes* – 22 October 1903

Log Books – handwritten
90/SCH/4/1   :   British Infants' School, later Southampton Street Infants' School: 1870 – 1907
1870 – 1923   :   Reading Girls' British School, later Southampton Street Board then Council School then George Palmer Girls' School
89/SCH/8/1   :   Southampton Street Boys' Log Book: 1905 – 1950
2001/SCH/3   :   George Palmer Infants' School: 1907 – 1996

Stock & Stores Accounts (Infants' School) – handwritten
        :   March – September 29, 1902

Reading Education Committee Minute Book 1 – handwritten
1903:   16 July   :   *Southampton Street School Headmaster* (page 60)
                   :   *Southampton Street School Playground* (page 78)
       17 December   :   *So'ton Str. Sch. Condition of Walls & Ceilings* (171)
1904:   14 April   :   *George Palmer Council School Purchase of site*
       19 May   :   *George Palmer Council School Architect* (p. 219)
       16 June   :   *George Palmer Council School Quantities etc* (233)
       21 July   :   *Southampton Street School Playground* (page 254)
                   :   *George Palmer School Instructions to Architect*
1905:   16 February   :   *George Palmer School Approval of Plans* (p. 378)

15 June	:	*Geo Palmer Sch. Tenders for erection of buildings*
	:	*Geo Palmer Sch. Appointment of Clerk of Works*
16 November	:	*Southampton Street School Tar paving* (page 531)
1906: 15 February	:	*Southampton Street School Housebreaking* (p. 578)

Reading Education Committee Minute Book 2 – handwritten

1906: 21 June	:	*Southampton Street School drainage* (page 21)
1907: 21 September	:	*Latest Addition to Reading's Splendid Elementary Schools*
17 October	:	*Matters arising out of Clerk of Works Report* (page 269)

Secondary Sources

Reading School Board Reports 1874 – 1902

1874:	9 March	:	*1st. Triennial Election*
1877:	13 February	:	*Elections of Members on Special Vacancies*
1878:	March	:	*School Treat*
1880:	February	:	*The Board*
1900:	31 December	:	*(page 6)*
1901:	31 December	:	*Transfer of the British School to the Board* (page 8)
1902:	31 December	:	*Southampton Street School (Late the British School)*

Reports of Reading Education Committee ending 31 March

1904	:	*Training of Teachers – new scheme* (p. 10 and 12)
	:	*Secondary School Scholarships* (pages 13 and 25)
	:	*Teaching Staff in Council Schools* (page 27)
	:	*Grants* (pages 33, 36 and 37)
1905	:	*New schools* (page 6)
	:	*Finance* (page 8)
1906	:	*Secondary School Scholarships* (page 5)
	:	*Elementary Education* (page 5)
	:	*Wokingham Road and George Palmer Schools* (p. 6)

Reading Education Committee Reports

| 1945 – 1950 | : | *The Education Acts 1944 – 1948* (Ch. 1 p. 7 – 11) |

Report of Royal Lancasterian Institution for the Education of the Poor

| 1812 | : | *Finance Committee and Trustees* |

Books or Booklets

Baker, T. F. T. (1976)	:	*Tottenham: Education, A History of the County of Middlesex: Volume 5*
Bassett, John (2000)	:	*A Brief History of the Reading British School*
Beecroft, Joseph (1882)	:	*Guide to Reading 1882*, p. 76 *The British Schools*
Billing, Richard (1846)	:	*Statistics of the Sanitary Condition of the Borough of Reading*
Bray, R. S. (2003)	:	*Reading's Forgotten Children* The story of Reading Board Schools, 1871 – 1902
Childs, W. M. (1910)	:	*The Town of Reading during the early part of the Nineteenth Century* Intellectual Life (i) Schools
Corley, T. A. B. (1972)	:	*Huntley & Palmers of Reading 1822 – 1972* Quaker Enterprise in Biscuits

Darter, W. S. (1888)   :   *Reminiscences of Reading by an Octogenarian*
Harman, Leslie (1946)   :   *The parish of St. Giles in Reading* (pages 82 – 83)
Harman, L. W. (1960)   :   *History of Education in Reading* (pages 83 – 85)
Marsh, Fredk. W. (1917) :   *Reading Communal Kitchen*

Censuses & Websites
1837 onwards   :   Births, marriages and deaths – *FreeBMD* website
1841, 1861, 1871, 1911   :   *Genes Reunited* website
1851   :   *MACH 2 – BERKSHIRE 1851 CENSUS (2003)*
1881   :   *Family Search* website
1901   :   *Ancestry.co.uk* website

Microfiches
Quaker Digest Registers   :   Berkshire Quarterly Meeting (Society of Friends)
MF678   :   Births 1612 – 1837

Newspapers
Berkshire Chronicle
    25 March   :   *Election results* (page 8)
1923: 2 February   :   *Cage Cure for Naughty Boys*
    9 February   :   *British Schools "At Home"; Tomorrow's Gathering*
                    :   *The British School Song*
    16 February   :   *British School Re-union* (Page 4)
                    :   *Mr Morley and the "Stick"; Absent Scholars:*

Reading Mercury & Oxford Gazette – General Advertiser of Berks, Bucks, Hants, Surrey, Sussex and Wilts (abbreviated to Reading Mercury)
1810: 30 July   :   *READING LANCASTERIAN SCHOOL*
    6 August   :   *To Builders*
    27 August   :   *Royal British System of Education*
17 & 29 December   :   *Donations*
1811: 5 January   :   *Opening of Lancasterian School*
1812: 30 January   :   *Religious Instruction*
    8 April   :   *Reading Lancasterian School*
1815: 4 December   :   *London News* (Page 4)
1817: 18 August   :   *Letter re proceeding with Girls' British School* (p. 4)
    25 August   :   *Conclusion of above* (Page 4)
    September   :   *Further donations towards erecting a Royal British Free School for Girls*
1818: 23 March   :   *Reading Boys' Free School on British System* (p. 3)
    30 March   :   *Reading Ladies' Free School Society for Girls on the British System Rules and Regulations (p 3)* 1820:
    1 May   :   *Reading British Free School* (Page 3)
1821: 19 May   :   *Reading British Free Schools* (P. 3 of XCIX 5139)
    28 May   :   (Page 3 of Volume XCIX Number 5140)
1822: 3 June   :   *Reading British Free Schools* (P. 3 of C no. 5193)
    10 June   :   (Page 3 of Volume C Number 5194)
1847: 18 December   :   *George Palmer's letter–Ragged school for Reading*

1869:	27 March	:	*Examination at Boys' British School* (page 5)
	2 July	:	*Treat to British School Children* (page 5)
	18 July	:	*Festival of the Reading Sunday School Union*
	23 October	:	*Reading and Basingstoke Turnpike Trust* (Page 5)
	13 November	:	*British Girls' and Infants' Schools*
	20 November	:	*New Wesleyan Chapel*
1894:	7 April	:	*Funeral of Mrs. George Palmer* (page 5)
1897:	21 August	:	*Death of Mr. George Palmer of Reading* (page 5)
	28 August	:	*The Funeral of Mr. George Palmer of Reading*
1923:	16 February	:	*The cage at the Old British School*

Reading Observer

1923:	9 February	:	*To-morrow's British Schools' Re-union*
		:	*Memories of the British School by a "Lankee Doodle" of former days*

Reading Standard

1907:	4 May	:	*The Children's Concerts*
	26 October	:	*The George Palmer Schools*
1911:	25 February	:	*The Children's Concerts*
1921:	22 January	:	*Reading Education Committee* (page 10)
1923:	27 January	:	At the British Schools fifty years ago (page 10)
	10 February	:	British School Reunion (Page 12)
	17 February	:	*British School Day*
	24 February	:	*Old British School* (Page 8)
	21 April	:	*British School reminiscences* (Front page)

Reading Street Directories

1826	:	Horniman's *Reading Directory*
1833	:	*Berkshire Commercial Directory*
1839	:	Yorke's *Reading Street Key*
1842 – 3	:	Snare's *Post Office Reading Directory*
1843	:	Rusher's *Reading Guide*
1845	:	Rusher's *Reading Guide*
1846	:	Rusher's *Reading Guide*
1847 – 49	:	Rusher's *Reading Guide*
1848	:	Kelly's *Berkshire Directory*
1852/3	:	Slater's *Directory of Berks, Cornwall, Devon . . .*
1855	:	Rusher's *Reading Guide*
1857	:	Rusher's *Reading Guide & Berks Directory*
1859	:	Macaulay's *Reading Directory*
1865	:	Macaulay's *Reading Directory*
1867	:	Macaulay's *Reading Guide*
1874	:	Webster's *Reading Directory*
1914	:	Kelly's *Directory of Reading*

Transcripts & Indexes of Registers for Reading Non Conformists

Baptist Burial Ground & Infants Register, Church Street, Reading

LANKEE DOODLE CHORUS
(To the Tune of "Marching through Georgia)

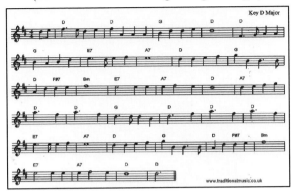

Sound the call to battle boys! The Britishers
are out,
Swell the mighty chorus; help "Lankee
Doodles" shout.
"Crowny Bobs" may do their worst and
"Centrals" sneer and frown,
But we go marching to vict'ry.

Chorus:
Hurrah! Hurrah! We're ready for the fray,
Hurrah! Hurrah! The "British" led the way,
Her scholars e'er did triumph and always
won the day.
Three Cheers for our Old British School.

From their lordy palaces the school board girls
crept out,
Thinking they were strong enough, the British
girls to flout,
British girls in hundreds rose and put them all
to rout,
And still go marching to vict'ry.

Often did the other schoolboys challenge
us to try,
With our orange-amber tunics their
"footers" to defy,
Our eleven good Britishers ne'er asked
The reason why,
But went on marching to vict'ry.

Oft they tried their level best our onward
march to stem,
Everything that we performed they'd
Instantly condemn,
Success embraced our efforts – ne'er
knuckled we to them,
And we went marching to vict'ry.

Britishers now rank yourself beneath our
wide-spread flag,
Sound alone the clarion call o'er valley,
Hill and crag,
Let Britonians live again – aye, live and
never lag,
And still go marching to vict'ry

These are the festive scenes through
which in life we pass
Homeward soon again we go – each old boy
and each lass
May Reunions such as these e'er lead us to
the mass
As we go marching to vict'ry

207

If you have enjoyed reading about Reading's British School, we are sure you will also appreciate the following books by Daphne Barnes-Phillips:

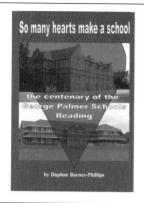

So many hearts make a school

Daphne, who was born and raised just a quarter of a mile from George Palmer Infant and Junior Schools, recalls her own memories, and also those of 50 other pupils and staff across the 100 years that are celebrated in this book.

Many hours of research at the Berkshire Records Office, Reading Central Library and on-line showed up facts and figures previously unknown to most pupils and staff throughout the century.

Fully illustrated with black and white photographs. 240 pages.

Price £12.95   ISBN 978 1 897715 07 2

George Palmer School in photographs 1907 to 2004

A photographic record of events in the life of George Palmer School, Reading, in its original buildings from 1907 to 2004.

Fully illustrated with black and white photographs. 40 pages.

Price £4.95   ISBN 978 1 897715 16 1

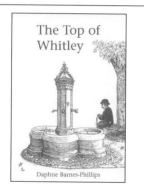

The Top of Whitley – A study of the Spring Gardens area of Reading

The Spring Gardens area of Reading may only be about half a mile square, but *The Top of Whitley* uncovers its history over a 160-year period, with reminiscences from twenty people who played, worked, lived or were educated there.

Fully illustrated book with black and white photographs. 160 pages.

Book: Price £8.95   ISBN 978 1 897715 01 3
CD based on A Walk around The Top of Whitley
     Price £4.95   ISBN 978 1 897715 02 1

**All books are available from: Corridor Press, 19 Portland Avenue, Exmouth, Devon, EX8 2BS – email: _corridorpress@yahoo.co.uk_ or phone: 01395 263494.
All Prices include postage & packing within UK.
Please make cheques payable to "Corridor Press".**